Dedicated to Ben and Alicia,

Children and Pals

A Smart Vacationers' Guide to Skiing, Dining and Adventures in the Vail Valley

By Ned R. Harley, M.D.

Board Certified in Psychiatry
Master of Architecture
Fine Artist (Painter)
Veteran Skier and
Former Ski Instructor

Library of Congress Catalog Card Number: 92-75298

This book produced in the U.S.A. by

🌸 Alpenrose Press
Box 499, Silverthorne, CO 80498

Book Editor: Mary Ellen Gililand, Alpenrose Press
Cover Design: Dannette Peterson

First Edition, 1992, published by Harley Press
Mail Orders: Harley Press
                 P.O. Box 4577
                 Vail, CO 81658
                 (303) 476-1521

DISCLAIMER OF LIABILITY

Skiing and other adventure activities are inherently risky sports. Each skier has a duty and a responsibility both to himself or herself and others on the mountain to maintain control of speed and direction at all times. Similarly each adventurer has a duty and responsibility to look out for his or her own safety and the safety of others at all times. The information contained in Exciting Vail represents the author's assessments and opinions with respect to the skiable terrain on Vail Mountain and Beaver Creek Mountain.

Similarly with leads to other activities, the author has presented information to the best of his ability regarding these adventures. Because of the variability of conditions both on the mountains, in the environment, and in each athlete's own physical and mental abilities, the author and publisher expressly disclaim any liability or responsibility for the consequences of any reader's activities. Issues of risk should be discussed with the proprietor or the proprietor's agents of each and every activity discussed in this publication for each and every person who will be involved in the activity.

Colorado State Law limits the liability of ski areas within the State. It is the duty of readers to familiarize themselves with the important features of this law. It is also the duty of skiers to read and understand the Skier's Responsibility Code. The law and the code are presented in the Cautions section of this publication.

The author and publisher disclaim any liability for incorrect telephone numbers. A best effort has been made to be correct. The proprietor of any restaurant or activity who believes the identifying information to be in error should contact the author by certified letter with the correct information for possible future editions. New businesses and changes of information should also be forwarded by certified letter. Write to: Harley Press, P.O. Box 4577, Vail, Co. 81658. This book is copyrighted as is the cognitive mapping Centers concept for describing a ski area.

CONTENTS

AUTHOR'S NOTE

EXCITING VAIL, the authoritative guide to skiing Vail and Beaver Creek as well as dining in the Vail Valley, will add a dimension of excellence to your Vail Valley vacation. A host of exciting adventures with phone numbers are listed to inform you of all the activities available on a Vail vacation.

I realized the need for this book when I first moved to Vail. I am a professional person, a physician and an avid, seasoned skier who has experienced numerous mountains and resorts. I gained insight as a ski instructor both at Vail and Keystone, although I am not now affiliated with either organization. My Colorado ski knowledge expanded when I owned a condominium at Copper Mountain and also made regular visits to Steamboat Springs to provide psychiatric consultation for the Northwest Colorado Mental Health Center. I know central Colorado ski country.

My 25 years of experience as a psychiatrist has taught me the importance of cognitive mapping. I am also an architect. These skills helped to create this book's organizing diagrammatic conceptual maps.

As a professional person, I am aware of what professional people want to enjoy on a ski resort vacation (winter or summer) and what they need to know to make it exciting. Having lived in this area for over two decades I am in touch with what is to be gained by everyone through living or vacationing in Colorado ski country. With this book I am at your side as well as on your side. **EXCITING VAIL** empowers you with the knowledge to cut through the mass of information you receive when arriving at Vail or Beaver Creek. While some of this other information is free, it is also self-serving. Neither Vail Associates, Vail/Beaver Creek Ski School, nor any of the restaurateurs in the Vail Valley, nor any of the adventure activity proprietors made any contributions to the writing of this book.

The cost of this book will seem cheap when you realize how much it enhances your experience of Vail and Beaver Creek. **EXCITING VAIL** will help you to save money and avoid awkward situations.

This book does not cover lodging accommodations, shopping, or equipment rental. For information on accommodations contact either the Vail Resort Association at (800) 824-5737 or Vail/Beaver Creek Reservations at (800) 525-2257, ext. 213; (800) 622-3131, ext. 258; or (303) 949-5750, ext. 4030. To contact the tourism and convention bureau call (303) 476-1000. FAX: (303) 476-6008. The rule is that lodging close to the mountain's base (or the golf course) is more expensive. For snow reports call (303) 476-4888 or 476-4889.

N.R.H.

VAIL: A BRIEF HISTORY

Vail has mushroomed over three decades from a meadowland for sheep to the largest ski resort in North America. Beaver Creek followed about fifteen years ago.

Like a number of Colorado ski resorts, Vail was spearheaded by World War II skiing soldiers from the U.S. Army's 10th Mountain Division. Prior to front line duty in Europe, this division of 15,000 men had trained in nearby Camp Hale, about 25 miles south of Vail. Peter Siebert, a 10th Mountain Division purple heart recipient, was guided to the back bowls by veteran skier Earl Eaton in 1959. The two developed the ski resort which opened (without snow) in 1962.

Vail Village was modeled after the European resorts of St. Anton, Zermatt and Megeve. Tyrolean architecture in pedestrian Vail Village reflects this influence. Many European immigrants established restaurants, shops and lodges in early-day Vail, creating a special ambiance.

Prior to the arrival of 1800s prospectors and homesteaders, the area had belonged to the nomadic Ute Indian tribe. Folklore suggests that the Utes created the treeless back bowls by setting a spite fire to foil their enemies.

In the 1850s Lord Gore, a wealthy baronet from Ireland, became the first European to actively tour the area. His purpose was to hunt. Lord Gore conducted his grand safari without regard for hunting ethics, frequently leaving dozens of carcasses to rot. He brought with him on this expedition fine liquors, china, silverware and a personal retinue of 42 men. Why the Gore mountain range and Gore Creek bear his name remains a mystery.

In 1873, William Henry Jackson photographed the Mount of the Holy Cross, which the poet Longfellow had made legendary. Pilgrimages to the mountain began and continue to this day.

Alfred Larzalere established Vail's first homestead in 1882. Vail was named after Charlie Vail, Colorado highway department chief engineer and Vail Pass road builder.

June Simonton's book, *VAIL, Story of a Colorado Mountain Valley,* is an excellent source for in-depth history. She has also written *BEAVER CREEK, the First One Hundred Years.*

Vail and Beaver Creek hosted the 1989 World Alpine Ski Championships and hope to do so again before the turn of the century.

EXCITING SKIING

INTRODUCTION TO THE ALPINE SECTION
(INCLUDING SNOWBOARDING AND TELEMARKING)

Vail Mountain and Beaver Creek Mountain provide a huge ski resort area with a wide variety of terrain. Vail itself is the largest single ski mountain in North America. Why waste valuable vacation time to puzzle over the slopes? **EXCITING VAIL** will simplify the complexity of these two major ski areas putting them into an organized conceptual framework. You will have more control over your ski vacation when you master the Ski Centers cognitive mapping concept which I have developed and utilized. Once you understand cognitive mapping of the Ski Centers, you will be able to navigate within a Center and from Center to Center with clarity and ease. You can coordinate with friends and family members in an organized manner (preventing the friction that comes from confusion).

From this Center perspective Vail Mountain has fourteen Ski Centers and Beaver Creek has eight. A major reason you choose to ski in the Vail Valley is the variety of terrain offered. But with that incredible variety comes immense size, sometimes overwhelming to visitors. This authoritative guide will provide you with an organizational framework to maximize your excitement and enjoyment while skiing Vail Mountain and Beaver Creek Mountain.

The diagrammatic maps I have developed will be of immense value to you, visually reinforcing the Center cognitive mapping process. However, they are not meant to replace the official ski area maps published by Vail Associates for Vail Mountain and Beaver Creek Mountain. The official maps are excellent and full of valuable information.

The helpful services of Vail/Beaver Creek Ski School and where to obtain these services (including those for skiing children and pre-skiing children) are discussed in this section.

Vail and Beaver Creek have designated certain areas as either Family Areas or Slow Skiing Areas. On the official ski maps these areas are easily seen. The Family Areas have a red dot covering; the Slow Skiing Areas have a yellow dot covering. On the slopes these areas are designated by banners. It is ultra important to ski slowly and with care in these areas, not only because you may lose your lift ticket or pass, but also because it is fair; the vast majority of skiable area is not designated as "slow." Be fair to those who need or choose to ski in a more relaxed space. Be aware, ski with care.

Snowboarders: note that there is a half-pipe in the Golden Peak Center.

Cross-country skiing is available at the Vail Nordic Center (the Vail Golf Course) as well as at Vail Mountain (Golden Peak Center) and Beaver Creek Mountain (McCoy Park in the Strawberry Park Center). Consult the Cross-

Country Skiing portion of the Adventures section and the Strawberry Park Center portion of the Beaver Creek Mountain section.

When skiing in Vail, don't forget Hot Winter Nights. If this wonderful event occurs during your stay in the Vail Valley, go to it for a real treat. What is it? The Vail/Beaver Creek Demo Team puts on a "skiing extravaganza" at Golden Peak starting at 7:00 p.m. one night per week. You will see spectacular skiing, telemarking, and snowboarding together with a magnificent lighting display, fireworks, music, and comedy.

Rarely it will be necessary to contact the Ski Patrol regarding an emergency. Find the nearest **red telephone box** and dial <u>1111</u>. Be prepared to give **clear** information as to location and extent of injury.

MAP KEY

Poma or Surface Lift	++++++++++++++++++++++++++++++++++++
Chairlift or Gondola	xxxxxxxxxxxxxxxxxxxxxxxxxxxxxxxxxxxx
Catwalk or Road	– – – – – – – – – – – – – – – – – .
Beginner (Green)	●●●●●●●●●●●●●●●●●●●●●●●●●●●●●●●●
Intermediate (Blue)	～～～～～～～～～～～～～～～～～～～～
Expert (Black)	★★★★★★★★★★★★★★★★★★★★★★★★★★★★★
Double Diamond (Double Black)	◆◆◆◆◆◆◆◆◆◆◆◆◆◆◆◆◆◆◆◆◆◆

Ski Tips

EXCITING VAIL MOUNTAIN

The best strategy to simplify the immense complexity of the ski terrain on Vail Mountain is my cognitive mapping organization of Vail's Ski Centers. As noted in the Introduction to Skiing, Vail has fourteen Centers, fourteen focal points to use in planning your ski experience.

VAIL MOUNTAIN CENTERS

1. GOLDEN PEAK
2. VAIL VILLAGE
3. LIONSHEAD
4. MINNIE'S MILE
5. AVANTI EXPRESS
6. MID-VAIL
7. NORTHWOODS EXPRESS
8. SOURDOUGH
9. DOUBLE DIAMOND
10. CHINA BOWL
11. TEA CUP BOWL
12. SUN UP BOWL
13. SUN DOWN BOWL
14. GAME CREEK BOWL

Vail is a big mountain, the largest single ski area in the United States. The mountain stretches more than seven miles wide and has more than 1,800 skiable acres. This is why you came to ski Vail. Add to you enjoyment of skiing Vail Mountain by putting a little thought into understanding the Ski Center concept. The placement of trails in Centers is designed for clear and easy cognitive mapping of Vail Mountain.

The ordering of these Centers is based on adjacencies. First I discuss the base areas from east to west; then the higher areas are discussed from west to east; finally the back bowls are discussed from east to west.

One area, Mountain Top/PHQ does not easily fit into a Center because it functions as part of three Centers. Mountain Top/PHQ is located at the summit of Vail Mountain where Chairlifts #4, #5, and #11 come together. Mountain Top Express Lift from Mid-Vail, Northwoods Express Lift, and High Noon Lift from the back bowls all bring skiers to the summit area, resulting in congestion. Then skiers fan out in all directions: Northwoods Express Center; Sun Up Bowl Center; Sun Down Bowl Center; Mid-Vail

VAIL MOUNTAIN'S CENTERS FOR SKIING

CHINA BOWL

TEA CUP BOWL

SUN UP SUN DOWN BOWL

GAME CREEK BOWL

SOURDOUGH

DOUBLE DIAMOND

NORTH-WOODS EXPRESS

MID-VAIL EXPRESS

AVANTI EXPRESS

MINNIE'S MILE

GOLDEN PEAK

VAIL VILLAGE

LIONSHEAD

Center; and even to Vail Village Center via Riva Ridge. Be careful. This is an especially important area to make use of the conceptual framework of cognitive mapping to guide you where you wish to go. Ski Patrol Headquarters is located here, hence the "PHQ" designation; the Ski Patrol can be very helpful. There is a large ski map for you to work with located here.

Vail Mountain can be crowded at certain times of the year. Usually this occurs over the Christmas holidays; President's Weekend; and Spring Break. Long crowds at Chairlifts #2, #4, #5, and #11 could dampen your spirits. My rule is to keep moving. However, you cannot keep moving if the maze is packed at High Noon Lift (Chairlift #5); so maybe you should avoid this situation.

If the maze is full at Avanti Express Lift (Chairlift #2), I often enjoy a short ski to the Vista Bahn Express (Chairlift #16); you will probably get to Mid-Vail just as fast.

If there is a long line at Mountain Top Express (Chairlift #4), you have a few choices. You could take the Hunky Dory Lift (Chairlift #3); ski Lion's Way or Spruce Face to the Avanti Express Lift (Chairlift #2); or take Gitalong Road to Riva Ridge and possibly continuing on TransMontane to the Northwoods Express Lift (Chairlift #11). If the Northwoods Express Lift is busy, I would ski over to Highline Lift (Chairlift #10) in the Double Diamond Center or even take Chairlift #6 out to Golden Peak Center or Vail Village Center.

If it is a totally crowded day the best bet may be to make use of Giant Steps Lift (Chairlift #1); Born Free Express Lift (Chairlift #8); Minnie's Lift (Chairlift #9); or the Gondola. It is more fun to be skiing on the lower part of the mountain than standing around at the summit or in the back bowls.

Vail Mountain does have light boards set up at various places which indicate what the crowd situation is at lifts around the mountain. A green light stands for short lines; a yellow light means you could be waiting up to 20 minutes; and a red light means the lift is shut down.

In powder most knowledgeable skiers head for the south facing slopes in the back bowls before the sun has a chance to "set up" the snow. If you want the real steep in powder, go for Straight Shot; Headwall; Rasputin's Revenge; or Prima Cornice. Not quite as steep suggestions are Morning Side Ridge; Widge's Ridge; Seldom; Apres Vous; Ouzo Glade; Wow; Windows; Yonder; and Bolshoi Ballroom. This list could go on and on. To avoid crowds on powder days try skiing north facing slopes. There is just one rule in fresh powder: "be first."

There are active plans and studies underway for additional Centers. These Centers will be located south of China Bowl. Keep coming to Vail for the great skiing its future will offer.

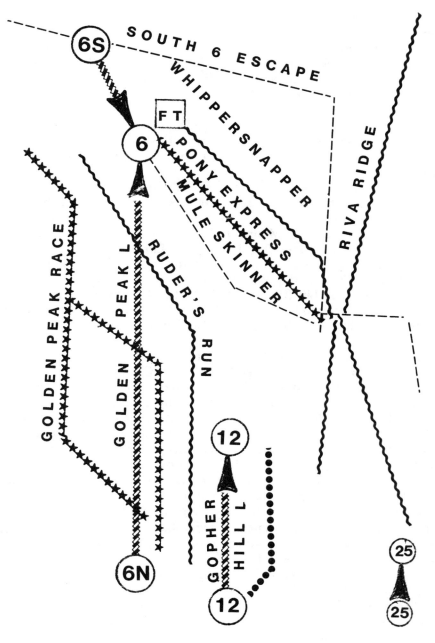

Front Side Centers On Vail Mountain

1. GOLDEN PEAK CENTER (Golden Peak Lift, Chairlift #6; Gopher Hill Lift, Chairlift #12; Golden Peak Surface Lift, Poma Lift #25)

INTRODUCTION

The Golden Peak Center, at the east end of Vail Mountain, is an interesting mixture of beginner skiing and advanced race skiing. Also, it is the site of the half-pipe for snowboarders. The base area contains the Golden Peak Restaurant, a cafeteria on the first floor, combined with an après ski bar on the second floor. There is a Vail/Beaver Creek Ski School Center operating out of Golden Peak. As well as arranging for alpine lessons, you can purchase snowboard lessons and cross-country ski lessons at this Center.

A beautiful Children's Center provides fun for your kids. The Small World Program takes care of small children

The Hot Winter Nights ski performances by the demo team of the Vail Ski School take place here in the evening, usually once a week. These are fantastic shows with great skiing, great jumps, great lights, and fantastic fire works. Do not miss the excitement of watching these performances.

ARRIVAL

Arriving at the Golden Peak is easy, if you are early. Turn south off South Frontage Road (east of the four way stop) onto East Meadow Drive (by the Tyrolean Inn). Otherwise you may need to utilize the Vail Village parking structure or Ford Park requiring a walk to arrive in time for your lesson.

THE LIFTS

There are two chairlifts and one surface lift in this Center. Golden Peak Lift (Chairlift #6) takes you to the top of Golden Peak. Interestingly this same lift brings people up the backside of Golden Peak. Ignore the early departure point on the front face which is for racers only.

The Gopher Hill Lift (Chairlift #12) is for beginners. It is more a part of the Ski School operation than a functioning lift for the public. For the "never evers" Vail has added a Golden Peak Surface Lift (#25) at the western end of this section.

THE RUNS

GOLDEN PEAK RACE (Black): To the east of the Golden Peak Lift and

15

directly under the lift lie runs mainly for racers. These are groomed and set up with flag poles to make a race course. They are roped off to the general public.

RUDER'S RUN (Blue):   Ruder's Run is the main intermediate route down Golden Peak. By skiing to the west you can ski directly over to the Vista Bahn in Vail Village. On Ruder's Run notice the half-pipe for snowboarders. You will also see Devil's Fork Mine; a teepee; and Dragon's Breath Mine. Give them a try.

FORT WHIPPERSNAPPER: This actually is not a run, but a place. If you take a few steps uphill as you get off of the lift, you can enter Fort Whippersnapper. The Fort looks quite real. It has a saloon, a general store, and a jail -- a great place for kids.

WHIPPERSNAPPER (Blue):   Whippersnapper is a relatively wide, intermediate run that is usually groomed and heavily used by the ski school.

PONY EXPRESS (Black): This is a somewhat steeper way down Golden Peak that you ski out of Fort Whipper Snapper.

MULE SKINNER (Green): This is a an easy run generally reserved for children. It provides a gradual rolling course between beautiful aspen trees.

LEAVING AND CONNECTING WITH OTHER CENTERS

If you get off at the top of Chairlift #6 and take Grand Junction Catwalk to the south you will reach the base of the Highline Lift (Chairlift #10). This way you can ski Double Diamond Center, an expert area. Or from the top of Highline Lift you can reach the Sourdough Center (Chairlift #14). From here you can ride up to Two Elk Restaurant and China Bowl; or you can mosey over to Northwoods Express Lift (Chairlift #11) on Flap Jack.

Additionally, if you come down the front face of Golden Peak on the left hand side (west side) you can ski directly over to the Vista Bahn Express Lift (Chairlift #16). Carry some speed, but not too much as here is a control gate. This control gate helps you find the short pathway over to the Vista Bahn Express Lift. The Vista Bahn Express Lift will take you directly up to Mid-Vail.

2. VAIL VILLAGE CENTER (Giant Steps Lift, Chairlift #1 and Vista Bahn Express Lift, Chairlift #16)

16

INTRODUCTION

The Vail Village Center contains a variety of runs for skiers of various levels from strong beginner to expert.

Vail Village is full of places to eat shops, galore, and places to rent or purchase ski equipment, together with all of the accessories. Aprés ski takes place up and down Bridge Street in the famous "Bridge Street Shuffle." Do not walk in the streets with open alcohol containers.

A Vail/Beaver Creek Ski School Center is located here. This outlet offers private lessons or Mountain Guide groups. It does not offer group lessons.

ARRIVAL

You arrive at Vail Village Center by walking south through Vail Village; either Bridge Street or Wall Street takes you to the base of Vail Village Center. From the Vail Village parking structure cross over the Covered Bridge; you are then on Bridge Street, heading towards Vail Mountain.

THE LIFTS

Actually, the Giant Steps Lift (Chairlift #1), a regular speed two passenger lift, runs infrequently. It usually runs only when the mountain is super crowded or when there is a race that ends (after a steep finale down Pepi's Face on International) in the Vail Village Center. You do get a good look at races on International when you ascend the Giant Steps Lift.

Most ski days you are committed to taking a high-speed quadruple passenger chairlift, the Vista Bahn Express Lift (Chairlift #16), to Mid-Vail Center when you start in Vail Village.

THE RUNS

BEAR TREE (Blue): Bear Tree is an intermediate trail reached by skiing down International from the top of the Giant Steps Lift. Its heaviest use comes from the base of the Avanti Express Center, a short distance above. Ski over to the left hand side and down. Do not go over the steep pitch. Be sure to take the left turn onto Gitalong Road. This trail goes west, cuts back to the east, and then heads back west onto Bear Tree. (Note that if you continue further west, beyond Bear Tree, on Gitalong Road, you will be heading for Born Free and the Lionshead Center). You will notice that some people are skiing a short run of steep moguls within the zig zag. However, you do not need to tackle these moguls; just stick to the zig zag catwalk.

Bear Tree is well groomed and seldom skied. It is a great place for the average intermediate skier to work on turns. It has pitches, but they are short

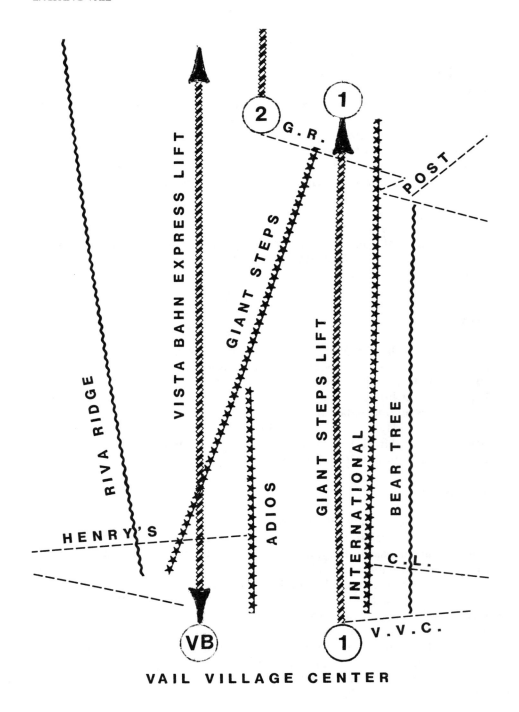

and lead into almost flat areas. At the base of Bear Tree, a right turn onto the Vail Village Catwalk will take you right back to the base of this Center.

So you are an intermediate skier and like this trail; how do you get there when Chairlift #1 is closed? Take the Vista Bahn, ski just beyond the Mid-Vail building, and then make a U-turn (now heading west on Lion's Way Catwalk); this will lead you to the Avanti Express Center while skirting its steep terrain. Then you can mosey over to the western side of International and begin the Bear Tree trek described above. For an even flatter course you could take Gitalong Road from Mid-Vail, heading initially to the east but turning west at Riva Ridge; Gitalong Road then goes in the same direction as Lion's Way, but runs below it. By using Gitalong Road you do not have to ski the intermediate section or the most difficult section of Avanti.

INTERNATIONAL (Black):   International is steep. It usually requires expert skiing. Since it is so low on the mountain, it may be hard packed or slightly icy. In powder International is a great place to make first tracks. It runs straight into the base of the Vail Village Center. The last steep pitch of International is now divided into Pepi's Face and Head First. Pepi's Face is named after Pepi Gramshammer, a local hero and proprietor of Pepi's Restaurant and the Gasthof Gramshammer Lodge in Vail Village.

GIANT STEPS (Black):   Giant Steps parallels International to the east. Giant Steps is left ungroomed most of the time. It is a mogul run. Check it out as you ride up the Vista Bahn to see if it is skiable. Observe the steepness of the slope, the quality of snow cover, and the size of the moguls.

ADIOS (Black):   Pick up Adios with a left turn off Giant Steps about one half of the way down. Like Giant Steps, Adios is steep and well moguled.

LEAVING AND CONNECTING WITH OTHER CENTERS

If you are at the base of the Vail Village Center, just walk into town and après ski. If you are at the top of Vail Village Center, you can ski either Bear Tree, International, or Giant Steps to reach Vail Village. Heading east from the top of Giant Steps Lift (Chairlift #1), when it is operating, will bring you to the Avanti Express Lift (Chairlift #2) in the Avanti Express Center.

You can ski to the Lionshead base from Bear Tree by sticking to Gitalong Road until it merges into Born Free. Or you can go further down Bear Tree and make a left turn onto Chicken Legs Catwalk which funnels into Lionshead Catwalk.

You can reach Golden Peak Center by making a right turn onto Gitalong Road until it connects with Henry's Catwalk. Giant Steps, Adios, and International run directly into Henry's Catwalk. From these trails, a right turn onto Henry's Catwalk will take you to Golden Peak Center.

3. LIONSHEAD CENTER {Lionshead Gondola (#19), Born Free Express (Chairlift #8), Little Eagle (Chairlift #15), Eagle's Nest Surface Lift (Poma lift #18), and Cascade Village Lift (Chairlift #20)}.

INTRODUCTION

Lionshead Center contains some excellent runs and is often uncrowded. A major exception: if you insist on taking the Gondola in the morning, there will be a line at the Gondola. But the line at the Born Free Express Lift will probably be minimal. However, at 10:00 a.m., when the more advanced Ski School groups start up the mountain, there will be a line at Born Free Express.

The trails in this Center are generally long, wide rolling runs. You can have a jolly time cruising in Lionshead Center, but be careful to honor the "family areas" on Simba and Safari. You may wish to avoid the few expert slopes near the bases of Simba, Safari, Bwana, and the Glades (if you are in a cruising mood or don't feel comfortable on expert terrain). How to reach or avoid these expert inclines is clarified below.

The Vail/Beaver Creek Ski School Center, operating out of Lionshead, takes beginner skiers to the top of Vail Mountain on the Lionshead Gondola. These skiers come down on the Gondola at day's end. There is a cafeteria and restrooms at the top of the Gondola, so beginners are never far from civilization while skiing the Chairlift #15 beginner area. This area at the top of the Gondola is called Eagle's Nest; it offers fantastic views to the north and west (Gore Range Wilderness) as well as to the south (Holy Cross Wilderness).

At Eagle's Nest you will find a cafeteria, sun deck, restrooms, ski accessory shop, and a sit down restaurant (The Wine Stube). There is a cabin near the Gondola building that houses a Vail/Beaver Creek Ski School Center. You can arrange private lessons or afternoon workshops at this cabin.

At the base, the Gondola building provides a variety of services. These include the Trail's End Restaurant, open for breakfast, lunch, and aprés ski with Don Watson providing entertainment. Don's performances are definitely fun. Restrooms are located on the bottom floor along with a video arcade, lost and found, and a basket storage area. Accessory ski equipment is available.

Surrounding the base area is a host of restaurants, ski stores, and shops.

ARRIVAL

You arrive at the Lionshead Center on foot, bringing your skis or snowboard from your car, bus, home, or condominium. The Lionshead parking lot is located off of South Frontage Road to the west of the four way stop at the I-70 Exit 176. There is an Information Center entrance to the parking lot with a guide and brochures.

THE LIFTS

Lionshead Gondola (Lift #19) is a six passenger lift which ascends over Lionshead Center to Eagle's Nest. It provides wonderful eagle eye views of a number of the slopes in this area as well as fantastic scenic views of the surrounding landscape.

Cascade Village Lift (Chairlift #20), a regular speed two passenger chairlift, ascends from Cascade Village to Post Road on the west side of Simba. From here you can ski to the base of Lionshead Center. Alternatively, you can ski Post Road east to Chairlift #9 in the Minnie's Mile Center or even over to Bear Tree in Vail Village Center.

Born Free Express (Chairlift #8), a high-speed quadruple passenger chairlift, takes you two/thirds of the way up to the top. It provides good views of lower Bwana and the Born Free.

Little Eagle Lift (Chairlift #15) at the top of Lionshead Center is the beginner chairlift. It is a regular speed two passenger chairlift. The Eagle's Nest Surface Lift (Poma Lift #19) carries more children than adults in Gitchee-gume Gulch. Adults are welcome.

THE RUNS

SIMBA (Blue and black): Simba is Vail Mountain's most westerly run except for the short pitch, Westin Ho, which takes skiers from near the base of Simba over to the Westin Hotel, Simba is a long, fun run. An intermediate slope, it holds snow and is frequently groomed. Almost all of Simba has been designated as a "Family Area" where slow controlled skiing has been mandated. Near the beginning of Simba, on the left, you may wish to visit the Old Silver Mine; kids love it.

There are two steeper faces. The first one (which is still intermediate) can be skied around by taking Post Road to the left which will swing around and bring you back to Simba below this steeper section. The other steep spot is a most difficult expert pitch. However, by cutting off onto Cheetah and then skiing Cheetah back to Simba you avoid this difficult pitch.

Aside from the steeper pitches, Simba is a great place to enjoy cruising or to work on your ski program. Reach Simba by skiing around the top of Eagle's Nest Gondola building to its west side. It can also be reached via a couple of catwalk connections if you start down Born Free; just remember to stay on the left/west side of Born Free to find the connections. Do not go too

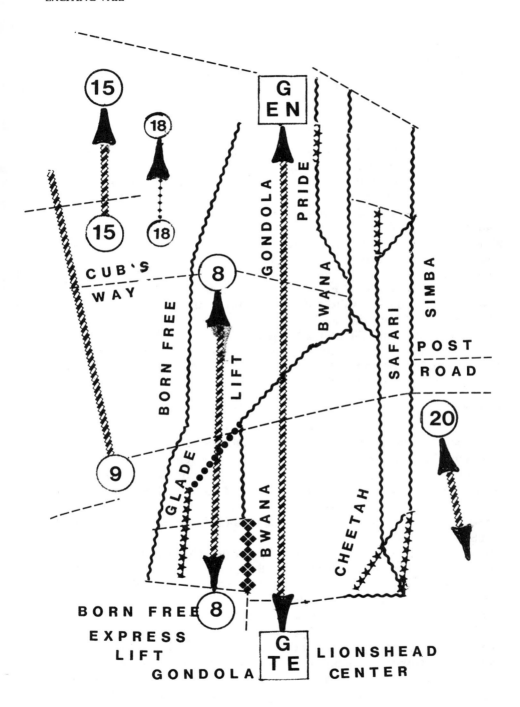

far down the mountain before trying to turn off or you will find yourself on a steep section of Born Free and unable to reach Simba. The beginning of Cub's Way is the last connector you can take off Born Free to reach Simba, as well as Bwana and Pride, before you are committed to upper Born Free, above the top of the Born Free Express Lift (Chairlift #8). Sticking to Cub's Way as it returns east to Born Free after taking you west to the other trails is the way to miss the steep section on upper Born Free.

BWANA (Blue and black): Bwana is an excellent intermediate cruiser run. It has some slightly steeper pitches and wonderful variety. It is an enjoyable run with one exception. The last pitch of Bwana down to the base is a most difficult, expert pitch. Most skiers avoid this path, usually by heading right/easterly to the Born Free trail. Note this is the section of Born Free which is crowded at day's end when so many skiers of varying abilities and sizes are finishing.

You can ski all of Bwana by starting at the top of the Gondola, Eagle's Nest. You can ski the lower part of Bwana from Born Free Express Lift if you head west as you get off of the Born Free Express Lift (Chairlift #8). Farther down Born Free there is another junction with Bwana (a fork in the trail with Bwana to the left while Born Free heads off to the right).

SAFARI (Blue and black): Safari is an interesting run which lies between Simba and Bwana. However, it does not start at the top of the mountain. It can be reached from either Simba or Bwana. Safari has three different entrances. First, skiers from Simba can use an expert route to access Safari. (Bwana skiers can also reach this advanced route by skiing the westerly road from Bwana to Simba.) A little farther down Simba, advanced intermediate skiers will find a second, more moderate entrance to Safari. Finally, a third entrance, this time from Bwana, allows skiers to access Safari over "more difficult" terrain. This last entrance to Safari is the only one you can take if you are skiing Bwana from the top of Born Free Express Lift. Safari is skied less than Simba or Bwana. Skiing Safari is a lot of fun. Examine the entrance pitches. If the entrance to Safari feels all right for you then the rest of the trail will be fun right up to the end where Safari does have a most difficult pitch. This is easy to avoid if you make a westerly/left turn onto Cheetah to reach Simba (below Simba's most difficult face).

CHEETAH (Blue): Cheetah is the way to avoid first the expert section of Simba by skiing over to the moderate section of Safari; then avoid the expert section of Safari by skiing Cheetah to the moderate section of Simba.

PRIDE (Black): Pride is fun. It is labeled a most difficult run. As with Safari, examine the entrance. The first pitch is quite steep. However, if you can get down this steep pitch, you will find the remainder a wonderful series of rolling hills. These hills will be skied less than the other Lionshead slopes, because of the expert labeling. So, go for it. Pride does merge back into Bwana, quite a ways before the Glade trails.

THE GLADE (Green and black):   The upper Glade slopes are great, moderate slopes. You generally enter the Glade from the east side of Bwana. You ski off into a glade of trees. Although you are in the trees, the trail has sufficient width to enjoy skiing wonderful gentle pitches. If you are skiing with a young child, be sure to take he or she into this magical area. You can enter the Glade from Born Free if you watch for the narrow trail on the left, slightly above Minnie's Lift (Chairlift #9).

The Glade does turn into a most difficult run after a while. So watch the signs. If you want to ski out of the Glade above the first expert section, head to the left back onto Bwana; then head back to the right to Born Free Express. If you ski the first expert section which is not too long or difficult, but wish to avoid the second section (which is longer and steeper), then head east on the catwalk to Born Free. On your map these trail changes are indicated by the label "Bwana Loop."

The most difficult sections of the Glade can be interesting tests for expert skiers. They are great pitches in fresh powder, but a problem is that the base is man made snow which can get slick and difficult to navigate when the powder is skied off.

BORN FREE (Blue and green):   Born Free is a long run from Eagle's Nest all the way to the base. It is a straight and therefore steeper than the runs which traverse around the mountain. Born Free is often groomed and makes for great cruising; be careful though, you can pick up a lot of speed on this run. The lower portion of Born Free is designated as a "slow skiing zone."

When you take Born Free from Eagle's Nest, eventually you will come to the section adjacent to the top of the Born Free Express (Chairlift #8). Be careful as there may be a significant grouping of people to avoid.

The section just below the top of the Born Free Express can be difficult, especially if it has not been groomed. It has a double fall line and can be slick.

Below this sometimes difficult section, Born Free eases up again into a great cruising area. You could turn onto Bwana here or ski to Minnie's Lift (Chairlift #9) on the right side of Born Free. Note there is a pathway to Glade if you watch carefully on the left just above Minnie's Lift. You can reach this path from Lion's Way as it reaches Born Free and from the base of Minnie's Mile.

Staying on Born Free, one last pitch needs to be watched carefully, especially at the end of the day when everyone, yes everyone, is sliding down its slick face at the same time. Take it easy; heed the GO SLOW signs. Be sure to honor the Ski Patrol and the control gates. This slope can be avoided by heading right onto Vail Village Catwalk and returning on Lionshead Catwalk. The ski school brings new skiers down in the Gondola to avoid this crowded situation; consider this, especially if you are tired.

LITTLE EAGLE LIFT (Chairlift #15):   This beginner area serves the students in Ski School. Beginners and instructors arrive here via the Gondola. While the Chairlift #15 beginner area fits in a relatively small space, it offers a wide variety of terrain for beginning adults and children. That's right. There are kids here too, and they often improve faster than the adults. In addition to Chairlift #15, Eagles's Nest Surface Lift (Poma Lift #18) operates in Gitchegumee Gulch. This area is near the teepees. The kids love this area. Your children may want you to race down the course set up here.

LEAVING AND CONNECTING WITH OTHER CENTERS

If you take the Gondola up you can have several choices. If you are anxious to get to the bowls, you can take Game Trail into Game Creek Bowl. This is not much of a run but basically a catwalk; nevertheless, it allows you to reach the bottom of the Game Creek Express Lift in a hurry. At the top of Game Creek Bowl you can choose to ski Sun Down Bowl; Mid-Vail Center; or Avanti Express Center as well as Game Creek Bowl Center. On a powder day this trail could be the quickest way to Sun Down Bowl.

Leaving Lionshead Center most skiers head east to the Avanti Express Lift (Chairlift #2). From the Gondola you have a variety of trails to choose from as you head to the Avanti Express Lift. You can ski down Born Free to Cub's Way and then head east (see below). Alternatively, you can ski through the beginners area on Owl's Roost, being sure not to frighten the novice skiers. You then have a choice of skiing Minnie's Mile, Ledges, Columbine, Lodgepole, or lower Berries to the Avanti Express Lift. All of these runs take off from Owl's Roost which traverses first east and back to the west across these trails. From Minnie's Mile and Ledges you need to make a right/easterly turn on Cub's Way

To leave from the top of Born Free Express Lift (Chairlift #8) take Cub's Way to the east. As you go down the catwalk, you will pass by Minnie's Mile and Ledges; this provides the opportunity to look up and down at these runs in Minnie's Mile Center. Ski past these trails. When you reach Columbine start heading downhill. Note that some people will call this short segment Lodgepole Gulch and others will see it as part of Lion's Way. Nevertheless, skiing over to the right side of the trail will bring you closer to the Avanti Express Lift(Chairlift #2) loading area. If you feel this section of the ski area is too difficult, stay to the left and you will be able to continue taking Cub's Way down to a catwalk section of Lion's Way.

As noted previously, Post Road will take you past Simba, Safari, and Bwana to Born Free a short way above the Minnie's Lift (Chairlift #9). Then you can ski Minnie's Mile Center or continue on Post Road until you reach Bear Tree in Vail Village Center.

4. MINNIE'S MILE CENTER (Minnie's Lift, Chairlift #9)

INTRODUCTION

Minnie's Mile Center is a small, two trail Center sandwiched between the Lionshead Center and the Avanti Express Center. It has its own unique personality. The runs are Minnie's Mile and Ledges. Here you can also find the Magic Forest, if you look carefully. The Center is north facing, resulting in flat light towards the end of the ski day. Unless you are excellent at bump skiing, it may be prudent to avoid Minnie's Mile for your last run of the day.

ARRIVAL

You can arrive at the Minnie's Mile Center a number of ways. You can take either the Gondola or the Born Free Express (Chairlift #8) and ski to the base of Minnie's Lift (Chairlift #9), entering the Center at the bottom.

Alternatively, you can head east on Cub's Way and catch the lower (and most difficult) parts of Minnie's Mile or Ledges. Cub's Way can be reached either from the Gondola or Born Free Express. Another choice is to leave the top of the Gondola and head east through the beginner area. On Owl's Roost, just before heading through the trees to Ledges, you will be able to enter Minnie's Mile. At this point, if you look uphill you will see the top of Minnie's Lift (Chairlift #9), the real top of Minnie's Mile. Likewise just after the trees at Ledges you can look up towards its start off of Eagle's Nest Ridge before skiing down.

You also can arrive at the top of the Minnie's Mile Center either from the top of Chairlift #9 or from the top of Avanti Express (Chairlift #2). From the top of Chairlift #9, Minnie's Mile will be the run that you have just ascended over while Ledges is one run over to the east. From the top of the Avanti Express Lift (Chairlift #2) you ski west down Eagle's Nest Ridge. You will pass a number of trail entrances. Then you will come to Ledges; and the next entrance is Minnie's Mile.

THE LIFT

Minnie's Lift (Chairlift #9) is a regular speed two passenger lift. It is slow

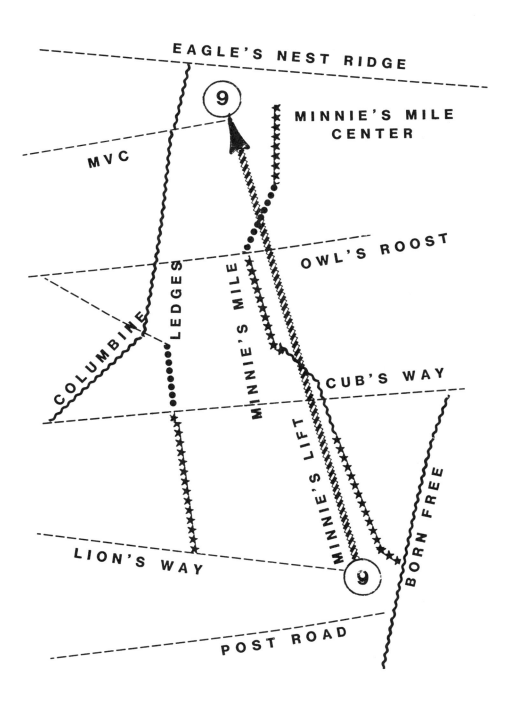

EAGLE'S NEST RIDGE

MINNIE'S MILE CENTER

MVC

OWL'S ROOST

COLUMBINE

LEDGES

MINNIE'S MILE

MINNIE'S LIFT

CUB'S WAY

BORN FREE

LION'S WAY

POST ROAD

but scenic as it passes through groves of aspen and evergreen. You are well protected from the wind by the trees, except for the very last section. There are virtually no lines on this lift except for the most crowded days. You get a good look at some of the difficult sections of Minnie's Mile as you go up this lift. If you are anxious about taking Minnie's Mile, you can still reach Minnie's lift. Ski Born Free either from the top of the Born Free Express Lift or from the Lionshead Gondola to reach Minnie's Lift. Now you have a chance to preview Minnie's Mile as you ride up the chairlift. Magical Forest, one of the Children's Mountain Adventure attractions, is in this Center.

THE RUNS

MINNIE'S MILE (Black): Minnie's Mile begins with a short, very steep pitch, often with a lot of moguls. Skiing can be best at the sides of this section, especially the side under the chairlift. Then you encounter a flat section, essentially the same terrain as the Chairlift #15 beginner's area.

The next section of Minnie's Mile is steep again with plenty of moguls. Here too, the best bumps can often be found under Chairlift #9; this is because there is a single fall line here. However, the whole trail can be fun, even where there is a double fall line. Enough width exists here to make for a number of entertaining runs, each one different in its own way. Remember, this is a north facing slope, so it should not get icy; however the light can be flat at the end of the day. (Magical Forest is off to your right at this time).

Minnie's Mile again becomes quite flat until you reach Cub's Way. From Cub's Way, you can get a look down at lower Minnie's; do not be fooled by the relatively easy terrain you see from here as it does get steeper and bumpier, for experts. When you do get to the mogul section, be ready with quick feet. The bumps initially do not have big drop offs, but they do require quick turns to hold your line. Gradually, the run becomes steeper and the bumps are bigger. This can be difficult skiing territory. If you ski far to the right, you will often find good crud snow. As you ski off to your left at the bottom of the run, you will be on Born Free just above Minnie's Mile Lift (Chairlift #9).

LEDGES (Green, blue, and black): Ledges is an interesting run in a couple of ways. First of all you will see Starter's Shacks on the run because this is where the World Cup races begin. This top segment is Ledges' intermediate section. Ledges is also interesting because it goes from intermediate to easy and then to most difficult. If you don't pay close attention to the signs, you could easily be skiing from intermediate Ledges onto intermediate Columbine; this is the way the racers ski on their way to International and the finish of the race in Vail Village.

However, by staying left and continuing past the yellow "slow" sign, you will be skiing the easy segment of Ledges. Look to your left and note the Magical Forest area for some fun skiing, especially with kids.

Soon you reach Cub's Way. The expert section of Ledges commences here. It will look pretty steep from Cub's Way, but there is an even steeper section just over the last visible lip. So be prepared. Ledges is groomed a great deal more often than Minnie's Mile, so it usually does not contain a lot of big moguls. As you complete the last section of Ledges you will come upon Lion's Way Catwalk leading to Born Free just above Minnie's Lift.

LEAVING AND CONNECTING WITH OTHER CENTERS

At the end of either Minnie's Mile or Ledges you will be on Born Free. You can ski down to the Lionshead base and start skiing Lionshead Center (maybe that last Gondola ride up to end the day with a cruiser). Just below Minnie's Lift you can get on the Post Road Catwalk to ski Bear Tree for a finish in Vail Village.

As you ski down Ledges several different cutoffs lead to the Avanti Express Center including Owl's Roost, Columbine, or Cub's Way. If you are skiing down Minnie's Mile, you can turn to the east on Cub's Way to reach the Avanti Express Center.

5. AVANTI EXPRESS CENTER (Avanti Express Lift, Chairlift #2)

INTRODUCTION

The Avanti Express Center is in the middle of Vail Mountain's front side, just to the west of the Mid-Vail Center. Consequently skiers use it to move from the west side of the mountain to the east side and vice versa. Usually skiers are moving east at the beginning of the day to get from the Lionshead side to Mid-Vail and beyond; at the end of the day these skiers are moving west in the Lionshead direction.

Though a good springboard to other centers, Avanti Express Center has its own array of fun, enjoyable, and even daring ski trails. Most of these runs tend to be cruisers which are frequently groomed. Nevertheless, if you want, there are plenty of moguls to be skied here. During the middle of the day if you stay in this Center you usually can ski with short lift lines. You can always move east to Mid-Vail or west to Eagle's Nest in order to eat or use the facilities. There is a superb Dog Haus gourmet hot dog stand at the base of this area, east of the lift with a number of picnic tables. Jebbie's Deck is located at the side of Avanti providing picnic tables (without a food stand) where you can rest or eat your own lunch.

Note there are two diagram maps for the Avanti Express Center; one is for runs to the west of the Avanti Express Lift (Chairlift #2) while the other is for runs to the east of the lift. Some might wonder why the runs to the east which end up in Mid-Vail are included in the Avanti Express Center. My reasoning is that people usually associate a trail with where it starts. Furthermore, utilizing Lion's Way (with or without Spruce Face and Gitalong Road) brings the skier back to the base of the Avanti Express Lift; this may be the right blend of trails for many people to ski.

ARRIVAL

You can reach the Avanti Express Center in several ways. You can take the Born Free Express Lift (Chairlift #8) and then ski east on Cub's Way until you reach the bottom of Columbine. Then head downhill in a northeasterly direction and you will find the base of the lift. If you find this path too challenging, stay to the left of Columbine and you will be able to take another section of Cub's Way to get down to the Avanti Express Lift base.

If you take the Gondola up to Eagle's Nest, you can head for the Avanti Express Center by skiing through the beginners area on Chairlift #15 (being careful not to bother classes). You could take Minnie's Mile down to Cub's Way, if you are an expert skier, or you could ski out onto Owl's Roost. From Owl's Roost you can take Ledges, Ledges to Columbine, Lodgepole, or Lower Berries.

When the Giant Steps Lift (Chairlift #1) is running out of Vail Village, it will bring you to the base of the Avanti Express Center. If you take the Vista Bahn, you can ski down Lion's Way to the Avanti Express Center. I will detail the different skiing opportunities other than the Lion's Way Catwalk later in this section.

From the top of Chairlifts #3 and #7 in the Wildwood area you will be able to ski Eagle's Nest Ridge to reach the top of the Avanti Express Lift.

THE LIFT

The Avanti Express Lift (Chairlift #2) is a high-speed quadruple passenger chairlift. It takes you from the base of the Avanti Express Center to the top, giving you an excellent view of Avanti trail. You can also see Cookshack and Pickeroon off to your right. On the left you can see the Bobsled run.

THE RUNS

Runs that are generally seen as part of the Avanti Express Center include upper Ledges, Columbine, Lodgepole, Berries, Pickeroon, Cookshack, Avanti,

Black Forest, Challenge, Over Easy, Mid Vail Express, Meadows, and Spruce Face. These runs can all be seen in the mid-mountain section of the front side Vail Mountain ski map on both sides of the Avanti Express Lift. For clarity of cognitive mapping they are divided into the runs which are west of Avanti Express Lift and those which head east. Note that while we consider Ledges as a whole run to be in the Minnie's Mile Center, upper Ledges (Blue and green) is frequently skied by intermediates who are sticking to the Avanti Express Center by switching to Columbine at the midway point or turning right on Cub's Way after the easy section.

Runs To The West Of The Avanti Express Lift

AVANTI (Blue and black):   Avanti is a fun run which is frequently groomed. Usually either Avanti or Pickeroon will be groomed on a given day. They are similar slopes with a gradual moderately difficult drop on a wide slope for a long distance. This is a great place to cruise and have fun. Eventually, you arrive at a steep face which can test your abilities. However, you can make a right turn onto Cold Feet and ski around the steep face. This run is relatively flat and easy the rest of the way back to the Avanti Express Lift (Chairlift #2). You also have the choice of taking Black Forest, just to the right of Avanti, which can be fun.

If you take Cold Feet down to Lion's Way you will pass by the top of the Bobsled Run.

BLACK FOREST (Blue):   Black Forest takes off from the right side of Avanti. Often its conditions are the same as the conditions on Avanti. However, it is less groomed. It can develop some playful moguls without steep drop- offs. This can help you with your mogul skiing. Also, on a powder day, Black Forest can remain untracked longer than Avanti.

PICKEROON (Blue and black):   Pickeroon, a moderately steep wide run making for great cruising, is frequently groomed. You will run into a difficult face, however, so be careful. On the other hand if you really want difficulty, take the cutoff to the right and ski Cookshack. If you ski Pickeroon, there is no escape from the very steep face as there is on Avanti.

COOKSHACK (Black):   Cookshack is a steep moguled run with good lines. It is an excellent place to work on mogul skiing. Usually there is a pretty good rhythm to the bumps. It can be a great playland when there is signifi- cant powder. You reach it by skiing the top of Pickeroon, and watching on the right hand side until you see the sign. Portions of Cookshack can be skied from Avanti if you watch for openings on Avanti's left.

31

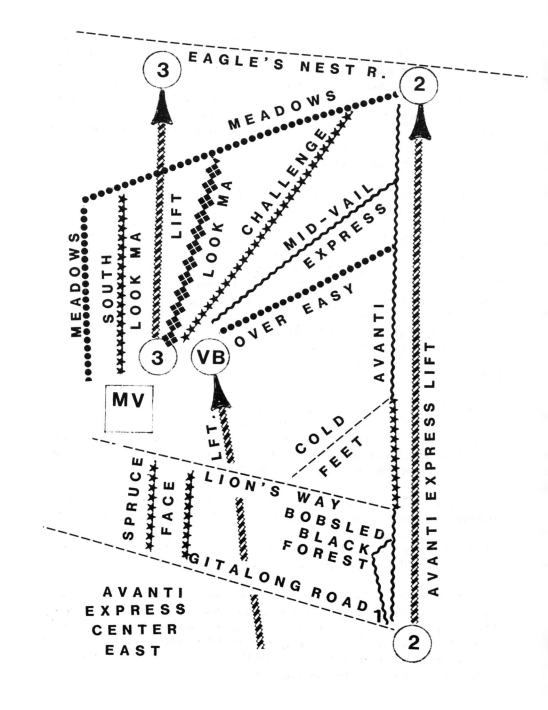

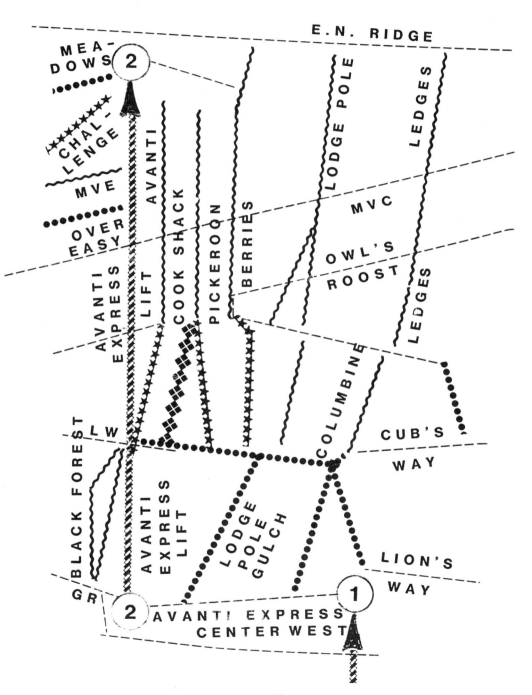

33

BERRIES (Blue and black): To the west of Pickeroon lies Berries. Berries gets its share of grooming. Upper Berries is not a difficult run. It parallels Pickeroon and frequently intermixes with it. Skiing to the left keeps you on Berries. However, the last pitch of Berries can be very difficult. You do have other choices. Since you are at Owl's Roost you can ski onto Lodgepole, Columbine or Ledges. But if you are up to the challenge, take on Berries' most difficult section. It will lead you to Lodgepole Gulch and Avanti Express Lift.

Runs To The East Of Avanti Express Lift

OVER EASY (Green): Over Easy is a run that takes you to Mid-Vail. It is frequently groomed and should be the beginner's choice. You start down Avanti to the right/east of the lift. Do not turn onto the Mid-Vail Express cut off as that will put you on more difficult terrain, less likely to be groomed. Even though this trail ends up in the Mid-Vail Center, I am mapping it as a part of the Avanti Express Center because you can head back to Chairlift #2 by utilizing Lion's Way or Spruce Face and Gitalong Road.

MID-VAIL EXPRESS (Blue): Mid-Vail Express is a slightly more difficult version of Over Easy. It cuts off from the right side of Avanti before Over Easy. This terrain presents more challenges, but if you are a solid intermediate skier you should be able to make it down. If you really hang to the right towards the bottom of this run, you can ski part way into Challenge and get some good bumps for a short distance. While the bumps are big, because mainly excellent skiers have skied the terrain, it is not real steep. As you ski down Mid-Vail Express, you may find some people skiing down through the woods towards you. These are the powder hounds and adventure skiers. As with Over Easy, you can ski back to Chairlift #2 by utilizing Lion's Way or Spruce Face and Gitalong Road.

CHALLENGE (Black): Challenge can be a little hard to find, but it is well worth it if you like bumps. Just ski northeast from the top of the chairlift and look for the Challenge sign. Keep heading that way. If you end up in the trees rather than strictly on Challenge, relax; this might be a lot of fun. Challenge is an expert, bumpy run. However, it is not as steep as Look Ma. The first couple of turns can look steep but the bumps are well rounded and generally easy to ski. Nevertheless, you might not want to make it your first run of the day. First do an Avanti or a Pickeroon (whichever is groomed) and get the blood pumping in your legs. By taking Challenge you will end up in Mid-Vail and can take Lion's Way or Spruce Face back to the Avanti Express.

THE MEADOWS (Green): If you head due east from the top of the Avanti Express Lift, you will be on an easy, wide trail, the Meadows. It will take you past Challenge, Look Ma, and South Look Ma. After this you should be able to locate an easy way down to Mid-Vail.

LION'S WAY CATWALK: Find Lion's Way Catwalk originating just east of the Mid-Vail building. Take it west to Avanti, passing by the cutoff to Spruce Face, the moguly lift line pitch, and the bobsled.

SPRUCE FACE (Blue):   I have skied with people who have been on Vail Mountain for over a decade and not recognized Spruce Face. They just ski by it on Lion's Way enroute to the Avanti Express Lift. Spruce Face is a great mogul run, especially for those who are a little afraid of moguls. You will frequently see kids on Spruce Face with their parents or on their own. They often go in in packs, either with a ski instructor or without one. The bumps tend to be small and quick. The fall line keeps moving you to the left, so be aware of this and perhaps make some stronger turns to the right.

If you do stay to the top of Spruce Face on the right you can burst through some trees to another, more narrow mogul alley. Also, if you stay on Lion's Way a little longer, you will find a rather wide lift line pathway with excellent large bumps. This is great skiing, too, but somehow just doesn't have the fun of Spruce Face.

Where does all this get you? It gets you to Gitalong Road (another catwalk) which will lead you to the base of the Avanti Express Center Lift (Chairlift #2.) The catwalk is long (you even pass the Vista Bahn twice) but you will get to Avanti. Just before Gitalong Road reaches Avanti, there is another short, steep section that you can take off to the right of the track. This can be fun to ski straight or with a lot of turns. It is an excellent practice spot; don't make it into just another ho hum short run. At the base of this short drop is the entrance to the wooded Indian Burial Ground. Kids will ski in it over and over as it has a multitude of pathways. You also can enter the Indian Burial Ground from Avanti or Black Forest.

LEAVING AND CONNECTING WITH OTHER CENTERS

Leaving the Avanti Express Lift from its base is essentially the same as skiing Vail Village Center from the top of Giant Steps Lift, Chairlift #1. Turn to that section for this information. You can take Lion's Way to the west and reach Minnie's Mile Center or Lionshead Center.

There are a few ways to leave the Avanti Express Center from the top. The first way is to ski the trails which lead to Mid-Vail: Over Easy, Mid-Vail Express, Challenge, and Meadows. Additionally, Look Ma and South Look Ma will take you to Mid-Vail. These two trails are described in the Hunky Dory portion of the Mid-Vail Center.

Alternatively, you can ski straight off the top of the Avanti Express Lift and enter the Game Creek Bowl Center, skiing on Faro, Ouzo, or Ouzo Glade. Check out the section on the Game Creek Bowl Center before you make the plunge because these are expert runs facing south where the sun can make the snow tricky.

Additionally, from the top of the Avanti Express Center you can ski west down Eagle's Nest Ridge into either Minnie's Mile Center or Lionshead Center.

6. THE MID-VAIL CENTER (Mountain Top Express, Chairlift #4 and Hunky Dory Lift, Chairlift #3)

INTRODUCTION

Mid-Vail the middle place on the front side of the mountain; hence, its name. It lies in the middle of the mountain from an east-west perspective and half way up the front side of the mountain.

Almost every skier from intermediate to expert will make a run each day in the Mid-Vail Center. This can be the place "to be;" it can also be the place to be avoided, since so many people are there. Riva and Riva Glade are discussed in this section. Even though these runs do not return you to Mid-Vail, they are most frequently skied out of Mid-Vail.

Many people make plans to meet at Mid-Vail, but it is easy for skiers to miss a meeting in big bustling Mid-Vail. Mid-Vail has two cafeterias as well as a sit-down restaurant. It also has a huge outdoor terrace with barbecue facilities for warm weather. The rule is to be very specific about where and when to meet.

The cafeterias are Look Ma on the third level and the Terrace on the second level. The Cook Shack on the first level is the sit-down full-service restaurant. The huge outdoor terrace is on the Terrace level. There is also a small terrace at the Cookshack level. On sunny days, enjoy the lounge chairs here. Also, there is a waiter/bartender serving the area. Remember to put on more sun screen before snoozing off.

Mid-Vail also has a Complete Skier outlet for accessories (sun screen, sun glasses, goggles, neck gators, hats). On the third floor, the Look Ma level, there is a Vail Ski School Center for arranging private lessons or afternoon workshops. At 11:00 a.m. each day, you can have a free run with a ski instructor. This is the Ski Tips program. A seasoned instructor will analyze your skiing quickly and let you know about fitting into the afternoon ski workshops for maximum improvement towards your skiing goal. Look for more information on afternoon ski workshops under the adult ski school section of this book.

Note two race courses in Mid-Vail Center. The pay-to-race is between Swingsville and Christmas. The NASTAR is next to Hunky Dory.

ARRIVAL

The simplest way to get to Mid-Vail is via the Vista Bahn Express (Chairlift #16), directly up from Vail Village. As you get off the chairlift you see the Mid-Vail building and two chairlifts rising out of Mid-Vail.

The two chairlifts are the Mountain Top Express (Chairlift #4) at left and the Hunky Dory Lift (Chairlift #3) to the right. Utilizing these two chairs you can ski a rainbow of runs which will bring you right back to the Mid-Vail area. These two lifts can also take you into other centers.

To reach Mid-Vail from Golden Peak you are best advised to take the Golden Peak Lift (Chairlift #6) and ski over to the Vista Bahn Express.

From Lionshead, you can take either the Born Free Express Lift (Chairlift #8) or the Lionshead Gondola to access Mid-Vail. In either case, head east to the Avanti Express Lift (Chairlift #2). From the top of Born Free Express (Chairlift #8) take Cub's Way to the east. From Eagle's Nest at the top of the Gondola you can select from different routes a path to the east to reach the Avanti Express Lift. Consult the section on leaving the Lionshead Center for more information.

From the top of the Avanti Express Center (Chairlift #2) there are various ways to ski to Mid-Vail, including Over Easy, Mid-Vail Express, Challenge, Look Ma, South Look Ma, and the Meadows. Consult the section on leaving the Avanti Express Center for additional information on this topic.

THE LIFTS

The Hunky Dory Lift (Chairlift #3) is a regular speed three passenger chairlift. It carries you from Mid-Vail up to Wildwood. Wildwood is where the Wildwood Restaurant is located. It is also at the top of the Game Creek Express Lift (Chairlift #7). While riding up the Hunky Dory Lift, you get a good look at Look Ma, the NASTAR Race Course, and Kangaroo Cornice.

The Mountain Top Express Lift (Chairlift #4) is a high-speed quadruple passenger chairlift which takes you from Mid-Vail to Mountain Top/PHQ. The Northwoods Express Lift (Chairlift #11) and the High Noon Lift (Chairlift #5) also top out at Mountain Top/PHQ. Riding up this lift, you only get a look at the unnamed lift line trail. A look at the cliffs will encourage you to take the named runs.

THE RUNS

Mountain Top Express (Chairlift # 4) Group Of Trails

From Mountain Top/PHQ you can start off skiing either Upper Swingsville or Ramshorn.

UPPER SWINGSVILLE (Green): Ski north from the summit onto upper Swingsville to reach a variety of trails that will return you to Mid-Vail.

These trails are off the left (west) side of upper Swingsville. (The runs off the right side of upper Swingsville are part of the Northwoods Express Center and discussed under that section.) First there is a cutoff to Powerline and Ramshorn which we will discuss later. Then there is an unnamed "lift line" run (which has the cliffs). Next comes Zot; then Whistle Pig; then Expresso; then Cappuccino; then Swingsville (itself), a designated family area; and finally Christmas. If you go beyond Christmas onto Riva Ridge or Prima you are heading into a different section which low intermediate and novice skiers need to avoid. Riva Ridge and Riva Glade will be discussed in this section, but they do not lead back to Mid-Vail; they take you to the bottom of Vail Mountain.

Skiing the runs discussed here will allow you easy access to the backside maze of Chairlift #4 which is often less crowded than the restaurant side maze. You can ski over to Chairlift #3 or into the Mid-Vail restaurant area.

CHRISTMAS (Green): Christmas is a easier run which can be friendly, although for a low intermediate skiers it will take some work. It is frequently groomed. Its pitch is moderate and steady. There are a few trees, giving the area a lovely glade feeling.

SWINGSVILLE (Blue and green): Swingsville is an easier slope of moderate pitch that Vail has designated as a safe, slow, family area. It is frequently groomed. Ski with your family or practice your moves, but don't ski fast. You will almost always see a person in a red coat from Vail Skier's Services perched at the bottom of the run looking out for your safety and the safety of others. This person has the authority to take away your lift ticket or ski pass for abuse of the "slow skiing" area.

Ironically, in this "slow area" there is a fenced off race course. This is a pay- to-race dual slalom course on which you can challenge your friend, mate or enemy. Your times will come up in lights at the bottom. You can also reach this race course from Christmas.

CAPPUCCINO (Blue): Cappuccino is a great, although slightly more difficult, glade run with a moderate pitch. The trees at the top make it a little difficult to find, so it is skied less than the other west facing runs. Also, it is frequently groomed. It is a good trail for getting in ski mileage while building up your strength and skiing skills.

EXPRESSO (Blue): Expresso is a more difficult run which is allowed to develop naturally without intensive grooming. Significant moguls may build up. Indeed, it may become a mogul field -- a great spot to work on your abilities in uneven terrain. The moguls are not as difficult as those on Whistle Pig or Zot. So begin here for bump experience. You can always go back to Swingsville to work on your fundamentals.

WHISTLE PIG (Blue and black): Whistle Pig is definitely a more difficult run. When its moguls are built up, it skis like an advanced mogul run. The drop-offs may not be huge, but there is a need to turn your skis quickly in rhythm with the bumps while also absorbing them. If you are moving ahead with your mogul skiing, this may be the place to be. Note that towards the end of the trail Whistle Pig merges into Zot.

ZOT (Black): The top of Zot looks oh so tempting to the beginner or intermediate skier. It is flat, and you may only see a few ripples. Don't be fooled. There is a steep pitch up ahead; Zot does deserve its most difficult rating. The steep face of Zot has big moguls. There may be some rocks lurking in the grooves of the first few bumps. This is an interesting pitch as you can see some people grooving down it, while others are hesitant and fearful. Everyone seems to complain about the lack of a consistent "line." Below the very steep pitch, there is still some very good mogul skiing. If you can handle this, you can move over even further to the left and catch some of the major bumps situated under Chairlift #4. At this point, you are below the cliffs, so it may be fun to ski in this unnamed section.

LIFT LINE (Black): Like Zot, the unlabeled "lift line" starts off gentle. Then you run into a sign which states "Cliffs Ahead." Sometimes it is roped off, barring entry. Often it is not roped off, especially on a powder day or a spring afternoon. If you are intelligent, you turn left over to Powerline and Ramshorn. But as you are coming up the Mountain Top Express, you will notice that people are jumping the cliffs. Isn't it wonderful that you get to share all of this vicariously? If you ski left from Zot at the bottom of Zot's steep face you will be able to ski "lift line" run below the cliffs and find some excellent moguls.

POWERLINE (Blue): You can reach Powerline two ways from the top of the Mountain Top Express (Chairlift #4). From Mountain Top/PHQ start down upper Swingsville. (1) Make a quick left and then a quick right onto Powerline. (2) Ski off to the west on upper Ramshorn, look for a very narrow trail through the trees, which can be fun but can also be intimidating. As you come out of the trees, look uphill to see if anyone is coming at you.
    If you are in a group, the first person through the trees should take on

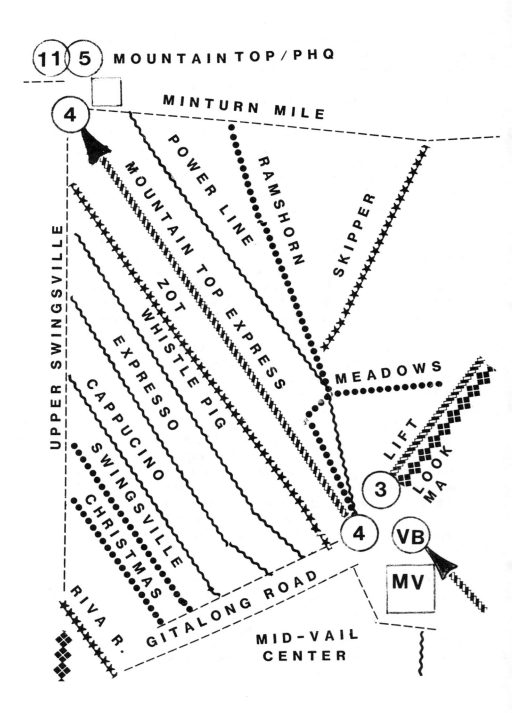

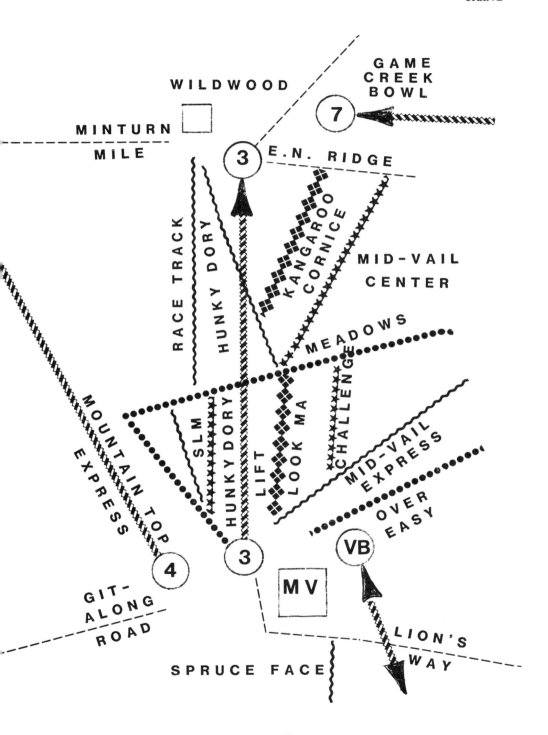

the lookout responsibility.

Here you are at the top of Powerline, a trail often left in a natural state. If you don't like what you see, you can keep heading west to catch Ramshorn. Powerline is usually fun. It often has small moguls. Occasionally it has big bumps, although this seems to be mainly during the beginning of the year when other major bump runs are not yet open (to keep the experts happy). If you look closely, during almost any part of the year you can find a few good bumps, often on the right hand side. Powerline does dovetail left (to the west) into Ramshorn about two thirds of the way down Ramshorn.

RAMSHORN (Green and blue): Don't let the green signage on Ramshorn fool you. If you are a novice, it is a long run. While it is frequently groomed, the groom gets skied off early in the day. If it is slick, novices may be overturning which takes a lot of energy. I'm not saying don't ski it; just be prepared to take a while to get down.

By the way, there are also two ways to get to Ramshorn. If you start down the upper Swingsville way, be prepared to make a quick left and then just ski by the top of Powerline. Or head directly west from the top of Mountain Top/PHQ and you will be on Ramshorn. Note that Powerline connects back into Ramshorn about two thirds of the way down Ramshorn.

Eventually Ramshorn gets more difficult, just before heading into Mid-Vail. If your mood is blue at this point, you can take a sharp right turn and ski the rest of the way into Mid-Vail on Meadows (Green). Or you might want to do some mogul skiing on the left side of South Look Ma. You can get over to steep and mogully Look Ma from here if you make a sharp left. Groomers often leave some bumps on the right of South Look Ma. Watch carefully for trees in the corner of the connection between Ramshorn and the Meadows. There will be a few interesting turns here for expert skiers.

SKIPPER (Black): One pathway to reach Skipper is to ski Ramshorn directly to the west, look for the Skipper sign on your left. While Ramshorn turns right (north), you can take a jog onto Minturn Mile, a catwalk that continues west. This is also the way to the two Windows openings into Sundown Bowl Center, discussed under the Sundown Bowl Center section. To access Skipper, take a right at the first fork in the trail. Another way is to ski east on Minturn Mile from the top of the Hunky Dory Lift (Chairlift #30. Most traffic comes from Mountain Top/PHQ.

Skipper is a broad, steep, heavily moguled slope. Enjoy wonderful skiing, especially with plenty of powder. Since only experts ski here, by and large, the dropoffs between turns are big and the flat spots are short, but well-placed for the expert. Skipper merges into Ramshorn about two thirds of the way down Ramshorn. As you come out from the trees, look uphill because a lot of skiers like to zoom down the left hand side of Ramshorn.

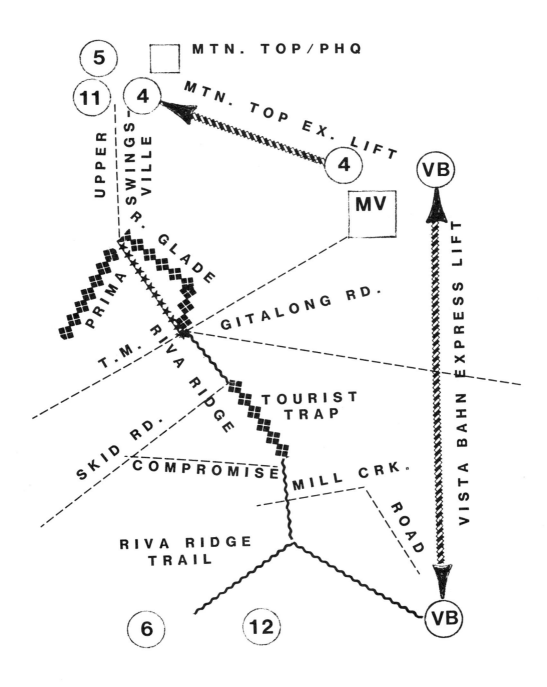

RIVA RIDGE (Black):   We will discuss Riva Ridge here. It belongs in this section because it comes off upper Swingsville to the left. However, it does not end up at Mid-Vail. It is a long run taking you to the bottom of Vail Mountain on the Golden Peak side. It is a wide, steep trail. Aptly named Tourist Trap is a steeper section of Riva Ridge about two thirds of the way down Riva Ridge. It is exciting. The conditions may be excellent, or there may be some big moguls, but it can also be very slick, leading to a "slide for life" on your butt down to the bottom. You can avoid Tourist Trap by skiing off to the right down Skid Road and then turning sharply left and cutting back to Riva Ridge on Compromise. You will return to the Riva Ridge trail below Tourist Trap. After a few more pitches, you will come to road area, which is flat. Do not take the turn to the left onto Mill Creek Road, even if it has a sign saying Vail Village, unless you want to take the slow route. Rather forge straight ahead. You will reach Golden Peak on its western side. Sometimes, the first steep section here in Golden Peak is icy or scraped off. Watch out for it. From here you can ski to the base of Golden Peak or over to Vail Village and the Vista Bahn Express.

If you had continued on Skid Road past Compromise you would reach Chairlift #10 at the base of Double Diamond Center. Along the way you would have had choices of turning back to Riva Ridge below Tourist Trap on North Face Catwalk or skiing the intermediate portion of Prima to Chairlift #6.

You can reach Riva Ridge skiing east from Mid-Vail on Gitalong Road. You are still above Tourist Trap on Riva Ridge. This is an excellent way to go if Chairlift #4 is crowded.

RIVA GLADE (Black):   First timers should enter Riva Glade with an experienced skier. It is in the trees to the southwest of Riva Ridge. It offers excellent bump and tree skiing for those who can handle such things. Eventually, it runs back into Riva Ridge. This book is not advising anyone to ski Riva Glade. We are just letting you know it is there; it is on the official ski map for Vail.

Hunky Dory Lift (Chairlift #3) Group Of Trails

HUNKY DORY (Blue):   Hunky Dory is a moderate trail heading down into the Meadows on the way back to Mid-Vail. It can be delightful, giving you a full view of this area of the mountain. Make a left turn as you get off Chairlift #3 to ski Hunky Dory. This is the Wildwood area and Wildwood Restaurant. Note that you are also at the top of the Game Creek Express (Chairlift #7).

NASTAR RACE COURSE (Blue):   There is a NASTAR Race Course set up just to the right (East) of Hunky Dory. Racing begins at 11:00 a.m.

KANGAROO CORNICE (Black):   Turn to the right (west) as you get off Chairlift #3 to get to Kangaroo Cornice. What a great name for a thrilling (if short) set of moguls that you can literally "hop down." For years skiers have noticed that the eastern pitch is very steep and that as you move west along this cornice the steepness decreases. Finally, Vail has actually put up signs labeling the most eastern section as suitable for level 9 skiers. The middle section is labeled as appropriate for level 8 skiers. The western section is labeled for level 7 skiers. A final option: you can ski around the cornice on easy terrain.

LOOK MA (Black):   After Kanagoo Cornice runs into Hunky Dory, you can ski sharply to the left (west) and enter Look Ma. You could also do this from the top of the Avanti Express (Chairlift # 2). I am placing Look Ma under the Hunky Dory Lift section because when you start up Chairlift #3 you get a great view of Look Ma. Professional mogul contests are held on steep and well moguled Look Ma. You really have to be on the trail to catch the close up action of these excellent bump skiers. You can ski it down one bump at a time, if you need to do so. At times I enjoy watching the contestants warming up on the sides more than the competition because you get a feel for how they ski the bumps naturally.
Try skiing Look Ma after a contest. The pros have skied some skiable lines into the midst of the bumps because they ski consistent turns.

SOUTH LOOK MA (Black):   South Look Ma has bumps, too. It is nice that you can ski in and out of some of these bumps onto Ramshorn. This way intermediates can get a feel for the bumps. However, this means that the moguls have some inconsistent lines. The farther you get to the left (west) and closer to the trees that separate Look Ma from South Look Ma, the bigger the bumps get.

LEAVING AND CONNECTING WITH OTHER CENTERS

Since Mid-Vail is a hub of activity and a central point, there are many interesting and exciting ways to leave. And leave it you should; don't get caught up spending a whole day just in Mid-Vail.
Without taking either of the chairlifts, there are two ways to leave the base of Mid-Vail Center. You can ski below it and to the west on Lion's Way. You will be skiing into the Avanti Express Center. If you ski to the east below the Mountain Top Express Lift (Chairlift #4), you will be heading first for Riva Ridge on the initial section of Gitalong Road. From here you can ski Riva Ridge or you can cross Riva Ridge, heading farther east on Trans Montane

Catwalk to either Prima (below the steep section) or farther on to the base of Chairlift #11 in the Northwoods Express Center. You could also stay on Gitalong Road, turning west at Riva Ridge to arrive at the base of Avanti Express Center (Chairlift #2).

From Mountain Top/PHQ at the top of the Mountain Top Express (Chairlift #4) you can ski into the Northwoods Express Center, Sun Up Bowl, and Sun Down Bowl. You can also head over towards Tea Cup Bowl, China Bowl, or Sourdough Bowl. As noted above, you can ski Riva Ridge to the base of Vail Mountain.

From the Wildwood area at the top of the Hunky Dory Lift (Chairlift #3) you can ski into Game Creek Center, over to the Avanti Express Center, and beyond to the Minnie's Mile Center and the Lionshead Center.

7. NORTHWOODS EXPRESS CENTER (Northwoods Express Lift, Chairlift #11)

INTRODUCTION

The Northwoods Express Center (Chairlift #11) is a popular skiing area, and rightfully so. It has great cruising terrain and expert bump runs. It offers the finest advanced skiing on the front side of Vail Mountain with significant portions being navigable by strong intermediates. A few runs (Log Chute, Choker Cut Off, and Northface Catwalk) are discussed under the Leaving Section because this is where they fit best as connectors between the Northwoods Express Center and other centers.

Pronto's Porch is a cabin with vending machines located on Flap Jack close to the base of the Northwoods Express Lift. Its name comes from its location at the bottom of Pronto.

ARRIVAL

The Northwoods Express Center (Chairlift #11) is reached by taking the Mountain Top Express Lift (Chairlift #4). This leaves you at the top Mountain Top/PHQ. Or, if you have skied in the back bowls, the High Noon Lift (Chairlift #5) will also get you to Mountain Top/PHQ.

THE LIFT

Northwoods Express Lift (Chairlift #11) is a high-speed quadruple passenger chairlift. Riding up the Northwoods Express Lift (Chairlift #11) you can preview most all of the trails in the Northwoods Express Center, except

Prima.

To preview Northwoods Express Center (if you are at least a strong intermediate skier) take the Northwoods trail (described below) down to the base of Chairlift #11. The ride on the chairlift will provide excellent views of a majority of the slopes, but not Prima nor the upper portion of Prima Cornice.

As you ride on the lift you will first notice Pronto on your right, which is followed by Prima Cornice. These are two steep, moguly slopes. If you see that these slopes are too difficult for you to ski, Prima is too difficult for you. After Prima Cornice comes Gandy Dancer. Gandy Dancer, although labeled an expert run, is easier to ski than the runs mentioned above.

Notice the unnamed lift line run under Chairlift #11. I do not advise skiing this path; note the rocks and double fall line.

As you approach the top of the Chairlift #11 you will get some good looks at North Rim Run and South Rim Run. These are great areas, sort of akin to the back bowl areas. They are wide and steep. South Rim Run is directly under the lift; North Rim Run is off to the right. First Step, to the left, is also visible as you approach the top of the Northwoods Express Lift.

Now you are back at Mountain Top/PHQ with a fair amount of knowledge about Northwood Express Center. From here there are two totally different paths to the trails that make up the Northwoods Express Center. (1) You can head east down Timberline Catwalk to reach South Rim Run, First Step, Northstar, Northwoods, Lower Snag Park, or Upper Snag Park. (2) You can head north down Swingsville to reach North Rim Run, Gandy Dancer, Prima, Prima Cornice, and Pronto.

THE RUNS

Runs Off Timberline Catwalk

TIMBERLINE CATWALK (Blue):   Timberline Catwalk goes off to the east from Mountain Top/PHQ leading you to First Step, Northstar and Northwoods and Snag Park. It then takes you through a wooded area to the bottom of Chairlift #14 at the base of the Sourdough Center.

Timberline Catwalk has an intermediate rating because if you head straight east on it, there is a difficult pitch, often moguly and/or scraped off. Skiing will be easier if you head south, almost as if you were heading for High Noon Ridge in the back bowls but make a left (eastern) turn on the flat catwalk just before you enter the back bowls. When it is crowded, Timberline Catwalk always provides some degree of difficulty. Adults should stay close to children, even if it means using the wedge technique.

SNAG PARK (Blue):   A short way past Northwoods, the skier reaches Snag Park. It is a broad slope, slightly more adventurous than Northwoods.

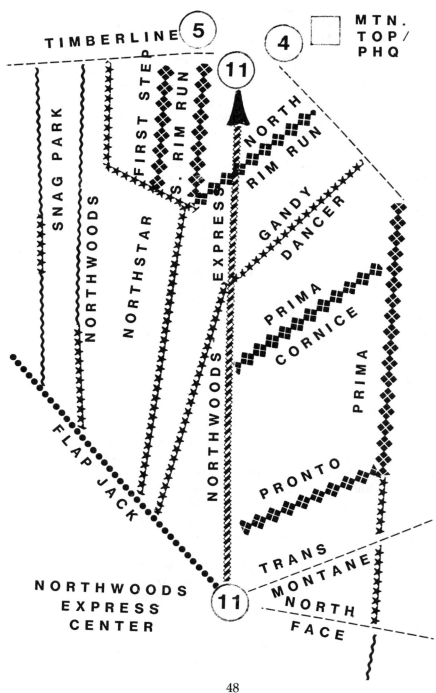

Eventually Snag Park merges with Northwoods and Flap Jack.

Snag Park is a new addition on the Vail Mountain ski map. But the name isn't new to Vail skiers. Between Northwoods and Snag Park, there is a stand of trees skiable by advanced skiers. This treed area used to be called Snag Park.

NORTHWOODS (Blue and black):   Northwoods is a cruiser run for the intermediate skier. It is a wide slope with a series of rolls from Timberline Catwalk to the bottom of the Northwoods Express Lift. At the end of each roll is a flatter section where the skier can stop and assess both technique and terrain. Northwoods is frequently groomed; this is when the cruising is excellent. At times, small bumps are allowed to build up on Northwoods, making it more of a challenge.

Where Northwoods turns into an expert slope, the merger of Northwoods, Snag Park and Flap Jack gives the skier a wide variety of terrain choices. It is easy to avoid this section by skiing off to the right onto Flap Jack, a beginner trail which leads directly to the Northwoods Express Lift.

NORTHSTAR (Black):   Northstar is just to the west of Northwoods; indeed you will get to Northstar first as you descend Timberline Catwalk. Northstar is labelled a most difficult run. Frequently at the top of Northstar a short section of large moguls will develop. After descending through the Northstar mogul field, the trail makes a sharp left turn, goes west for a ways, and then makes a sharp right turn through a little canyon as it resumes its proper downhill, northerly direction. Head to the right and slightly uphill as you come out of this canyon to stay on Northstar and avoid the lift line run. Northstar is similar in many ways to Northwoods, except it is steeper. Also, it is not groomed as often. The final steep pitch on Northstar can be difficult, especially without recent grooming. Good size moguls can often be found here. You do not have a way to avoid the steep section on this trail as you do on Northwoods.

As you go down Northstar, there are opportunities to ski under the lift line of Chairlift #11. This is a moguled pathway with a double fall line which has rocks and small cliffs. A suggestion: when you are on the chairlift enjoy the antics of those who daringly ski this lift line. I do not advise skiing this way.

FIRST STEP (Black):   First Step is located to the east of South Rim Run. It is a steep trail, well deserving its most difficult rating. It is highly moguled, and you have to deal with some rock outcroppings. An exciting run, First Step provides a test of your skiing ability. It merges into Northstar after its short but steep descent.

SOUTH RIM RUN (Black): South Rim Run is a highly moguled steep pitch that runs under the Northwoods Express Lift. It is a most difficult run; however, it is broad and there is room to maneuver.

Runs Off Upper Swingsville

UPPER SWINGSVILLE (Green): This ridge trail is a relatively flat section of Swingsville that lies between the Mid-Vail slopes and the slopes of Northwoods Express Center. Don't confuse it with the lower portion of Swingsville that heads left down to Mid-Vail. This discussion covers the runs that come off upper Swingsville on its right (eastern) side: North Rim Run, Gandy Dancer, Prima, Prima Cornice, and Pronto. Upper Swingsville is flat and easy; the problem here may be the crowds.

NORTH RIM RUN (Black): North Rim Run is a steep, highly moguled section that runs west of the Northwoods Express Lift. Please note that there are cliffs here which you may not want to jump. A suggestion: you can get your thrills watching others do the jumping as you ride safely up Chairlift #11. If you take the second entry into North Rim Run, you will avoid most of the rocks, but it will still be steep.

GANDY DANCER (Black): What a great name, for a great run. Gandy Dancer is just plain fun. Though it deserves its most difficult designation, Gandy Dancer has pitches and rolls which end in flat areas. Each pitch or roll can be an adventure. Upper intermediate and lower advanced skiers can delight in the different opportunities and adventures. Some moguls must be negotiated, and occasionally they are difficult. However, with the rest areas at the end of each of the more difficult sections, there is time to enjoy and meditate. When Gandy Dancer is groomed, it can be a real thrill to cruise. This is also an excellent run for powder days.

PRIMA (Double black diamond): Prima is primo. A double diamond, mogul studded course for experts to enjoy. Skiers cannot preview the run from any chairlift. Do not be fooled by how flat it looks at the top.
Prima begins with a relatively flat section which is still heavily moguled. It gradually gets steeper and steeper with the moguls falling off more and more. This section is called Brown's Face. Staying on top of your skis (versus sitting back) becomes more difficult as the need to finish turns but then start new ones becomes quick, precise, and exacting.
Eventually Prima does level off somewhat to allow for intermediate skiing.

PRONTO (Double black diamond): For skiers who love steep bumps, skip the moderate lower part of Prima. Rather, take the right turn at the bottom of Prima's steep face and start down Pronto. This is as steep and moguly as Prima. And, guess what? Now the people on Chairlift #11 can see you, as can the people in the Chairlift #11 maze. So, turn it on. Remember, the gullies are often quite dug out; so be ready with your absorption-extension technique.

PRIMA CORNICE (Double black diamond): Oh, yes, we skipped Prima Cornice. Actually Prima Cornice takes off to the right from the initial relatively flat part of Prima, before Brown's Face. We usually do skip by Prima Cornice, venturing in only when there is a lot of snow. If you want to do Prima Cornice, be ready for moguls, sharp drop-offs, rocks, trees. In other words, I am not advising you to take Prima Cornice. The best preview of upper Prima Cornice is from Roger's Run in the Double Diamond Center. It is the upper portion of Prima Cornice that is most difficult with rocks and trees as well as moguls.

LEAVING AND CONNECTING WITH OTHER CENTERS

Skiers can exit the Northwoods Express Center via a number of different routes. First of all, at the top of the Northwoods Express Lift you are at Mountain Top/PHQ. There are a variety of ways of heading off from here in different directions. You can enter Sun Up Bowl; Sun Down Bowl; or Mid-Vail Center directly. You can also head over to Riva Ridge and ski to the base of the mountain.

Runs Leaving Northwoods Express Center

CHOKER CUTOFF (Blue): Choker Cutoff starts below the bottom of Northwoods Express Lift (on its right/east side). It is an intermediate way to get to the Double Diamond Center (Chairlift #10). Skiing past Chairlift #10 you can reach the backside of Chairlift #6 which will lift you to the top of Golden Peak Center.

LOG CHUTE (Black): Follow Northface Catwalk from the base of Northwoods Express Lift until you reach Log Chute, an expert slope connecting Northwoods Express Center and the Double Diamond Center. Initially, Log Chute has some steeper, more difficult bumps, with deep grooves, often reaching down to rock level. However, once you get below this section, Log Chute becomes an excellent bump run with generally well rounded moguls and excellent lines. It gets a little more dynamic again towards the bottom, but by then your rhythm should be grooved and flexible.

Maybe you haven't noticed that you can ski Prima to Pronto to Log

Chute, all major mogul runs, without riding a lift. And you end up in steep moguled Double Diamond Center. Who says downhill skiing is not much exercise?

Continuing down the trail below Chairlift #10 (on its left/west side) will get you to the south side of Chairlift #6 which will take you to the top of Golden Peak Center. Remember this for days when the Highline Lift is crowded, for instance when Blue Ox has been groomed.

If you do not wish to take Log Chute, you can continue on Northface Catwalk until you reach Prima again. You can ski this very lowest section of Prima either down on the right via Skid Road to Highline Lift (Chairlift #10) in the Double Diamond Center or farther down to Chairlift #6 and the Golden Peak Center.

If you continue on Northface Catwalk past intermediate Prima, you will be skiing over to Riva Ridge below Tourist Trap. This is the best way to leave Northwoods Center if the lifts are closed down.

8. SOURDOUGH CENTER (Sourdough Lift, Chairlift #14)

INTRODUCTION

The Sourdough Center offers novice runs. It is a great place for beginners to practice. There is one intermediate run, Whiskey Jack, which has more natural terrain and some moguls to challenge a skier. What is especially nice about the Sourdough Center is the Two Elk Restaurant which is just yards away from the top of Chairlift #14. This huge new restaurant is receiving raves as the place to eat on Vail Mountain. Additionally, from the top of the Sourdough Lift you get a great view of Holy Cross Wilderness.

ARRIVAL

You can arrive at the Sourdough Center from the top of the Highline Lift (Chairlift #10) by skiing either Flap Jack or Tin Pants. You can also get to the Sourdough Center from Mountain Top/PHQ by continuing down the Timberline Catwalk past Northwoods until it runs into the base of the Sourdough Lift.

THE LIFT

The Sourdough Lift (Chairlift #14) is a regular speed three passenger chairlift. It ascends over the Sourdough trail. When you get off the lift, you will be facing one of the most magnificent views in the ski world. Take a good

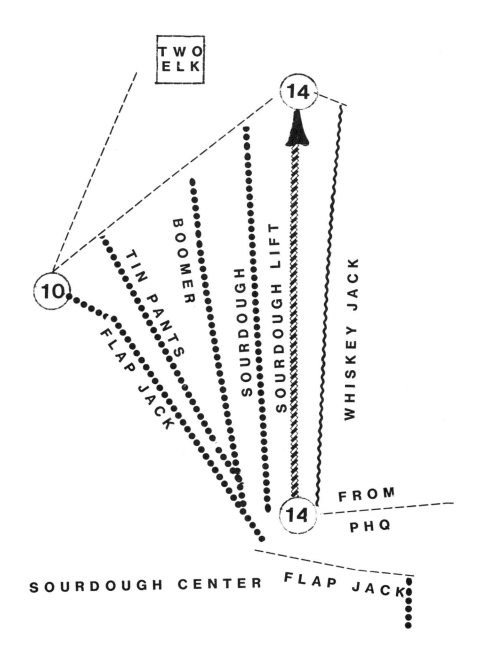

look; enjoy yourself.

RUNS

FLAP JACK (Green):   Flap Jack is a mighty long run, all the way down to the Northwoods Express (Chairlift #11). However, skiers do not have to take it that far. While skiing in Sourdough Center area just go as far as Chairlift #14 and ride back up. This initial part of Flap Jack in the Sourdough Center is an easy beginner trail.

TIN PANTS (Green):   Tin Pants is another novice run in this area.

BOOMER (Green):   A little more adventurous than the others, Boomer is another novice run in Sourdough Center. Work your way up to it.

SOURDOUGH (Green):   Sourdough runs right under the Sourdough lift. In general it is easy groomed terrain. With powder it can be quite fun. If you go directly under the lift line you will find a short section of steep terrain just before the chairlift base. It is easy to ski around this pitch; but think about giving it a try.

WHISKEY JACK (Blue):   Whiskey Jack is allowed to be more natural and to develop some moderate size moguls. It is a great trail for the ready beginner to sample intermediate skiing. I have always enjoyed runs on this trail. There is a bail out road back into Sourdough about half way down.

LEAVING AND CONNECTING WITH OTHER CENTERS

To leave the Sourdough Center from its top you can enter China Bowl, Sun Up Bowl, Tea Cup Bowl, and Double Diamond Bowl.

Alternatively, reach Northwoods Express Center by skiing on Flapjack past Chairlift #14 and all the way down to the Northwoods Express Lift (Chairlift #11). Beginner skiers leaving the Sourdough Center may find that even sticking to the easier Flap Jack run can be a lengthy and tiring experience, especially if the weather is adverse. Feel free to take rests along the way. You can stop at Pronto's Porch for a break.

9. DOUBLE DIAMOND CENTER (Highline Lift, Chairlift #10)

INTRODUCTION

Double Diamond Center is part of the Northeast Bowl on the front side of Vail Mountain. An expert bowl, it's the place for working over your body and your knees on the moguls. This is bump city. Skiing here makes for a good night's sleep.

ARRIVAL

The Double Diamond Center is often reached from the Northwoods Express Center by skiing past Chairlift #11 to the difficult Log Chute run. Taking the mogul packed Log Chute run will lead you right to the base of the Highline Lift (Chairlift #10). Alternatively, you can ski past Log Chute to the bottom section of Prima. Ski a little way down this bottom section of Prima, staying to the right. You will notice a turnoff which will get you to Chairlift #10. Another option is to ski Choker Cut-Off, an intermediate trail which will take you from the base of the Northwoods Express Lift (Chairlift #11) to the base of the Highline Lift (Chairlift #10).

From Golden Peak you can reach Double Diamond Center by taking the Golden Peak Lift (Chairlift #6). Then ski Grand Junction Catwalk to the south which will lead you to the base of the Highline Lift.

Another way: from the top of Sourdough Center and Two Elk Restaurant ski the farthest east trail on the front side of the mountain. Try to gain some speed on the last pitch before skiing off to the right onto a wide, flat trail through the woods. You will probably have to walk a short ways but you will eventually come to the top of the Highline Lift.

THE LIFT

Highline Lift (Chairlift #10) is a regular speed two passenger chairlift. It takes a while to get to the top of this Double Diamond Center from its base. However, some people enjoy the added rest when skiing the expert runs in this Center. Also, the pause may be necessary if you just skied a Prima to Pronto to Log Chute bump extravaganza.

The good news for the newcomer is that you can preview some of Vail Mountain's steep, moguled runs before skiing them. As you start up the Highline Lift, you can look off to your right and see Log Chute from top to bottom. Then, after a short ride through the trees, you will get an excellent look at Highline which is considered to be the steepest and most difficult of the three runs in Double Diamond Center. If Log Chute or Highline seem too difficult for you, be sure to make a right turn at the top of the chairlift, heading west into the Sourdough Center on Tin Pants or Flap Jack. If you turn left into the heart of Double Diamond Center, there is "no easy way out."

THE RUNS

HIGHLINE (Double black diamond):   This is the steepest and usually the bumpiest of these three double black diamond runs. None of the three slopes are groomed much but Highline is groomed the least; its moguls grow into huge mounds of snow. Even if you do not ski Highline, the ride up the Highline Lift (Chairlift #10) gives you a great view of this bump paradise. From the top of Chairlift #10 there is an easier section at the top of Highline. Sometimes this is flat and groomed. Other times it presents a series of smaller bumps with which you can begin to get your rhythm. Just before Highline gets steep there is a cutoff to the left to Roger's Run. Good signage marks this juncture.

When Highline steepens, the moguls begin to drop off rapidly. However, there is usually a small bit of flat after each drop off, giving you some time to prepare for the next drop off. If you are just getting started at this, I think it is usually somewhat easier to start off way at the far right side. The bumps are a little kinder here, and you are farther away from the lift (and the thought that everyone is watching you). Down lower the skiing is a little easier on the left side; think about making a transition. Highline is a thrill. Remember if you can catch it with fresh snow or soft spring conditions, it will be more forgiving.

BLUE OX (Double black diamond):   Blue Ox is a fun run and usually somewhat easier than Highline. If you ski Blue Ox you will end up back at the bottom of Chairlift #10. This means that you either have to come back up Chairlift #10 or else ski down farther to catch Chairlift #6 which leaves you at the top of Golden Peak. This latter choice is great if you are staying near Golden Peak or Vail Village; but to return to Lionshead, you will need to take a bus.

To reach Blue Ox, just stay to the right of the top section and you will find yourself on Blue Ox. There is a short area with a few bumps followed by a long, long, long flat area. This flat segment can be the hardest section to ski if it has thick powder or numerous little bumps like frost heaves. You eventually come to the expert part of Blue Ox. The first incline is actually not too steep; it is an excellent place to either warm up or let yourself go. There is generally only a single fall line and the bumps are pretty round with a reasonable "line" through the bumps. Eventually Blue Ox does get steeper but the bumps do not get outrageous like Highline and Prima. Sometimes Blue Ox gets icy, especially in the middle. Then it often makes sense to ski the

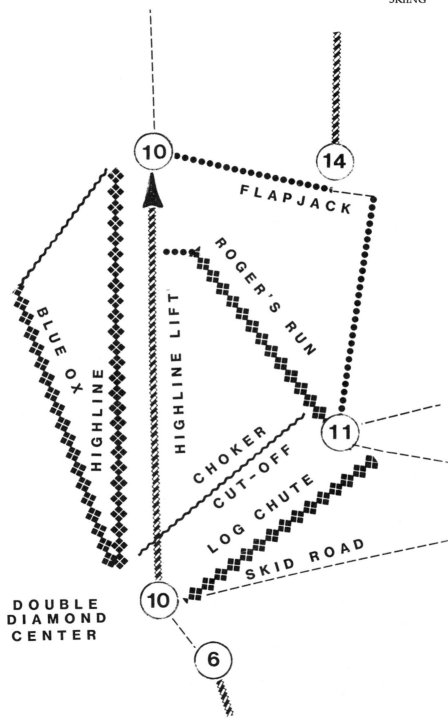

sides. Neither side is preferable.

Once you have gotten off the steep, you have two choices. The right side is generally smooth, while the left side often offers some smallish but very quick bumps. If you like quick bumps and still have the energy, choose the left.

Blue Ox is groomed occasionally. Pay attention to the grooming reports. Advanced intermediates can ski here when it is groomed. Expert skiers can have fun with big round turns. However, there may be long lines at the Highline Lift when Blue Ox is groomed, as a lot of intermediate skiers take advantage of this opportunity to ski Blue Ox.

ROGER'S RUN (Double black diamond):   This is an excellent mogul run which should be enjoyed for this challenge alone. However, it is also important to note that this trail takes you to Chairlift #11 rather than Chairlift #10. Therefore, it is the advanced skiers route to move west on the mountain. You can still get back to Chairlift #10 via Log Chute or by Choker Cutoff.

To get to Roger's Run stay to the left at the top and you will see the cutoff from Highline to Roger's.

At the top of Roger's, skiers will initially find difficult passage because of a cluster of trees. Once you get past the trees, the skiing is enjoyable. Stop and take a look across the valley for one of the very best views of Prima Cornice (not Prima itself). Based on this look you can appreciate the steepness that some skiers tackle. Below the first grove of trees there is another cluster but the whole slope is wider here. When there is fresh powder, go for Roger's.

When you get to the bottom of the steep, rest a bit, because this is not the end of the steep. First you negotiate a narrow chute with its own set of quick bumps and then go uphill a ways before you see the last challenging pitch. Here, too, there are more trees. Go to the right if you want to ski some smaller bumps before hitting the steep; if you wish to get into the steep right away, go left. You arrive at the Northwoods Express Lift (Chairlift #11). This is a way to leave the Double Diamond Center. You could also ski down Log Chute to the Double Diamond Center again for more bump runs (hoping the hot tub is fired up).

LEAVING AND CONNECTING WITH OTHER CENTERS

As indicated above, most people leave this Center by taking Roger's Run to the Northwoods Express Lift (Chairlift #11) and arriving at Mountain Top/PHQ. You could also ski past Chairlift #10 down to the back side of Chairlift #6 which will take you to the top of Golden Peak. You could then either ski Golden Peak slopes or head directly over to the Vista Bahn for a return to Mid-Vail. If Chairlift #6 is not operating there is a South 6 Escape Catwalk which will take you to the front of Vail Mountain.

You can leave this Double Diamond Center at the top of Highline Lift (Chairlift #10) as well as at the bottom. By skiing over to the Sourdough Center you will be able to access Two Elk Restaurant or China Bowl Center. Alternatively, ski the Sourdough Center for relaxing cruises. Another choice: ski past the bottom of Chairlift #14 on Flapjack to the Northwoods Express Lift (Chairlift #11).

Vail's Back Bowl Centers

10. CHINA BOWL CENTER (INCLUDING SIBERIA AND MONGOLIA BOWLS) {Orient Express Lift (Chairlift #21), Mongolia Surface Lift (Platter Lift #22), the Two Way West Wall Lift (Poma Lift #23), the Wapiti Lift (Poma Lift #24), Sun Up Lift (Chairlift #17)}

INTRODUCTION

China Bowl is a vast skiing area. On the runs near the Orient Express Chairlift (Chairlift #21) and the popular Two Elk Restaurant you feel you are at a popular ski resort. When on Outer Mongolia, you feel you are in God's Country, away from it all. Adding China Bowl a few years back actually almost doubled Vail's skiable terrain. Vail already was North America's largest single ski area.

Popular Two Elk Restaurant has great food. Try to get there before 11:15 a. m. or after 2:00 p.m. to avoid the long rush hours. At the base of China Bowl east of the Orient Express, enjoy yakitori, a wonderful chicken on a stick delight, or hamburgers at the Wok 'n' Roll Express

ARRIVAL

One way to arrive at the China Bowl area is to take the Sourdough Lift (Chairlift #14) up to the top. Approaching the top you will be amazed at the panoramic view awaiting you. The Two Elk Restaurant is to your left (farther east).

For another way to reach China Bowl (from Mountain Top/PHQ), start down Sleepytime Catwalk, which traverses around Sun Up Bowl. After you pass Yonder, you will come to a turnoff to the left/east. Take this turnoff and ski in a traverse over the top of Tea Cup Bowl. This will bring you to the Genghis Kahn section of China Bowl, a difficult area. Or, you can ski down the Tea Cup Bowl runs to a lower portion of the Sleepytime Catwalk, where you can continue on down to the base of China Bowl. Another option: do not make the left turn off of Sleepytime Catwalk but continue on down the catwalk. You will have a slow but beautiful run to the base of China Bowl.

An additional way to get to China Bowl is to take Sun Up Lift (Chairlift #17) from the base of Sun Up Bowl. From here you can ski down Jade's Glade, as well as skiing into Sun Up Bowl.

THE LIFTS

There are a number of lifts in China Bowl. Starting at the west end, the Sun Up Lift (Chairlift #17) brings you to Jade's Glade and provides a wonderful view of the Yonder runs in Sun Up Bowl. The two way West Wall Lift (Poma Lift #23) connects the Sun Up Lift and Two Elk Restaurant. The Wapiti Lift (Poma Lift #24) connects the Orient Express Lift with Two Elk Restaurant. The Orient Express Lift (Chairlift #21) is a high-speed quadruple passenger chairlift which rises from the base of China Bowl to the top provides an excellent view of the Poppyfields runs and Shangrila. The Mongolia Surface Lift (Platter Lift #22) takes you from the top of Siberia Bowl to the top of the Mongolia Bowls.

THE RUNS

China Bowl

POPPYFIELDS, WEST AND EAST (Blue): Poppyfields is the intermediate way down. Using either of these trails followed by The Orient Express will afford a good view of the pathways in China Bowl. When coming from Two Elk Restaurant you are starting on west Poppyfields. The east side starts at the top of Orient Express Lift (Chairlift #21).

SHANGRILA (Black): Shangrila is a beautiful area to ski, as indicated by the name. There is a wide variety of skiing available in the Shangrila area with small bump areas, glades, and clearings. Shangrila is east of the Poppyfield runs. Traverse east from the top of the Orient Express Lift up to, but not through, the control gate which indicates that you are entering Siberia Bowl. You can turn downhill practically anywhere you choose off this catwalk into the Shangrila area. Your general direction will either be south towards the bottom of the lift or westerly descending back into the East Poppyfield area. Take your time, have some fun; this is intermediate skiing at its grandest. You get a taste of expert skiing without intense speed or fear. For strong and expert skiers this is a blast. There are open runs, moguled runs, and tree runs which allow almost anything. Although this area is labeled black on the ski maps, it can be skied carefully by strong intermediate skiers.

DRAGON'S GLADE (Black): Dragon's Glade is fun because you don't have to climb, as you do for Jade's Glade or the top of Genghis Kahn. Watch out for the cliffs near the top. Once you are past these, you can have a great run into Poppyfields.

JADE'S GLADE (Black): Hiking up the ridge which you can see heading

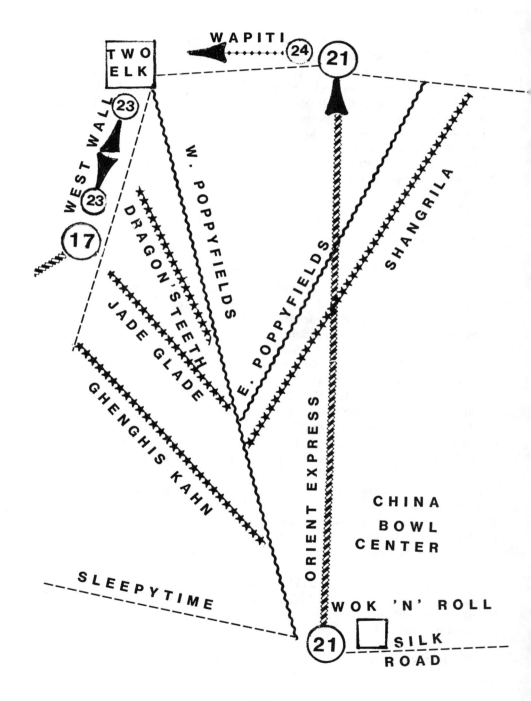

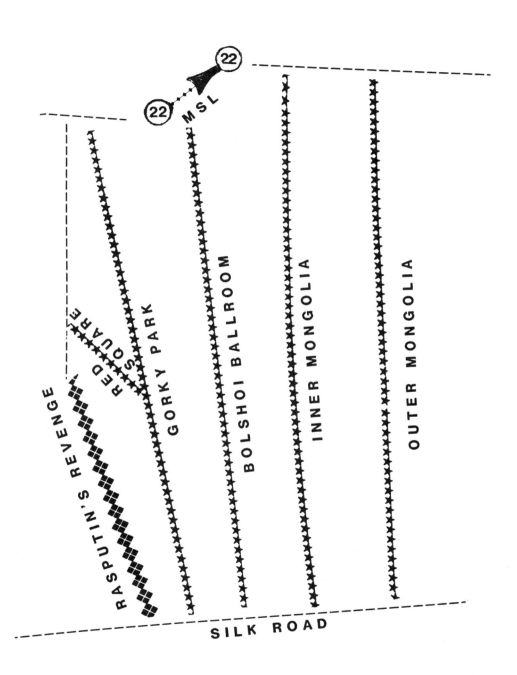

off southwest of Two Elk Restaurant, you come to a place just beyond some trees below. You will usually see some tracks, unless you are the smart one who gets "first tracks." This is Jade's Glade and it is fun for the expert. Here you need to be more careful for rocks near the bottom, just before Jade's Glade merges into Poppyfields.

GENGHIS KAHN (Black):   Hiking farther to the summit of this ridge, you have a vast, steep expanse of snow to ski. It is definitely expert skiing. Since it is a broad face, there is room to maneuver whether the conditions are powder, crud, bumps or a mixture. This run also ends up at Poppyfields. You have to ski through and up a little ravine to get onto Poppyfields, so watch for tracks to guide you and make this easier to accomplish.

Siberia Bowl

When people talk of China Bowl they are often including Siberia Bowl plus Inner and Outer Mongolia Bowls. These bowls are way out there. Siberia Bowl can be reached by traversing to the east from the top of the Orient Express Lift (Chairlift #21), past Shangrila and through the control gate. Siberia Bowl includes the areas labeled Rasputin's Revenge, Gorky Park, and Bolshoi Ballroom. (The Bolshoi Ballet Company often visits Vail in the summer).

RASPUTIN'S REVENGE (Black):   A sharp right turn after the control gate into Siberia Bowl takes you to Rasputin's Revenge. This run should probably have a double black diamond rating. It is steep, moguly, and has rocks/cliffs to negotiate. It makes sense to take one of the other runs in Siberia Bowl. Then take the opportunity to preview Rasputin's Revenge as you are returning to the lift on Silk Road.

RED SQUARE (Black):   Turn east prior to Rasputin's Revenge for Red Square, a broad expert run which you can ski into Gorky Park.

GORKY PARK (Black):   Reach Gorky Park by continuing on the catwalk almost to the bottom of the Mongolia Platter Lift. Take a right turn and head down the slope onto a broad area of advanced skiing terrain. The cats hardly ever groom this area. There is often a mixture of crud and bumps to give you plenty of exercise. The acreage is vast; you will have room to maneuver.

BOLSHOI BALLROOM (Black):   To get to Bolshoi Ballroom continue on the catwalk past the bottom of the Mongolia Surface Lift. Get off the catwalk whenever and wherever you want. Here the skiing includes trees and glades, but they are neither tight nor dangerous for an expert skier. You will probably work your way back west as you follow the southerly descent. Adventurous skiers can head easterly, moving towards the Mongolia Bowls.

Mongolia Bowls

When you go past Siberia Bowl and take the Mongolia Surface Lift (Platter Lift #22) you reach the Mongolia Bowls. On top of the Mongolia Bowls you feel way out there with a wonderful sense of wilderness skiing. I will never forget my first run here. Visibility was poor but the powder was great. The person showing me the way gave a whoop which I assumed was a whoop of joy. However, when I got to the spot of the whoop I realized that I was falling straight down through space. It was only a four to five foot drop into soft, deep powder but I didn't expect to be going off a jump. With decent visibility, this jump is obvious and avoidable.

The Mongolia Bowls are wonderful. The acreage is huge. The Inner Mongolia Bowl area starts just as you get off of the platter lift. There is a catwalk track heading farther east to Outer Mongolia Bowl. There is a lot of terrain to be skied, and generally it is not too steep. You can head east or west as you work your way south down to Silk Road. Some complain of the length of the catwalk returning you to the Orient Express Lift. However, I feel it is a small price to pay for an experience of God's Country on downhill skis.

INNER MONGOLIA (Black): The top of Inner Mongolia is where skiers get off the platter lift. Watch out for the road cuts at the top. If visibility is bad, be aware of the dropoffs. Be kind to your skis by being careful here. After this short space, it is a grand ride down to Silk Road, the catwalk that will take you back to the Orient Express. Depending on the snow conditions, skiing in this area can be great, ridiculously easy or ridiculously hard. Try to find out before you go. At times, when the snow is cruddy (heavy, wet and clumpy) there will be a narrow groomed run created by one of the cats. The more you ski to the right (to the west) the shorter your catwalk run back to the China Bowl base area. As you come off of the steep onto Silk Road carry some speed, but be careful.

OUTER MONGOLIA (Black): Reach Outer Mongolia by continuing east on the catwalk beyond Inner Mongolia. There is a small sign, indicating the top of the run. It appears to begin where there is a clearing beyond some tree limbs and rocks. Stop and look around. It's magnificent. Pause to stop and look around several times as you descend. It's a great feeling. However, skiers can lose your bearings in this vast landscape. Go with a friend, hopefully one who has been there before.

LEAVING AND CONNECTING WITH OTHER CENTERS

Leaving China Bowl Center means heading west on the catwalk at the top of the Orient Express. The Wapiti Lift will help you out here, especially if you are heading for a well deserved snack or lunch at the Two Elk Restaurant. If you intend to keep skiing you have some options. One is to make a right turn and pass the east side of the restaurant. You will be entering the Sourdough Center on its eastern side. You can ski into the Double Diamond Center by watching for a right turn out of the Sourdough Center. Try to carry some speed and hold the tuck position for as long as you can in order to shorten the walk to the Double Diamond Center. Remember if you stay on Flap Jack and go past Chairlift #14, you will be entering the Northwoods Express Center.

Alternatively, you can hike or take the West Wall two way lift over to Sun Up Bowl.

11. TEA CUP BOWL CENTER

INTRODUCTION

Tea Cup Bowl is a Vail Mountain back bowl located between Sun Up Bowl and China Bowl. Powder skiers savor Tea Cup Bowl. It is a great place to ski in deep powder, just plain heavenly.

ARRIVAL

You can reach Tea Cup Bowl by skiing down the Sleepytime catwalk from Mountain Top/PHQ. Just after Yonder you make a left turn to the east at the posted sign. You will quickly see Tea Cup Bowl.

Or, you can take the Sun Up Lift from its base in Sun Up Bowl or take the West Wall surface lift from Two Elk Restaurant. Then you can ski down the ridge, Emperor's Choice.

THE RUNS

MORNING THUNDER (Black):   As you make the left turn off Sleepytime, you will be at the top of the Morning Thunder run. Enjoy some great turns here when there is powder.

RED ZINGER (Black):   To ski Red Zinger traverse past Morning Thunder until you feel like you are right at the apex of the bowl. Again, with

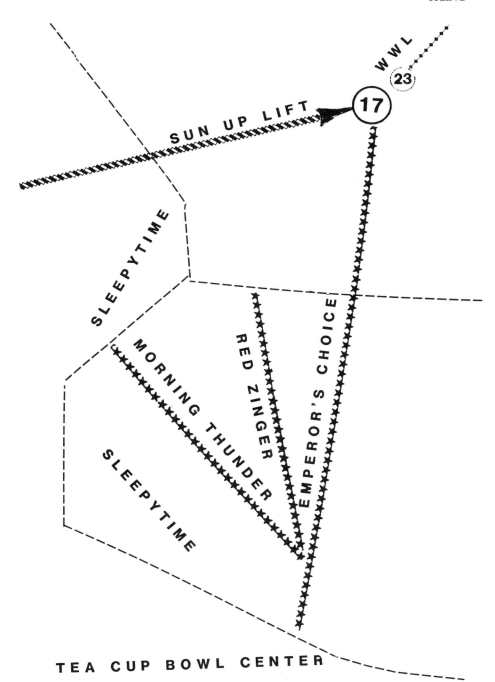

WWL

23

17

SUN UP LIFT

SLEEPYTIME

RED ZINGER

MORNING THUNDER

EMPEROR'S CHOICE

SLEEPYTIME

TEA CUP BOWL CENTER

powder conditions, go for it.

EMPEROR'S CHOICE (Black): If you are skiing from the top of Sun Up Lift, you can ski down the ridge, Emperor's Choice. Another way to reach Emperor's Choice is to continue past Red Zinger on the traverse across the top of Tea Cup Bowl.

LEAVING AND CONNECTING WITH OTHER CENTERS

One way to leave Tea Cup Bowl is without skiing it. That is you stay on the traverse across the top of the bowl; this is a way of skiing from Sun Up Bowl over to the Genghis Kahn area of China Bowl.

Alternatively, if you ski down into the bowl, keep going until you reach the Sleepytime catwalk again. This will take you to the base of the Orient Express Lift (Chairlift #21).

12. SUN UP BOWL CENTER (High Noon Lift, Chairlift #5, and Sun Up Lift)

INTRODUCTION

Sun Up Bowl is truly a tremendous place to ski. Its views are awesome; its terrain is marvelous and varied. You can choose to ski the bumps, the trees and/or the steep. You can start into Sun Up Bowl from Mountain Top/PHQ. You ski to the left (east) of High Noon Lift (Chairlift #5). For your initial introduction to this skier's paradise, I recommend skiing down the Slot from Mountain Top/PHQ. When you do so, you can take a look at all of the side wall slopes to the east and the west which Sun Up Bowl offers you. Also, if you are an intermediate/advanced skier the Slot may be all you want to ski. In the Sun Up Bowl Center you will have to choose between the Sun Up Lift (Chairlift #17), the first one you will reach, or the High Noon Lift (Chairlift #5). Note that whether you utilized the High Noon Lift or the Sun Up Lift, you will be able to keep skiing the Sun Up Bowl Center.

ARRIVAL

You reach Mountain Top/PHQ which provides access to the majority of runs in Sun Up Bowl Center by taking up either Mountain Top Express Lift (Chairlift #4) or Northwoods Express Lift (Chairlift #11). You can also ski into Sun Up Bowl by taking the two way West Wall surface lift from Two Elk Restaurant over to the top of the Sun Up Lift.

THE LIFTS

High Noon Lift (Chairlift #5) is a regular speed three passenger chairlift which takes you from the base of Sun Up Center to the top at Mountain Top/PHQ. Your views from this lift are essentially of Sun Down Bowl, not Sun Up Bowl.

The Sun Up Lift (Chairlift #17) is a regular speed three passenger chairlift. It ascends from Sun Up Bowl over the Yonder trails taking you to the top of Yonder in Sun Up Bowl and Jade's Glade in China Bowl.

THE RUNS

Slot And Runs West Of Slot

THE SLOT (Black):   To get to the Slot start on Sleepytime catwalk; but then immediately make a right onto the Slot trail. The Slot is a broad trail that you can ski back and forth across. There is no need for tight turns or gathering a lot of speed. Most likely the fast expert skiers are on the other runs in Sun Up Bowl, so they won't be buzzing you.

Take your time and look left (west) at the Yonder runs; these include Yonder Gully, Yonder, and Over Yonder. Do these look inviting or scary? Make an informed decision about this. Also, look right (east) at Milt's face; this is usually a mogul covered beauty with plenty of early morning sun as it faces east. You can ski up a little way onto Milt's Face to get a feeling for how it skis. Once again, make an informed decision as to whether you want to tackle Milt's Face. You will reach the base of the Sun Up Lift which will be heading uphill over the Yonder runs.

As you ski the Slot, to the right (west) you will gradually see Milt's Face turn into Campbell's and then into Cow's Face. Continuing down the Slot you will be headed to High Noon Lift (Chairlift #5) on the Sun Up Bowl Catwalk. Skiers from Sun Down Bowl end up at this same High Noon Lift, so a crowd may develop here.

MILT'S FACE (Black):   Again to the left (east side) of Chairlift #5, ski through the control ropes into the section labeled Milt's Face. Ski along High Noon Ridge. After a while you will notice some tracks turning left toward the east. You are probably in the right area. Anyhow, if you notice the Apres Vous sign on the right, this is a good time to turn left. You will find great, steep skiing as you head down Milt's Face. The slope is broad though, and in that manner forgiving. Bumps are usually excellent. Have fun. If it looks like you are getting close too soon to the Slot (the bottom), make a sharp right traverse as you may be able to pick up a few more lines on Campbell's Face or Cow's Face before you reach the catwalk. Skiing here can be so tremendous that you do not want it to stop at all; have fun skiing to the Slot.

CAMPBELL'S (Black): Campbell's face is similar to Milt's Face; just continue a while longer down High Noon Ridge before turning left to head east and down the slope. As Campbell's is skied a less frequently, it often keeps its powder longer. Here again, you can traverse to your right (south) to reach Cow's Face.

COW'S FACE (Black): Keep heading straight down High Noon Ridge, and soon it will become a downhill run which will probably have great powder and or great bumps. It is a thrilling run, not very difficult for expert skiers. Enjoy the powder and the sun; remember you face south as you ski this slope. As you ski Cow's Face you will be able to ski to Sun Up Lift (Chairlift #17) as you ski the eastern side and angle to the lift.

APRES VOUS (Black): To ski Apres Vous stay close to the control rope on the right/west side of High Noon Ridge. You will come to a control gate, hopefully open, with a sign saying Apres Vous. Apres Vous is its own little south facing bowl. It is a wonderful place to ski on the right day. (When it is too icy, the ski patrol closes off the entrance gate). You can make some great turns on Apres Vous while enjoying the wonderful southern vista. Eventually, the trail begins to funnel, however, and the skiing becomes more difficult. Finally, there is a fairly tight section between some outcroppings before you reach the Sun Up Catwalk. You should be an expert skier before entering Apres Vous; and go with a friend. If you want, ski close to the rope on your left. There is an opening where you are allowed to ski out to Cow's Face without going through the funnel. If you ski Apres Vous you will be able to reach only to High Noon Chairlift, not Sun Up Chairlift.

CHICKEN YARD (Black): Ski to the west over the top of Apres Vous to another control rope. Watch closely and you will find another gate, labeled Chicken Yard. Think twice about going in here, but if there is great powder, don't think too long. Chicken Yard descends to the south. As with Apres Vous, the slope funnels out through a small opening to get back to the Sun Up Bowl catwalk. Remember that the powder will stay soft here for a longer time because it takes the sun longer to get here than on the eastern facing slopes off of High Noon Ridge.

Runs East Of Slot

HEADWALL (Black): We are beginning to talk here about skiing east past the Slot on the Sleepytime Catwalk. You may want to miss Headwall, as most people do, except on deep powder days. It is a steep pitch. Facing south it has better visibility on gray days; however there is not much of a treeline to help you keep your bearings if the atmosphere is really "souped in."

YONDER GULLY (Black):   Yonder Gully is a favorite slope. It develops "practice" moguls that advanced skiers love. Skiers notice it from Sleepytime Catwalk past the Headwall because of its mogul line. Yonder Gully turns off before you reach the trees; if you get above the trees you are on Yonder rather than Yonder Gully. Yonder Gully is a very regular slope with no surprises. It is fun anytime. It can especially be an ego booster for your last Bowl run of the day, allowing you to put together all of the things you have been working on during the day. From Yonder Gully you will have a choice of either Sun Up Lift or High Noon Lift (Chairlift #5). Note that if you take the Sun Up Lift, you will be able to ski Yonder Gully again from higher on the ridge.

YONDER (Black):   Yonder is a steep slope with trees. The trees are not formidable because there are numerous pathways through them. From Yonder you will have a choice of either Sun Up Lift or High Noon Lift (Chairlift #5). Note that if you take the Sun Up Lift, you will be able to ski Yonder again, but you will begin higher on the ridge.

OVER YONDER (Black):   If you keep skiing the traverse in Sun Up Bowl and do not make a left turn into the Tea Cup Bowl Center, you will reach Over Yonder. It is similar to Yonder except the trees are somewhat denser and it begins to face more northerly rather than easterly.

WTFOT (Black):   It's not on the map, and don't ask.

SUN UP CATWALK: It is not always easy; it can be bumpy or icy. Look for a large pine tree in the middle of the Sun Up Catwalk. Glance to your right and you will see an opening. Generally there are about five or six excellent bump turns here which you can take or avoid.

LEAVING AND CONNECTING WITH OTHER CENTERS

There are several ways to leave Sun Up Bowl. First, the Highnoon Lift (Chairlift #5) leaves you at the top of Mountaintop/PHQ. From here you can head into Mid-Vail Center; Northwoods Center; Sun Down Bowl; Tea Cup Bowl; or China Bowl (Genghis Kahn).
Another way is to take Sun Up Lift (Chairlift #17) which will enable you to ski China Bowl (Jade's Glade) or Tea Cup Bowl. Also, you can reach Two Elk Restaurant by taking the two way West Wall surface lift from the top of Chairlift #17.

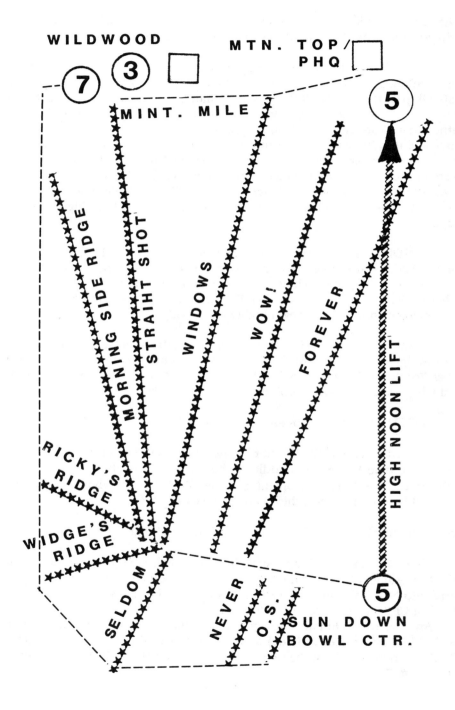

WILDWOOD

MTN. TOP/
PHQ

(7) (3) ☐ ☐ (5)

MINT. MILE

MORNING SIDE RIDGE

STRAIHT SHOT

WINDOWS

WOW!

FOREVER

HIGH NOON LIFT

RICKY'S RIDGE

WIDGE'S RIDGE

SELDOM

NEVER

O.S.

(5)

SUN DOWN
BOWL CTR.

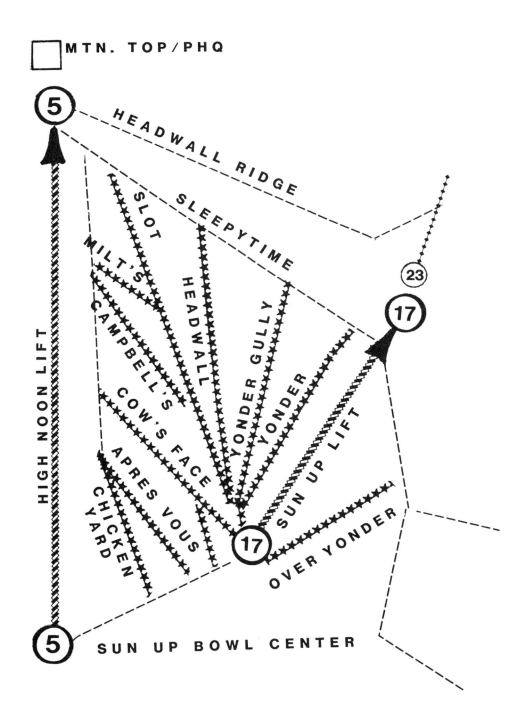

MTN. TOP/PHQ

13. SUN DOWN BOWL CENTER (High Noon Lift, Chairlift #5)

INTRODUCTION

Sun Down Bowl is huge and spectacular. The vistas are wonderful. The expert skiing is great. The bowl offers well over 180 degrees of walls for you to ski down into the base. Enjoy the skiing; enjoy the scenery.

ARRIVAL

You can arrive at Sun Down Bowl by first reaching Mountain Top/PHQ at the top of Mountain Top Express Lift (Chairlift #4) or Northwoods Express Lift (Chairlift #11). From here you can ski Forever, Wow, and Windows.

You can also arrive at Sun Down Bowl by reaching the Wildwood area at the top of the Hunky Dory Lift (Chairlift #3) or the Game Creek Express Lift (Chairlift #7). From here you can ski Straight Shot; Morningside Ridge; Ricky's Ridge; Ptarmigan Ridge; Widge's Ridge; Seldom; Never; and O.S.

THE LIFT

The High Noon Lift (Chairlift #5) is a normal speed three passenger lift. As you take it up to Mountain Top/PHQ you get an excellent view of Sun Down Bowl. Take out your map and notice Widge's Ridge; Rickey's Ridge; Ptarmigan Ridge; Morning Side; and Straight Shot. You can also see Windows and Wow as they break out of the Woods. You will be riding the lift above Forever.

If all of this is new to you, take Slot in Sun Up Bowl for an initial run to the base of the High Noon Lift. Then as you ride up you will get a good look at Sun Down Bowl before skiing it.

Note that only some of the runs in Sun Down Bowl are directly accessible from the top of Chairlift #5 at Mountain Top/PHQ (Forever, Wow, and Windows).

THE RUNS

Runs From Mountain Top/PHQ

FOREVER (Black): Forever actually begins slightly to the Sun Up side of Chairlift #5. Its entry/control gate is to the east of Chairlift #5. However, this trail quickly turns west into Sun Down Bowl. Forever gets its name honestly. It is wide and long, the trail most exposed to view from the High Noon Lift. It is also very exposed to southern sun. It can be bullet proof, ice hard; soft

74

powder; difficult crud; moguled or unmoguled. While it is never groomed, it is skied so frequently that it tends to be skied out or "skier groomed." Towards the bottom, there are some decent mogul lines just before reaching the Sun Down Catwalk which will take you back to the High Noon Chair.

WOW (Black): Moving to the west, you come to a control/entry gate for Wow. Wow is one of my favorite runs. It begins as a rather wide trail through the woods. This section of the trail is heavily moguled but without steep dropoffs. It is fun mogul skiing (for the expert) and then "wow!" You arrive out in the open with a magnificent view of the Holy Cross Wilderness. There is a direct line down from here to the Sun Down Catwalk. You can also swing east to ski on Forever or swing to the west to ski the Windows slopes. Usually you will move toward Forever if you prefer the more skied out terrain. On great powder days you will thoroughly enjoy moving towards Windows.

WINDOWS (Black): Arrive at the Windows entrances by heading west down Minturn Mile Catwalk off Ramshorn. If you want my suggestion, do not take the first ("upper") Windows entrance. You will find yourself in thick woods that seem more for cross-country skiers. However, in the second ("lower") Windows entrance you can quickly get through the tree section and experience the panorama of slope and view that lies ahead. It is a steep drop down to the catwalk; in powder it can be heavenly.

Runs From Wildwood

Note that once you ski into Sun Down Bowl from this peak, there is no chairlift to bring you straight back up to this same starting point. You need to ski down to the Hunky Dory Lift (Chairlift #3) on the front side of Vail Mountain to return to this Sun Down Bowl starting point.

STRAIGHT SHOT (Black): Straight Shot is a steep pitch, beginning just to the south of Wildwood Shelter. It is steep and has big moguls. The moguls are generally well placed, as only expert skiers take the plunge down Straight Shot.

MORNING SIDE RIDGE (Black): Morning Side Ridge, an east facing slope, receives the first morning sun in Sun Down Bowl, as it is an east facing slope. Here you can have a fantastic powder run on a powder day and some excellent crud skiing when conditions change. Morning Side Ridge also gets moguled up, and the moguls are usually pretty round and smooth. You ski down to the Sun Down Catwalk and then over to the High Noon Lift.

RICKY'S RIDGE (Black): Everyone talks about Ricky's Ridge, so here is the scoop. You ski past Morning Side on a traverse track that may be very, very bumpy. Keep looking down, and when you see a long narrow ridge heading out into the depths of the bowl, you have reached Ricky's Ridge. Note that this is an east facing slope, also. At first Ricky's Ridge is quite steep with big moguls. Then when you ski down onto the spine of the ridge, you will find smaller but very quick moguls. You really need to keep your feet moving here. When the spine ends, you then get another chance to ski left (north) down some steep moguls to the Sun Down Catwalk. Note that if you ski to either side of the moguled spine, you can find some great powder or crud.

PTARMIGAN RIDGE (Black): If you hike up a ways you can ski down Ptarmigan Ridge onto Ricky's Ridge or the other runs mentioned below. You will be able to see the hike-up trail, which is usually groomed, just as you are approaching Morning Side Ridge.

WIDGE'S RIDGE (Black): Ski past Ricky's Ridge on this grand traverse below Ptarmigan's Ridge, (which does get less bumpy once you pass Ricky's Ridge because fewer skiers continue the traverse), and you will find Widge's Ridge. It is a great ridge, usually smoother than Ricky's. Great in powder, Widge's may be tough in crud. It narrows down into a little valley. There are some good sized moguls down in this lower section. This is still an east facing ridge.

SELDOM (Black): Skiing past Widge's Ridge, the traverse curves to the left, heading to Seldom. Seldom is a north facing slope, protected from the rays of the sun. Seldom is fun. It is steep but also rolling. There are some worrisome cliffs indicated by a rope. If you ski down the right (east) side of the cliffs, you can cut under the wooded area and reach the bottom part of Never for some nice steep moguled turns to finish off the run.

NEVER (Black): Well, how did it get this name? Probably because you have to enter negotiate a densely wooded section once you pass Seldom in order to access Never. Some skiers never do it. If you choose to do it, look at the white spaces between the trees; do not look at the trees themselves. As you come out of the trees you can do some turns on steep runs with steep bumps. This too is a north facing slope.

O.S. (Black): O.S. is on the map. However, this is not the place to explain what the initials stand for. Go at your own risk.

SUN DOWN CATWALK: It isn't always easy. It can be bumpy or icy.

LEAVING AND CONNECTING WITH OTHER CENTERS

To leave Sun Down Bowl Center you need to take the High Noon Lift (Chairlift #5) to Mountain Top/PHQ. From here you can ski into Sun Up Bowl Center, Mid-Vail Center, or Northwoods Center. You can also get over to China Bowl, Tea Cup Bowl, Sourdough Bowl, or down to the base of Vail Mountain via Riva Ridge.

14. GAME CREEK BOWL CENTER (Game Creek Express, Chairlift #7)

INTRODUCTION

Game Creek Bowl is an inviting place to ski. There are a variety of runs in this bowl for the strong beginner, intermediate, and expert. Game Creek Bowl has a relaxed, fun atmosphere.

ARRIVAL

You can enter the Game Creek Bowl from the top of the Lionshead Gondola in the Eagle's Nest area directly or indirectly. The direct way takes you down a flat road down into the bowl.

The indirect way is to ski down to the Avanti Express Lift (Chairlift #2) and take it up. From here you can enter a few of the relatively steep, south facing slopes: Faro, Faro Glade, Ouzo and Ouzo Glade plus Deuces Wild. These expert faces are relatively similar to the Sun Down and Sun Up back bowl experiences.

Another way to get to the Game Creek Bowl Center is to ride the Hunky Dory Lift (Chairlift #3) from Mid-Vail. The Hunky Dory Lift and the Game Creek Express Lift (Chairlift #7) practically meet together in the Wildwood area, where the Wildwood Restaurant is located. Reaching the Hunky Dory Lift (Chairlift #3) is easy. You can ski down from the top of the Avanti Express Center (Chairlift #2). See the section on the Avanti Express Center for guidance here. Another way is to take the Vista Bahn Express Lift (Chairlift #16) up from Vail Village.

THE LIFT

Game Creek Express Lift (Chairlift #7), a high-speed quadruple lift, whisks you to the top of Game Creek Bowl Center in 4.5 minutes. From the lift enjoy excellent views of the majority of the trails in the bowl. To your right you can observe Lost Boy; Deuces Wild; Baccarat; the Woods; and Wild Card. Show Boat is beneath you. To your left you can see Ouzo; Faro; and Deuces Wild. If you feel unsure in this bowl, take Lost Boy down to the base; on the way back up you will be able to observe the skiing opportunities and challenges.

THE RUNS

LOST BOY (Green):   Lost Boy is the beginner run in the Game Creek Bowl Center. It is a long and relatively flat run. It is frequently groomed. However, to the beginner skier, the first face does look a might steep. Use your wedge. With well controlled turns you can take on this short face. After you have handled this, the upcoming cruising terrain will seem quite easy. Then you can work on your higher level exercises. Towards the bottom of the run, it gets a little steep again. However, now you will be ready to handle the pitch. Go right back up and do Lost Boy again. It is a great place for getting ski mileage under your belt. By the way, look around at the views. The scenery from Lost Boy is spectacular.

DEALER'S CHOICE (Blue):   To reach Dealer's Choice, ski the steeper first section of Lost Boy and then make an immediate right turn. Dealer's Choice is similar to Lost Boy and is also often groomed. Though Dealer's Choice has a more difficult rating, skiers who can handle Lost Boy need not be intimidated. However, do not mistakenly make a second right turn as that will put you on Baccarat.

BACCARAT (Blue):   Baccarat is reached by a right turn off of Dealer's Choice. It is left in a more natural condition than Lost Boy or Dealer's Choice. Therefore, it can be more of a challenge to ski, and deserving of its more difficult rating. It finishes up intermixed with the Woods trail. Because Baccarat is more natural, you might encounter powder, crud, bumps, whatever. Generally, it is not too steep, except for a very short section before it runs into the Woods. Baccarat provides a good introduction to those who feel ready to handle different and more challenging terrain.

WOODS (Blue):   Woods is a long slope with an even drop. It has a more difficult rating. Woods is groomed every once in a while, preventing it from becoming a mogul field. However, it is generally left in its natural state. It is a great trail for the upper intermediate to early advanced skier, as skiers will need to use a number of different skiing skills to get down. There are skiers who love skiing the Woods because it gives a great feeling of skiing in the wilderness between its deeply forested sides.

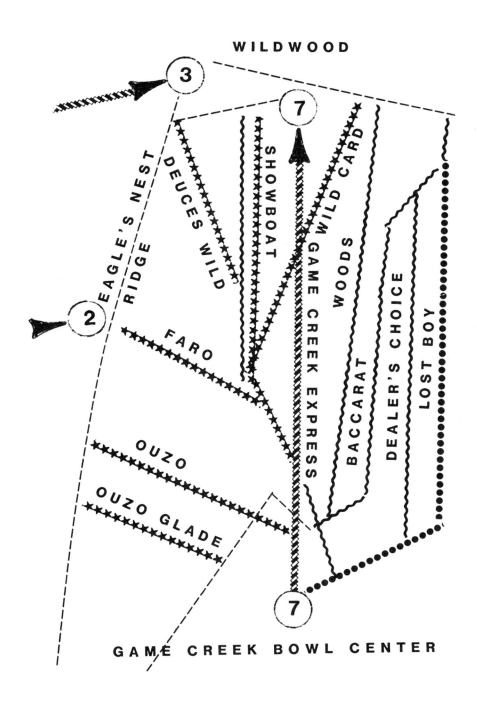

WILDWOOD

EAGLE'S NEST RIDGE

DEUCES WILD

SHOWBOAT

WILD CARD

GAME CREEK EXPRESS

WOODS

BACCARAT

DEALER'S CHOICE

LOST BOY

FARO

OUZO

OUZO GLADE

GAME CREEK BOWL CENTER

WILD CARD (Black):   Then, of course, there are skiers who are not satisfied with skiing natural conditions. They wish to ski supernatural mogul fields. Wild Card is one of the best in this category. Wild Card has a rather easy entrance, but then the mogul field develops quickly. Gradually it gets steeper with deeper drop offs. Finally, it levels off but still remains full of moguls. The whole experience is a challenge of balance, strength and mobility. Noteworthy, the moguls in the middle steeper section of Wild Card seem to run to the left. It is easier to make a turn to the left than a turn to the right. Therefore, unless you are careful you will keep drifting to the left. It is not necessarily bad to go left with the drift, especially when you are first learning to ski difficult bumps. When you do reach the bottom mogul area, you should be able to set a fairly direct line. This builds ego, allows you to feel better, and tempts you to go up and try again.

SHOWBOAT (Black and blue):   Showboat is a wide trail which runs directly under the Game Creek Express Lift. In fact it is often divided into two runs. On the north side (right side facing downhill) it is frequently groomed and smooth; however, small moguls will sometimes develop on this side. On the south side (left side facing downhill) it is allowed to develop moguls. At times it is difficult to tell the lower end of Wild Card and the lower end of this left side of Showboat apart. Showboat has a more difficult rating; obviously it tends to be a little more like an expert run where the moguls have built up.
One nice thing about Showboat: skiers on Chairlift #7 above the run can get a good look at varied styles of skiing the moguls.

DEUCES WILD (Black):   If you ski around to the left as you get off of the Game Creek Express you can first reach Deuces Wild, labeled a most difficult run. It is one of the several steep south facing runs that lead into the Game Creek Center. Facing south, like the back bowls, the snow on these trails can be soft in the afternoon, then icy in the morning. Be careful. However, do note that Deuces Wild is groomed at times, often when the north side of Showboat is not. Intermediate skiers can handle Deuces Wild when it is groomed.

FARO (Black):   Faro, labeled a most difficult run, faces you when you get off the Avanti Express Lift (Chairlift #2). It is also reached by skiing even farther around to the left off Game Creek Express past Deuces Wild. Faro is a south facing slope. Therefore, the thaw/freeze cycle can affect this slope too. Faro is a broad slope. You may encounter a variety of conditions before you end up at the bottom in Showboat. Frequently moguls are encountered in the lower steeper section.

OUZO (Black):   Ouzo is another south facing slope dropping down into

Game Creek Bowl Center to finish on Showboat. It starts off gently, but then becomes steep. Be sure you want to ski a most difficult run before heading down. Often there are moguls towards the bottom. As Ouzo is a south facing slope, it is subject to the thaw/freeze cycles.

OUZO GLADE (Black):   To the west of Ouzo, there is a rather dense clump of trees. Ski in these trees and you are skiing Ouzo Glade. Under the right conditions, this can be fantastic. Watch out though as you approach Game Trail, the catwalk that brings people down from Eagle's Nest directly into Game Creek Bowl Center. It can be a real surprise to come out of deep powder onto a groomed catwalk. People, including yours truly, have been known to leave their skis on the catwalk with a hockey stop but find their bodies propelled down the hill, unable to control their momentum. This glade is protected from the sun by the trees. Powder will last longer here and so will crud. Be aware, ski with care

LEAVING AND CONNECTING WITH OTHER CENTERS

You can leave the Game Creek Bowl Center by skiing to the left as you get off the chair. There is a short path through some trees leading to the top of the Hunky Dory Lift (Chairlift #3) on its western side and Eagle's Nest Ridge. Now you are at the top of Kangaroo Cornice, should you wish to accept this challenging assignment. After skiing the cornice or around it, you can ski into Mid-Vail Center or Hunky Dory Center. Or you can travel west down Eagle's Nest Ridge towards the top of the Avanti Express Center (Chairlift #2). Heading further down Eagle's Nest Ridge will take you to Minnie's Mile Center, Eagle's Nest, and the Lionshead Center.

On the other hand, you can take a right turn at the top of the Game Creek Bowl Center to enter Sun Down Bowl. This is the way to reach runs like Straight Shot; Morningside Ridge; Ricky's Ridge; Widge's Ridge; Seldom; Never; and O.S. (that is what is shown on the trail map). Read the section on Sun Down Bowl Center before taking the plunge into this expert area.

BEAVER CREEK MOUNTAIN'S CENTERS FOR SKIING

STUMP PARK

DRINK OF WATER

ROSE BOWL

CENTENNIAL EXPRESS

BIRDS OF PREY

GROUSE MOUNTAIN

LARKSPUR

STRAWBERRY PARK

Ski Tips

EXCITING BEAVER CREEK MOUNTAIN

The best way to introduce you to the excitement of skiing Beaver Creek Mountain is my cognitive mapping organization of Beaver Creek's Ski Centers. In this conceptual framework Beaver Creek has eight Centers.

BEAVER CREEK CENTERS

1. CENTENNIAL EXPRESS
2. STUMP PARK
3. ROSE BOWL
4. DRINK OF WATER
5. BIRDS OF PREY
6. GROUSE MOUNTAIN
7. LARKSPUR BOWL
8. STRAWBERRY PARK
   INCLUDING McCOY PARK

The order of these centers extends from the mountain's base up and then from east to west. While Beaver Creek Mountain is not as difficult to organize in your mind as Vail Mountain, the Centers concept will make skiing more enjoyable through organized cognitive mapping of the mountain. Beaver Creek is a beautiful ski area, rarely crowded. Snowboarders and telemarkers have fun here, too. Cross-country skiers enjoy wonderful McCoy Park, high up on Beaver Creek Mountain with great vistas to the north and east.

Beaver Creek is a small mountain in comparison to Vail; nevertheless, it provides quality skiing for experts as well as intermediates and beginners.

Beaver Creek is beautifully set into its mountain. With narrower trails than Vail, it has a touch of the New England look. Yet, there is plenty of trail width for maneuvering. The skier does not feel hemmed in. The only exception to this is Golden Eagle in the Birds of Prey Center.

One drawback to Beaver Creek at this time is the slow speed of the majority of the chairlifts. Beaver Creek Mountain does have two high-speed quadruple passenger lifts, Centennial Express Lift (Chairlift #6) and Grouse Mountain Express Lift (Chairlift #10). Skiers think that the lack of long liftlines offsets the slowness of the lifts.

My preference is to arrive at Beaver Creek early, if you are not already lodging there. This way you can park on the mountain in an underground parking lot. There is a charge during ski season, but worth it. If you do not arrive early enough, you may be turned around at the security gate and asked to park in the free parking lots at the base of the mountain. You get a free bus ride up to the ski area base when you park in these parking lots.

If you are lodging in the Beaver Creek Resort Village you will have parking provided at your accommodation. If you are coming up in the evening for dinner or entertainment, you'll find post-ski parking is more plentiful.

Beaver Creek Resort Village is a beautiful assemblage of traditionally constructed buildings with a post-modern flair. It is an experience to see the public spaces shared with a spectacular sculpture collection. Enjoy.

1. CENTENNIAL EXPRESS CENTER (Centennial Express Lift, Chairlift #6; Haymeadow Lift, Chairlift #1; and Highlands Lift, Chairlift #2)

INTRODUCTION

The Centennial Express Center covers all the terrain between Spruce Saddle and the base of Beaver Creek Ski Area. This terrain has varying degrees of difficulty. Within this Center you can ski a road all the way to the base or catch some pretty steep bumps. Even if you don't ski this Center all day, you finally have to ski this Center to end your day at the base.

Facilities at the base of the mountain include the Hyatt Regency operated McCoy Cafeteria; Vail/Beaver Creek Ski School for adults and children; and a wonderful Small World nursery. Enjoy the popcorn wagon.

At Spruce Saddle (at the top of the Centennial Express Lift) find Spruce Saddle Cafeteria; Rafters, a sit-down full-service restaurant; and a Ski School Center for arranging private lessons or afternoon workshops.

ARRIVAL

The Centennial Express Center is located at the base of the Beaver Creek Ski Area where the Centennial Express Lift (Chairlift #6) is easily seen. It requires a short walk east to reach Haymeadow Lift (Chairlift #1) in the beginners area. Highlands Lift (Chairlift #2) is also in this beginner area.

THE LIFTS

The Centennial Express Lift (Chairlift #6) is a high-speed quadruple passenger chairlift which takes you from the base of Beaver Creek Mountain to Spruce Saddle, ascending over Centennial trail. Haymeadow Lift (Chairlift

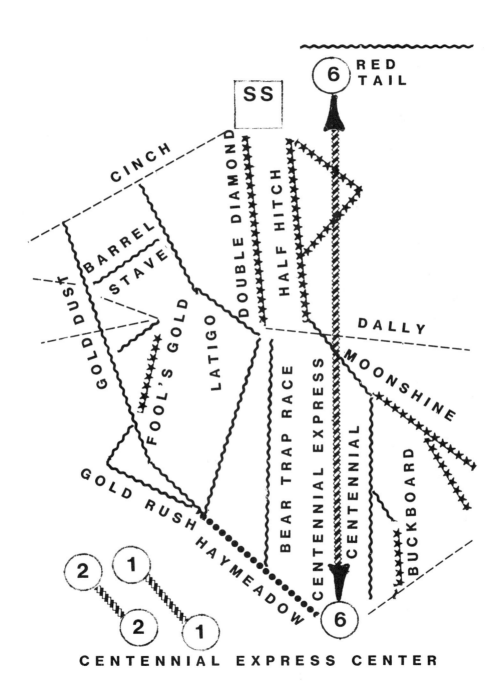

CENTENNIAL EXPRESS CENTER

#1) and Highlands Lift (Chairlift #2) are regular speed two passenger chairlifts which service the beginner area at the base of the mountain.

THE RUNS

CINCH (Green): Cinch is a catwalk that begins at the summit. It reaches Spruce Saddle and then runs through the east side of the Centennial Express Center. Look for it on your trail map; the comments about its intersection with the following trails will be easier to understand.

LATIGO (Blue): Latigo is a friendly run reached by heading east from Spruce Saddle on Cinch. Latigo takes off downhill to the left. You can stay on Latigo all the way until it reaches Haymeadow at the base. Alternatively you can ski to the left onto Bear Trap Race (where the NASTAR race course and the pay-to-race course is located) or onto Centennial.

GOLD DUST (Blue): Gold Dust is an amiable run. You reach Gold Dust by heading east on Cinch from Spruce Saddle and going a short way past Latigo. Gold Dust also ends up in Haymeadow. However, it has a few wrinkles different from Latigo. If you watch carefully to your left, you can catch a short expert run, Fool's Gold. To the right you can find Assay. Gold Dust is labeled a Family Area, which also distinguishes it from Latigo.

BARREL STAVE (Blue): If you start on Latigo and then decide you would prefer Gold Dust, make a right turn on Barrel Stave. Then say, "Mission accomplished." You will be skiing Gold Dust.

FOOL'S GOLD (Black): By watching and skiing to the left on either Gold Dust or Barrel Stave you catch a short piece of Cinch to reach the top of Fool's Gold. Fool's Gold is steeper than the other terrain in the area.

GOLD RUSH (Blue): Gold Dust and Fool's Gold flow into Gold Rush which leads into Haymeadow.

ASSAY (Blue): If you go east on cinch, avoiding Gold Rush, you will have a couple of chances to ski Assay (as Cinch goes back and forth). Assay also merges into Haymeadow.

HAYMEADOW (Green): Haymeadow is the name of the wide beginner area at the base of Beaver Creek Mountain to the east of the Centennial Express Lift.

DOUBLE DIAMOND (Black): If you ski straight down from Spruce

Saddle you will run into some expert mogul runs. The one farthest to the east is Double Diamond. It is short but challenging.

HALF HITCH (Black):   This is another expert mogul run reached by skiing straight down from Spruce Saddle. Half Hitch runs under the Centennial Express Lift (Chairlift #6).

CENTENNIAL (Black and blue):   Centennial is a long run which begins at the summit and runs through the Stump Park Center before entering the Centennial Express Center. It is designated as an expert run for about one-third of the way down from Spruce Saddle to the base, then it becomes an intermediate run.

BEAR TRAP RACE (Blue):   As Centennial crosses Cinch, switching from expert to intermediate, the intermediate run Bear Trap Race takes off to the right. Located on Bear Trap Race are both the NASTAR race course and the pay-to-race slalom course. Take on your friend, your enemy, or your spouse. Go for it.

DALLY (Green):   Another catwalk, Dally begins in the Centennial Express Center and heads west through the woods to Red Tail Camp. From Red Tail Camp it cuts back to the north and east to the base of Beaver Creek.
      If you miss the Westfall Lift (Chairlift #9) at the end of the day, you will need to take Dally back to the base. It is a flat run; be prepared.

MOONSHINE (Black):   Moonshine offers another chance to ski expert, mogul terrain. When you ski the upper expert runs in this Center under Spruce Saddle, you can still get to Moonshine. Stay to the left on Centennial. Moonshine is a fun run with lots of bumps, but not a great deal of vertical drop. It runs into Dally as Dally is making its final stretch to the ski area base.

BOOTLEG (Black):   Bootleg is an offshoot of Moonshine. It takes off from the right side of Moonshine. There is essentially no difference between Moonshine and Bootleg as they run parallel into Dally.

BUCKBOARD (Black):   Buckboard diverts left from Centennial after the Moonshine cutoff. Its terrain is similar to Centennial.

LEAVING AND CONNECTING WITH OTHER CENTERS

      At the end of the day you exit the Centennial Express Center by leaving the Ski Area.
      Connect with other centers from the top of Centennial Express Center by

skiing east to the Rose Bowl Center on C1 Prime or Stone Meadow; up to the Stump Creek Center on Chairlift #8; or west on Red Tail to the Birds of Prey Center. From these Centers you can access other Centers.

2. STUMP PARK CENTER (Stump Park Lift, Chairlift #8)

INTRODUCTION

The Stump Park Center provides a number of trails for the strong beginner to the strong intermediate. Look for some advanced bumps above Spruce Saddle. Stump Park also serves as a pathway to a number of other centers. These include the Birds of Prey Center (by staying to the west on the Flat Tops trail); the Drink of Water Center (by skiing to the east); and the Rose Bowl Center (by skiing down Powell).

ARRIVAL

You reach Stump Park Center by riding the Centennial Espress Lift (Chairlift #6) to Spruce Saddle. Ski to the east, past the Spruce Saddle building; look to your right for the Stump Creek Lift.

THE LIFT

The Stump Creek Lift (Chairlift #8) is a regular speed three passenger chairlift.

THE RUNS

POWELL (Green): When you get off of the Stump Park Lift, ski to the east. Looking down the mountain you will see Powell on your right. It runs close to the Drink of Water Lift (Chairlift #5). Powell is a long, relatively easy run. It intersects Cinch twice. The first time it meets Cinch, Cinch is heading east over to the Drink of Water Lift. The second time it runs into Cinch, the run is heading west back over to the Stump Park Lift. You will notice a control gate and a moguled expert trail, Spider, a run in the Rose Bowl Center. To stay on easier terrain in the Stump Creek Park Center, make this left turn onto Cinch.

CENTENNIAL (Green and blue): Centennial runs under the Stump Park Chair. It starts off easy, then gets a little more difficult. Just above Spruce Saddle, decent moguls develop. If you ski to the west you can skirt the

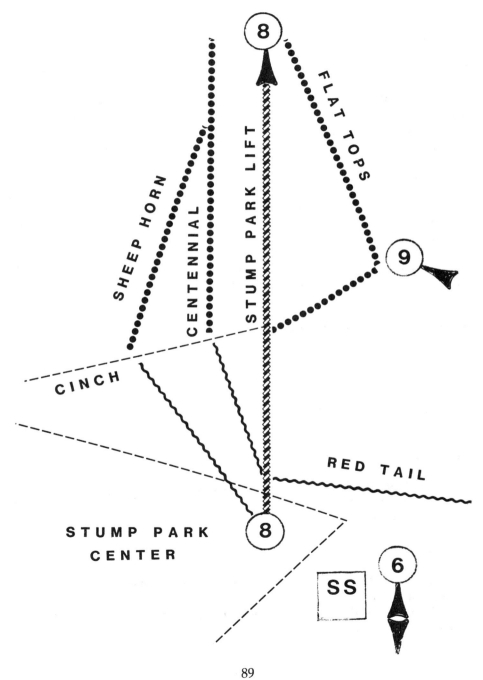

moguls. Centennial does continue down to the base of Beaver Creek Mountain. The remainder of the trail is discussed in the Centenial Express Center section.

SHEEPHORN (Green and blue):   As you ski down Centennial, stick to the right. You will see Sheephorn take off from Centennial near the top. Like Centennial which it parallels, Sheephorn starts off easy and then gets steeper.

FLAT TOPS (Green):   Ski Flat Tops for easy, fun skiing and/or to access the Birds of Prey Center. Flat Tops is the farthest trail to the west from the summit. Flat Tops eventually cuts back onto Centennial above Spruce Saddle. Flat Tops is the trail you take from the top to enter the Birds of Prey Center.

LEAVING AND CONNECTING WITH OTHER CENTERS

Stump Park Center serves as a pathway to a number of other centers. From the top, directly to the east you can ski into the Drink of Water Center. By skiing directly down Powell you can head into the Rose Bowl Center. If you stay to the west on Flat Tops, you can ski over to the Birds of Prey Center. Ski all the way down to Spruce Saddle to access the Centennial Express Center to the base of Beaver Creek Mountain.

3. ROSE BOWL CENTER (Rose Bowl Lift, Chairlift #4)

INTRODUCTION

Rose Bowl is not as sweet and calm as it may sound. It has excellent mogul runs.

ARRIVAL

To ski into the Rose Bowl Center base, head east from Spruce Saddle. To reach the Rose Bowl at the top, ski down Powell from the summit of Beaver Creek Mountain.

THE LIFT

The Rose Bowl Lift (Chairlift #4) is a regular speed three passenger chairlift. It ascends over Spider, allowing a clear view of this slope. It also provides views of Ripsaw, looking uphill to your left, and Cataract, looking downhill to your right.

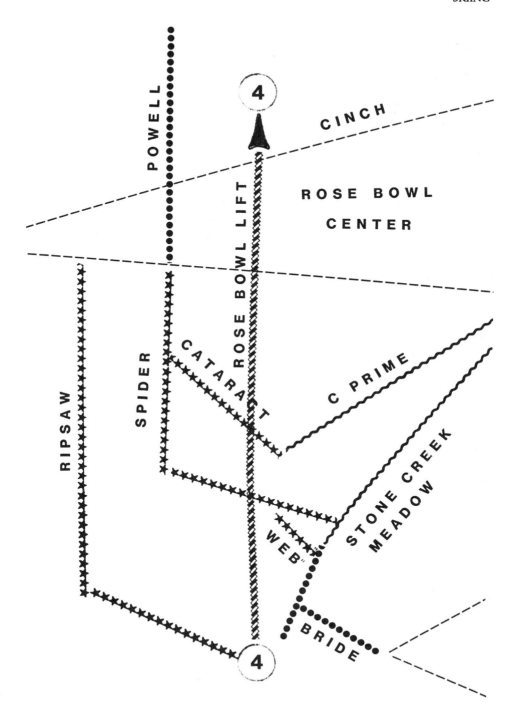

THE RUNS

Runs From Spruce Saddle

STONE CREEK MEADOW (Blue): This intermediate run takes you from Spruce Saddle to the Rose Bowl Lift (Chairlift #4). If you don't like all the moguls, you can ski down the easy section and then head west on Cinch. This will put you back at Spruce Saddle.

C1 PRIME (Blue): Although similar to Stone Creek Meadow, C1 Prime is steeper and has some nice moguls. If you have trouble here, you can easily ski down onto Stone Creek Meadow. An intermediate skier can give this a try. If you don't feel up to the bumps, there is the escape route downslope to Stone Creek Meadow.

Runs From The Top Of Rose Bowl

RIPSAW (Black): To enter the Ripsaw run you have to ski a little bit to the east on Cinch. For a while it is relatively flat. Gradually, it gets steeper and the moguls get bigger. Where the moguls get big, the trail is wide. Skiers who like wide open spaces when they are in the bumps will find lots of room to maneuver. Ripsaw ends at the base of the Rose Bowl Lift.

SPIDER (Black): Reach Spider by skiing Powell (green), either from the summit or from the top of the Rose Bowl Lift. If you reach the entry to Spider, and do not want to ski it, make a left turn onto Cinch and head back to Spruce Saddle. Spider is a wonderful bump run. You can get have the excitement of the people on the Rose Bowl Lift watching you. Spider ends up on Stone Creek Meadow and takes you back to the base of the Rose Bowl Lift (Chairlift #4).

CATARACT (Black): Cataract takes off from the left side of Spider. It is somewhat steeper, so be prepared for a faster line and bigger moguls. It, too, ends up on Stone Creek Meadow, funnelling into the Rose Bowl Lift.

WEB (Black): Web takes off from the right side of Spider, near the bottom. It, too, ends up in Stone Creek Meadow.

LEAVING AND CONNECTING WITH OTHER CENTERS

To leave from the top of Rose Bowl Center, take Cinch over to Sheep Horn, and you will end up at Spruce Saddle. Otherwise, ski down the left side of Stone Creek Meadow and make a left turn onto Bride which will take you over to Gold Dust in the Centennial Express Center.

4. DRINK OF WATER CENTER (Drink of Water Lift, Chairlift #5)

INTRODUCTION

Drink of Water Center is an excellent place for strong beginner skiers to get a feel for the mountain. Here even at an early stage in your skiing, you can get high on the mountain and enjoy the vistas. This entire Center is indicated as a slow skiing area. If you are having difficulty, the Ski Patrol Cabin is located at the top of the Drink of Water Lift (Chairlift #5). In the cabin there is a public warming hut available to you.

The views from the Drink of Water Center are spectacular. Look over to Vail Ski Resort and the Game Creek Bowl to the east. The Gore Range is seen in its magnificence.

ARRIVAL

First take the Centennial Express Lift (Chairlift #6) to Spruce Saddle. Ski to your left. Then take the Stump Park Lift (Chairlift #8) to the summit. Ski to the east. You will be entering the Drink of Water Center from the top. The top of the Drink of Water Lift and the Ski Patrol Cabin will be there as guideposts.

THE LIFT

The Drink of Water Lift (Chairlift #5) is a regular speed two passenger chairlift.

THE RUNS

RED BUFFALO (Green): Red Buffalo, an easy run in a "slow ski zone," can be lots of fun. Enjoy it. This is a lengthy run on which beginners can get in lots of mileage.

BOOTH GARDENS (Green): Booth Gardens is also a fun easy run on a "slow ski zone" trail. It is pleasantly terraced.

POWELL (Green): See Stump Park Center description. This is a beginner slope which can take you from the top of Drink of Water Center to its base. However, it is not a slow skiing zone. Also, be careful to make the right turn onto Cinch to get back to Chairlift #5 or you will be out of the

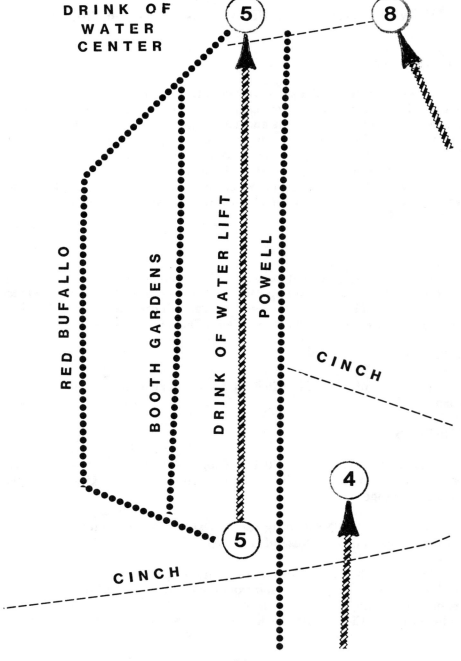

Drink of Water Center.

LEAVING AND CONNECTING WITH OTHER CENTERS

If you are a beginner, the easiest way down is to take Cinch from the bottom of the Center. Taking Cinch you can ski either to Spruce Saddle or to the base of the ski area. Expert skiers may prefer skiing into the Rose Bowl Center from the bottom of the Drink of Water Center. Intermediate skiers might like to ski from the top of the Drink of Water Center into the Stump Park Center.

5. BIRDS OF PREY CENTER (Westfall Lift, Chairlift #9)

INTRODUCTION

Beaver Creek has become famous for its own difficult, double diamond Birds of Prey Center. This Center has impressive, steep runs with plenty of moguls. At the base, you will find Red Tail Camp, a small public restaurant with restrooms.

ARRIVAL

You reach the Birds of Prey runs, except for Red Tail, by taking the Stump Park (Chairlift #8) up from Spruce Saddle. Then ski the west side on Flat Tops, looking for the entry points to Golden Eagle, Peregrine, and Goshawk. Alternatively ski west down Red Tail from Spruce Saddle.

THE LIFT

Westfall Lift (Chairlift #9) is a regular speed two passenger chairlift. It ascends over Peregrine. Preview Peregrine by taking Red Tail down to the base of Birds of Prey Center and then riding up this lift.

THE RUNS

GOLDEN EAGLE (Double black diamond):   I do not recommend anyone take Golden Eagle, except possibly on a powder day. It is steep, narrow, and hard to find amidst the trees.

PEREGRINE (Double black diamond):   Peregrine is a wonderful run when the conditions are ripe. It is steep, full of moguls, and lengthy. It runs

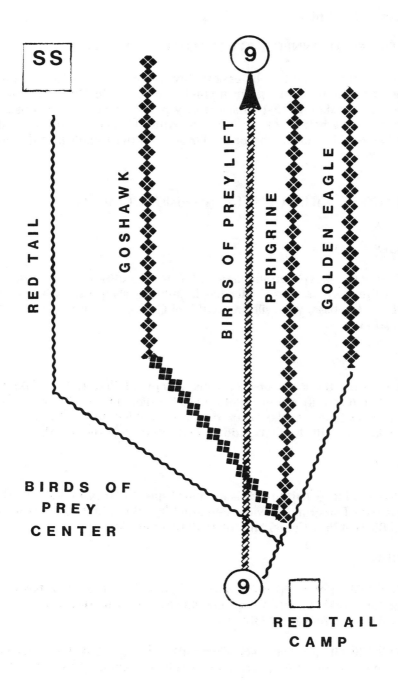

under the Westfall Lift (Chairlift #9).

GOSHAWK (Double black diamond): Goshawk may be easier than Peregrine but it is still a well-moguled steep run for expert skiers.

RED TAIL (Blue): Ski west from Spruce Saddle down Red Tail, the intermediate way to the base of Birds of Prey Center and Red Tail Camp. This is a fun run.

LEAVING AND CONNECTING WITH OTHER CENTERS

Leave Birds of Prey Center at the top by riding up the Westfall Lift (Chairlift #9) and skiing down to Spruce Saddle. At the bottom of the Birds of Prey Center, you have a choice of two other centers. One is the difficult Grouse Mountain Express Center serviced by the Grouse Mountain Express Lift (Chairlift #10). The other is the Larkspur Bowl Center serviced by the Larkspur Lift (Chairlift #11). You can ski Dally to the base of Beaver Creek Mountain.

6. GROUSE MOUNTAIN CENTER (Grouse Mountain Express Lift, Chairlift #10)

INTRODUCTION

Grouse Mountain Center is an expert center, although there are two intermediate ways down. Red Tail Camp is a small cabin with food and restrooms, located near the base of this Center.

ARRIVAL

Arrive at the Grouse Mountain Center by way of the Birds of Prey Center. Ski the more difficult runs of Birds of Prey by taking the Stump Park Lift (Chairlift # 8) up to the top of the Stump Park Center. Then head down on Flat Tops, looking for the entrances to Peregrine or Goshawk. Or head down to the Grouse Mountain Express Center on intermediate Red Tail.

THE LIFT

Grouse Mountain Express Lift (Chairlift #10) is a high-speed quad chair which initially ascends over Ruffed Grouse. Preview the expert sections of Raven Ridge and Ptarmigan. Near the top take a good look at the intermediate section of Raven Ridge.

THE RUNS

SCREECH OWL (Black and blue):   Screech Owl is initially very steep. The turns between bumps are big drops, as mostly expert skiers take this route. It turns into an intermediate trail connecting with the intermediate section of Golden Eagle in the Birds of Prey Center as it heads back down to the base of Grouse Mountain Center.

RAVEN RIDGE (Blue and black):   Raven Ridge starts out as an intermediate run. Half way down it turns left into an expert run. You can avoid the expert section by connecting up with the intermediate section of Golden Eagle and Screech Owl.

CAMP ROBBER ROAD (Blue):   This trail cuts back and forth along the path of Raven Ridge and a number of other expert runs providing an opportunity for a close look at the steep moguled runs without much risk. It eventually runs into the intermediate section of Screech Owl. Take a good look at this run on your official Beaver Creek Ski Map.

PTARMIGAN (Black):   Ski onto this is expert run coming off the left side of Raven Ridge. It is steep and moguled.

RUFFED GROUSE (Black):   This is the expert trail that you viewed on the Grouse Mountain Express Lift. It is a lift line run which branches off Raven Ridge.

OSPREY (Double black diamond):   This expert trail can be reached from Ruffed Grouse or Camp Robber Road. It is steep and moguled, deserving its expert designation.

FALCON PARK (Double black diamond):   This expert trail can be reached from Ruffed Grouse or Camp Robber Road. It, too, is steep and moguled.

BALD EAGLE (Double black diamond):   Access this expert trail from the top or reach its lower sections from Camp Robber Road. It is the steepest trail in this center and well moguled.

LEAVING AND CONNECTING WITH OTHER CENTERS

You can only leave the Grouse Mountain Express Center from its base.

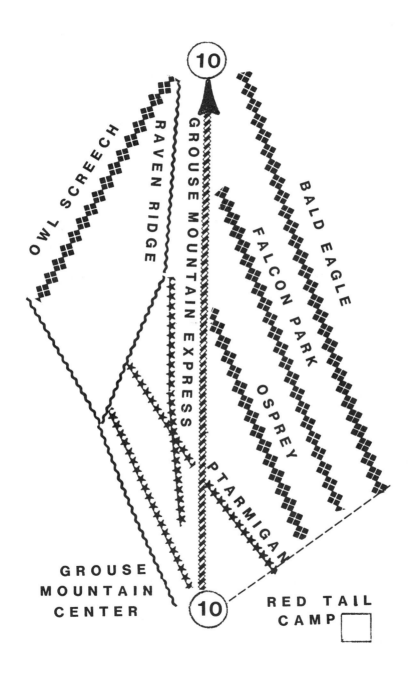

Larkspur Lift (Chairlift #11) in Larkspur Center is located near the base of the Grouse Mountain Express Center. Likewise, Westfall Lift (Chairlift #9), near the base of Grouse Mountain Center, can whisk you to the top of the Birds of Prey Center. Then ski either Birds of Prey Center or head down to Spruce Saddle, on Stump Park Center trails (starting on Flat Tops and finishing either on Centennial, Sheep Horn, or Cinch).

7. LARKSPUR BOWL CENTER (Larkspur Lift, Chairlift # 11)

INTRODUCTION

Larkspur Bowl is a fun bowl. It is U-shaped with intermediate skiing down the middle of the bowl and moguled expert runs down its sides. It faces east and receives morning sun. Red Tail Camp, a small, public restaurant, is located at the base (with restrooms). Beano's Cabin is also in this area, but signs indicate it is private, for members only, during the day. In the evening it is open to the public, a moderately expensive restaurant requiring reservations. Read about it in the Restaurant section.

ARRIVAL

Reach Larkspur Bowl by skiing down any of the Birds of Prey runs, including intermediate Red Tail. Using Red Tail, you do not need to ride up Stump Park Lift (Chairlift #8).

THE LIFT

Larkspur Lift (Chairlift #8) is a regular speed three passenger chairlift. It ascends over Larkspur trail. You can get a good look at the mogul runs, Loco, Star, and Lupine to your left. Yarrow can be seen off to the right.

THE RUNS

LARKSPUR (Blue): Larkspur is the intermediate way down. It sits under the chairlift. From this trail, as well as from the chairlift, you will have a view of all the advanced mogul runs that descend into the bowl. On your map you will notice two other runs in this neighborhood, Blue Bell and Paintbrush. To a skier they all look like the same run.

LUPINE (Black): Looking back down the mountain, ski southeasterly to Lupine. North facing Lupine is a fun mogul run.

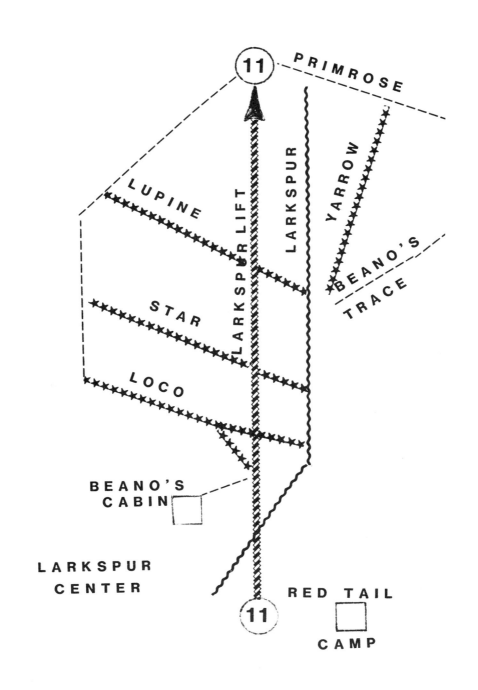

STAR (Black):   Past Lupine, you come to Star, another enjoyable mogul run. It is a short but sweet north facing mogul run.

LOCO (Black):   Past Star you come to Loco, a highly enjoyable mogul run. First bump down and then bump off to the right. The moguls get easier as you move to the right which is ego boosting as well as fun.

YARROW (Black):   To get to Yarrow traverse to the north. Yarrow is an advanced run that is left natural; it does not get as moguled as the trio of runs on the other side. You are more likely to encounter crud. On fresh powder days it is a fantastic run to ski. Eventually funnelling into Larkspur, Yarrow is a southeast facing run.

PRIMROSE AND BEANO'S TRACE: Located past Yarrow, Primrose takes you to the top of Strawberry Park Lift and the base of McCoy Park. Beano's Trace will bring you back to Larkspur Bowl. Neither of these traverses is very exciting in itself, but you can get a look at McCoy Park, Beaver Creek's Mountain Top Cross-Country Ski Center.

LEAVING AND CONNECTING WITH OTHER CENTERS

Leaving Larkspur Bowl is relatively easy. You can switch over to ski Grouse Mountain by taking the Grouse Mountain Express Lift (Chairlift #10). You may choose the Westfall Lift (Chairlift #9) up over the Birds of Prey. From the top of the Westfall Lift, you can ski the Birds of Prey Center or you can head down to Spruce Saddle. Another choice you have is to pick up speed towards the end of Larkspur and catch the Dally Catwalk to the base of Beaver Creek Mountain. Via Primrose you reach Strawberry Park Center.

8. STRAWBERRY PARK CENTER (Strawberry Park Lift, Chairlift #12)

INTRODUCTION

Strawberry Park Center contains McCoy Park which is Beaver Creek's Cross-Country Ski Center, a nordic delight. What is unique about McCoy Park is its location on top of Strawberry Park Center (approximately 10,000 ft. above sea level). Within McCoy Park there is a 30 kilometer track system with 18 trails of machine-set double track and a skating lane.

Snuggle up in the warming room at the top of the Chairlift #12 if you get cold or need a rest. Have a gourmet picnic lunch in the spring. Some alpine trails run from the top of the Strawberry Park Lift to the base of Beaver Creek Mountain. You can download on the Strawberry Park Lift.

Cross-country lessons are available. Tickets need to be purchased in the Vail/Beaver Creek Ski School Center at the base of Beaver Creek Mountain. Review the Cross-Country Skiing Section of this book.

ARRIVAL

The Strawberry Park Lift (Chairlift #12) is across the road to the west from the base area of Beaver Creek Mountain. It is directly across the road from the Village Bus Stop.

THE LIFT

Strawberry Park Lift is a regular speed three passenger chairlift. It ascends over Pitchfork and takes you to the base of McCoy Park, the cross-country ski area on the mountain.

THE RUNS

Nordic Runs Within McCoy Park

Easier runs include Meadows; Cabin Loop; Polaris; and Discover. Intermediate runs include Sanctuary; Morning Star; Aurora; Black Diamond: and Sunshine. Expert runs include Discovery Overlook; Sluice Box; Cabin Ruins; and The Wild Side.

There is a Citizen's Biathlon Course in McCoy Park as well. You may note the private Trapper's Cabin if you are on Meadows. Contact the Activity Center at Beaver Creek if you wish to make use of Trapper's Cabin. Look it up in the Restaurant Section.

Alpine Runs In Strawberry Park Center

PITCHFORK (Black and blue): This intermediate trail runs under the Strawberry Park Lift. You view it on your way up the chairlift. The expert section can be skirted.

STACKER (Black and blue): This trail has an expert section which cannot be avoided. It is west of Pitchfork.

BEANO'S TRACE (Green): The easy way down starts on Beano's Trace which guides you to Paint Brush in the Larkspur Center. Taking Paint Brush down to Dally leads you to the base of Beaver Creek Mountain.

LEAVING AND CONNECTING WITH OTHER CENTERS

You can download on Strawberry Park Lift (Chairlift #12). Otherwise, any of the trails listed under Alpine Runs direct you to the base of Strawberry Park Center or Beaver Creek Mountain.

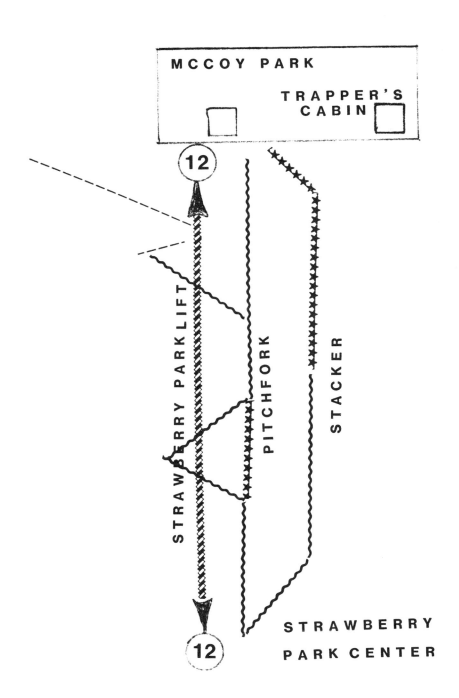

SKI SCHOOL

THE EXCITEMENT OF IMPROVING YOUR SKIING
THROUGH VAIL/BEAVER CREEK SKI SCHOOL

ADULT SKI LESSONS
    476-3239 for Vail Mountain
    949-2300 for Beaver Creek

Vail/Beaver Creek Ski School is an enormous ski school dedicated to teaching ski techniques for everyone from the frightened beginner to the confident mogul masher or ski racer. Vail's system of teaching is the same as the Professional Ski Instructors of America (PSIA) system. With either group or private lessons, students use the "express lift lanes" which are reserved for the Ski School. This privilege extends to snowboard, cross-country, and telemark classes.

Group lessons are available at Golden Peak Ski School Center at the eastern end of Vail Mountain; Lionshead Ski School Center at the western end of Vail Mountain; and Beaver Creek Ski School Center at the base of Beaver Creek Mountain. Adults need to be in the appropriate "Ski School Yard" by 9:45 a.m. for group lessons. Lionshead Ski School Center does not offer cross-country or snowboard lessons.

Classes are grouped by age and ability. Vail uses a number system from level one (for the "never-ever" brand new beginner skier) to level nine (an expert skier who is working on a focused area). These levels have descriptions to help you to place yourself in the correct level. At the base and at the on-mountain Vail/Beaver Creek Ski School Centers, videotapes show demonstrations of each ski level to make it as clear as possible which group level you would like to join.

You can enjoy a free Ski Tip, a critiqued ski run on a gentle slope with an instructor to help you to see which group level is for you. This on mountain Ski Tip is especially valuable if you are thinking of taking an afternoon ski workshop. Ski Tip sessions are held at 11:00 a.m. everyday at Mid-Vail and Spruce Saddle.

All day classes run from 10:00 a.m. to 3:45 p.m. daily. Though you must check in by 9:45 a.m., it's better to be at the lesson area around 9:30 a.m. or even earlier to get through the registration format without anxiety about being late.

In addition to classes, there are also Guide Programs for levels seven through nine which help you to experience the Vail ski mountain with only light coaching from the instructor/guide. "Mountain Guides" is for intermediate skiers. "Super Guides" is for advanced and expert skiers.

Afternoon workshops for levels five through nine provide focused attention by an instructor on a subject of your choice. The Style Workshop is for intermediate and advanced skiers. Instructors help you with form and technique. In the Race Workshop skiers learn how to run gates. They also learn strategy. The Bump and Powder Workshops provide input to more advanced skiers to improve technique and confidence in these areas.

Vail/Beaver Creek Ski School offers Breakthrough Groups for levels five through eight. Students ski with the same instructor for three days with the goal of really making a breakthrough to another level of skiing. These Breakthrough Groups have become very popular.

Thinking about a private lesson? You pick your instructor and the time of day that you wish to start. From one to five people can enjoy a private lesson, including children or a family. With private lessons you learn in your own way and at your own pace. Private lessons are available at the Vail Village Ski School Center as well as all of the other Ski School Centers. All day private lessons usually begin at 8:30 a.m.

In addition to the base Ski School Centers, other Centers where you can purchase private lessons include the cabin at Eagle's Nest; the Look Ma Restaurant on the third floor of the Mid-Vail building; Two Elk Restaurant; and Spruce Saddle Restaurant.

A complimentary Meet the Mountain tour for intermediate and advanced skiers is a wonderful way to learn about the mountain ranges, local history, wildlife, and future plans. Vail tours start at 1:00 p.m. at Wildwood Shelter on Sunday, Monday, and Tuesday. Learn about Beaver Creek Mountain at 1:00 p.m. on Monday and Tuesday, starting at Spruce Saddle.

CHILDREN'S SKI LESSONS
479-2040 for Golden Peak
479-2042 for Lionshead
949-2304 for Beaver Creek

SKI LESSONS FOR CHILDREN AGES SIX TO TWELVE

Group lessons from Vail/Beaver Creek instructors for children from ages six to twelve are available at Golden Peak Ski School Center at the eastern end of Vail Mountain; Lionshead Ski School Center at the western end of Vail Mountain; and at Beaver Creek Ski School Center. The children are grouped by ability levels, and off they go. The same nine levels of skiing performance are utilized with this age group as with adults. Children in this age group do need to be at the appropriate Ski School Yards, ready to go, at an earlier time than the adults. They should be there at 9:15 a.m.

In addition to skiing regular terrain, children also go to special areas,

Children's Mountain Adventure attractions, which provide entertainment while developing special skiing skills. Maps of Vail and Beaver Creek Children's Mountain Adventure attractions are available to help adults find these areas. These maps are not as exact as the official Vail Ski Map.

On Vail Mountain watch out for the **Lost Silver Mine** off of Simba in the Lionshead Center. Also, in this Center you can check out **Gitchegumee Gulch** next to the Chairlift #15 beginner area. There is also a little park, **Lionshead Park**, located near the base of this Center, just to the east of Born Free which can be utilized in winter as well as summer.

Magical Forest with **Jackrabbit Joe's Camp** can be reached from Minnie's Mile but probably more easily from Ledges. This path through the woods can be challenging.

Indian Burial Ground is located in the Avanti Express Center to the east of Avanti. It is enjoyable. The pitch of the slope is not as steep in this wooded area as it is in Magical Forest. Indian Burial Ground is a walk through "forest."

Golden Peak Center features **Fort Whippersnapper** with a true "old fort" look. A general store, saloon, and jail are featured. Look out for **Devil's Fork Mine** in Golden Peak Center, as well.

At Beaver Creek, check out **Tombstone Territory**, just to the east of Spruce Saddle; it is great fun. **Buckaroo Bowl Snow Park** is located very close to the base of the mountain. Off Gold Dust you will be able to find the **Hibernating Bear Cave**. An **Indian Burial Ground** is located off of Red Buffalo in the Drink of Water Center. An **Indian Village** is located off of Latigo in the Centennial Center.

If your child wants to take you to one of these fabulous, imaginative attractions, be sure to go with enthusiasm. After all, there is the "inner child" in all of us needing to be nourished with such memorable events.

You can get special Children's Adventure Maps at the Children's Ski School Centers, which will provide some help in locating the attractions. They are not meant, however, to take the place of official Vail or Beaver Creek Ski Maps in terms of being accurate guides to the trail systems. Check out the maps. Ski with your kids (as long as you can keep up). Have fun!

SKI LESSONS FOR CHILDREN AGES THREE TO FIVE

Vail is a great ski area for young children's lessons. Lessons for children are available at Golden Peak Ski School Center on the eastern end of Vail Mountain; at Lionshead Ski School Center on the western end of Vail Mountain; and at Beaver Creek Ski School Center. Children usually take all day group lessons which include lunch. Programs for children too young to take official lessons take place at the Small World Play School. Yes, the Disney World is available (in part) at Vail. Children as young as three months receive day care in the Small World program. Small World Play School is available at

Golden Peak or Beaver Creek.

Once a child is willing to learn to ski and is potty trained, there are several levels of programs available. The Mini Mice program is an early introduction to skiing through games and snow-related play. The Mogul Mice program is for four year olds and up who can stand on their skis but are not yet able to stop. Once children can stop on their own they can be in the Super Star program.

In the Super Star format, the children go up on the mountain, first to beginner areas. When their skiing ability allows, they venture onto the green trails. They also make use of the Children's Adventure Mountain attractions. Refer to the previous section on Ski School for ages six to twelve for more information about these attractions.

Even at this young age the one to nine level system is utilized because the skiing skills are technique related and not necessarily strength related.

CAUTIONS

Vail Valley is a wonderful, beautiful, exhilarating place to live or vacation. However, when people engage in so much vigorous activity at Vail's high altitude, they need to observe some cautions.

Overview

ALTITUDE

If you are from a lower altitude, it will take a while for your red blood cells to increase to the level necessary to bring sufficient oxygen to your muscles and brain. You need to take it easy. Listen to your body. If it is giving you signs of fatigue, dizziness, breathlessness, or headache, take it easy. There is a report on Altitude Sickness later in this section for more details.

SUN

With higher altitude there is a substantial increase in the intensity of the sun rays because there is less atmosphere to filter them. You will need sun screen and sun glasses (or ski goggles). So will your children. Be prepared for the sun. Wear sun block of at least SPF 15. Make sure your sun glasses or goggles filter out ultraviolet light. It takes a few hours for your skin to get pink or red; once that happens, it is already too late

DEHYDRATION

The mountain air is dry. Your body fluid loss is two times greater at this altitude than at sea level. The decreased amount of oxygen will cause you to breathe more rapidly and lose additional body water. Furthermore, you will breathe more rapidly because you are exerting more energy than in a sedentary job. Adults need to drink eight glasses of non-alcoholic fluid daily. Limit your alcohol intake. Alcohol, while a liquid, is also a diuretic.

WEATHER CHANGEABILITY

While preparing for the sun, take note that you also have to prepare for wind, snow, and/or rain. Weather in the Rocky Mountains is variable and changes rapidly. To deal with this tricky situation, dress in layers so that you will be able to take garments off or add them on as the weather changes.

FROSTBITE

Frostbite results from cooling of tissues in a body part followed by destruction of these tissues. If you experience frostbite do not rub the affected areas as this worsens tissue injury. Re-warm tissue in water between 100 and 106 degrees (common hot tub temperatures). The best cure is prevention. Have your warm layers ready to put on when indicated. And do this for your children, too!

LIGHTNING

Among the most dangerous weather changes is a lightning storm. People do die from lightning strikes in the mountains. You can be struck by lightning on the ski trail, on the golf green, or on a horseback ride. If a thunderstorm with lightning develops, get off of ridges as soon as possible. Be sure to get off of Eagle's Nest Ridge. Vail and Beaver Creek will shut down the lifts when thunderstorms occur, but only after everyone is off the lift at the top. If you cannot get to a building, try to get into a wooded area, if possible. However, do not stand right next to a tree.

INJURY AND WORSE

Common injuries involve the knee or thumb. Do not ignore pain in these areas; have it checked out medically. If you aggravate the injury, this will lengthen the recovery period or make the condition chronic. Feel free to utilize the services of the Vail/Beaver Creek Ski Patrol if you have any questions at all about your health while on the mountains.

People have been seriously hurt or killed while participating in alpine activities. Skier collisions have led to death. Colliding with a tree has caused death. People have been known to suffocate when their head buries in a tree well (where neither skiers nor groomers pack the snow down). Be careful. Read the Skier's Responsibility Code and the Colorado Skier Safety Act.

If you leave the designated ski area, you are on your own. If you need to be rescued, it will not be by the free Ski Patrol system, but by other rescue resources which will be costly and billed to you.

AVALANCHES

Avalanches are not much of an issue if you are skiing in bounds on the designated open section of Vail Mountain or Beaver Creek Mountain. However, if you are downhilling in out of bounds chutes or ski touring in the backcountry, avalanches are a real potential hazard. Learn how to avoid them and learn how to survive them.

111

ALCOHOL AND DRUGS

Your usual tolerance of alcohol may not hold at this high altitude. Do not drink heavily. Be aware that some people drink heavily or take drugs on the mountains and on the streets. Alcohol deaths are among the greatest tragedies in the Vail Valley, just as they are throughout the country. Drive defensively, especially in the late evening. Don't drive drunk or let a friend drive drunk!

I personally have a hard time dealing with the fact that alcohol consumption is not only allowed on the mountain but that it is also encouraged through the sale of beer and wine at restaurant locations on the mountains.

Altitude Sickness

Altitude sickness is a real entity, as any of you who have had this ailment can testify. Often it is a vague lethargic feeling, almost like having the flu. Low oxygen is the culprit. The level of oxygen at Vail's altitude is probably 40% lower than the oxygen level at sea level. Altitude sickness can be dangerous and life threatening when someone develops High Altitude Pulmonary Edema (HAPE) or High Altitude Cerebral Edema (HACE). These two conditions are rare. But physicians do believe that roughly 25% of the visitors suffer from Acute Mountain Sickness with headaches, nausea, loss of appetite and insomnia.

The best recommendation is to go easy for the first two days at altitude. Go easy on exertion, on how high you go up the mountain, and how much alcohol you consume during this critical 48 hour period.

It is important to stay hydrated to alleviate the effects of altitude illness. This also means that you should stay off alcohol. Although alcohol is served as a liquid, its main effect is to act as a diuretic which will dehydrate the consumer. Also, the visitor from a lower level should pay attention to the feeling "I just don't feel like it today." Look out for symptoms such as headache, nausea, fatigue and shortness of breath; then take it easy. Those who push themselves anyway (perhaps believing that their ill feelings are just psychological and it will ruin their vacation if they give in and take some time off) are not paying close enough attention to the body's warning of a physiologic syndrome.

A possible remedy, now in the research process, involves placing the patient in a pressurized bag; then air is pumped in to increase the atmospheric pressure, relieving the altitude sickness. But this is not presently available.

Oxygen condensors can be prescribed so that the patient can "go home" rather than spending a costly night with an oxygen hook up in the hospital.

The Skier's Responsibility Code

1.) Ski in control so that you can stop or avoid other skiers or objects.
2.) When skiing downhill or overtaking another skier you must avoid the skier below you.
3.) Do not stop where you obstruct a trail or are not visible from above.
4.) When entering a trail or starting downhill, yield to other skiers.
5.) All skiers must wear retention straps, ski brakes, or other devices to prevent runaway skis.
6.) Keep off closed trails and posted areas, and observe all posted signs.

The Colorado Skier Safety Act

Safety first! Only in this context can skiing maintain the excitement of a healthy invigorating sport. It is your duty to obey the law. The Colorado State Legislature has recognized that dangers are inherent in the sport of skiing, regardless of any and all reasonable safety measures that can be implemented. The Colorado Skier Safety Act of 1979 as amended, contains provisions that are important to all skiers, snowboarders, etc. Copies of the Act are available at tickets offices or the Ski Patrol facilities.

Highlights include:

1.) You are responsible for using a lift safely. Ask the operator for assistance if you are unfamiliar with lift loading or unloading.
2.) Do not throw objects from the lift. Do not bang your skis together while riding the lift.
3.) Each skier solely has the responsibility for knowing the range of his or her own ability to negotiate any ski slope or trail and to ski within the limits of such ability.
4.) Each skier has the duty to maintain control of his speed and course at all times when skiing and to maintain a proper lookout so as to be able to avoid other skiers and objects.
5.) Use of lifts or trails while impaired by alcohol or drugs is unlawful.
6.) If you are involved in a collision with another skier, you are required to give your name and address to the Ski Patrol.
7.) Do not ski on slopes or trails posted closed by sign or rope.
8.) It is your responsibility to obey all posted information and warnings.
9.) You must refrain from acting in any manner which may cause or contribute to your injury or the injury of others.

Medical Help

(In extreme emergencies call 911)

AVON MEDICAL CENTER
949-3222

DOCTORS ON CALL
949-5434

ORTHOPAEDIC SURGERY

STEADMAN HAWKINS CLINIC
476-1100

VAIL ORTHOPAEDICS & SPORTS MEDICINE
476-7220

VAIL INTERNAL MEDICINE
476-7600

VAIL MOUNTAIN MEDICAL
476-5695

VAIL MOUNTAIN RESCUE
Contact through Eagle County Sheriff
911

VAIL PSYCHIATRIC
Ned R. Harley, M.D., P.C.
"Hey that's me!"
476-1521

VAIL VALLEY EMERGENCY PHYSICIANS
476-8065

EXCITING DINING

A wide selection of restaurants with variety in pricing exist in the Vail Valley. **EXCITING VAIL** will help you sort this out before you come to Vail or before you head out on your evening sojourn. Arriving in Vail, you will discover an abundance of restaurant advertising in the newspapers *(Vail Daily, Vail Trail, Avon Beaver Creek Times)*; on television; and in various other media. The Restaurant Section in **EXCITING VAIL** gives an unbiased point of view. I have personally eaten at and thoroughly reviewed almost 150 restaurants in the Vail Valley to bring you this information.

The restaurants are located in a variety of places. Beside restaurants in Vail Village and Lionshead, there are dining establishments across Vail Valley and in West Vail. Surprising enough there is a restaurant in residential East Vail. Beaver Creek has excellent restaurants. You will also find wonderful dining in Avon, Minturn, Red Cliff, Eagle-Vail, and Edwards.

I present my findings as a professional person, not a gourmet, although I do like gourmet food. I have eaten in many ski resorts in the Rockies, from Jackson Hole, Wyoming, throughout Colorado, and down to Taos, New Mexico. I have also traveled in France, Italy, Mexico, and Costa Rica.

In addition to commenting on the quality of food, I make observations to help you avoid an awkward financial situation. The $ signs that go along with the description of each restaurant and its food indicate roughly how expensive a particular establishment is. A single $ stands for inexpensive. $$$$ stands for expensive, but within reason. There are restaurants which have more than $$$$, but most fit between $ and $$$$.

EXCITING VAIL is dedicated to helping you have an enjoyable vacation dining experience. I offer one caveat: guidebooks cannot account for change. Menus change, chefs change, restaurants come and go. Information could change after the printing of this book (and probably will). Look for future editions.

The restaurants are presented alphabetically with special attention to their dinner menus. The on-mountain restaurants which are open for breakfast and lunch only are presented after the alphabetical section, while Beano's Cabin, Trapper's Cabin, and Anderson's Cabin (on-mountain and open evenings) are presented in the main selection. The restaurants are also listed by food type and by location. Where you are staying and your transportation situation may influence your choice of eating establishments.

If you would like to provide specific comments about your restaurant experiences, please feel free to write me: Ned R. Harley, P.O. Box 4577, Vail, CO 81658.

DINNER RESTAURANTS IN VAIL VALLEY
Which May Serve Breakfast, Lunch, And Apres Ski

ALFIE PACKER'S $$
Lionshead Mall
476-9732

Alfie Packer's is a great après ski spot. It has a wonderful, sunny deck, looking directly at the mountain. If there is sun and a crowd on the deck, it is easy to find. They call their afternoon après ski the Bad Attitude Cafe but then quickly claim that Alfie's is Vail's friendliest bar.

Alfie Packer's also offers food. Appetizers include shrimp quesadilla; BBQ shrimp wrapped in bacon; fried zucchini; hot chicken wings; muchos nachos; mozzarella fingers; javelin steak; ravioli stuffed with chorizo sausage and cheese; and guacamole galore. Their salads include Caesar; spinach; grilled chicken; and pasta. They have a salad bar. They also serve burgers; pastrami; turkey; tuna; BLT and veggie sandwiches.

For Mexican favorites choose among fajitas; burritos; enchiladas; and a tamale plate. You have your choice of beef or chicken with most of these entrees.

North of the border entrees are excellent. I have enjoyed their black a

Angus New York strip steak and grilled shrimp fettuccine. Other items such as cajun-style catfish and Alaskan crab legs sound delicious. Chicken breasts come in a variety of styles. Alfie Packer's serves them with tequila lime sauce; marsala; or with dijon mustard.

For dessert try a Fudge Packer, a fudge brownie topped with Cherry Garcia frozen yogurt and smothered with chocolate fudge syrup. Other desserts include cheesecake and a caramel granny apple pie.

Live entertainment is frequently available. Check the newspapers.

Alfie Packer's accepts Visa, MasterCard, and American Express. A children's menu is available with cheese enchiladas; cheeseburgers; chicken wings; grilled cheese; hot dogs; and bacon cheese hot dogs.

ALFREDO'S $$$$
Westin Hotel
Cascade Village, Vail
476-7111

If quiet elegance and excellent food is what you are searching for, consider Alfredo's. Alfredo's is located in the Westin Hotel. It's in a wonderful setting. You can look out at the Gore Creek through big picture windows. Settle yourself into the comfortable upholstered chairs and luxuriate in the rich, dark paneling. Enjoy Peter Vavra playing the piano.

Wonderful baked rolls and herbed garlic bread served with rich olive oil let you know up front that this evening's meal is not on your diet plan.

Alfredo's combines Northern Italian and New American cuisine, making for a creative culinary style.

I had a wonderful pheasant soup to begin, a specialty of the house. Appetizers range from seared Wyoming venison medallions to California snails to Alaskan snow crab cakes.

My first entree at Alfredo's was a Maple-Bourbon Duckling roasted crisp with pistachio crust. This certainly was creative and delicious. The fettuccine alfredo contained reduced cream, sherry, scallions and mild seasonings. Once I tried a special rib eye of veal. This was one of the best veal meals I have ever eaten.

Other choices include fresh seafood such as salmon (gently broiled with whole grain mustard and dill pickle cream); seared fresh swordfish; and roulades of fresh lemon sole (poached in a dry Cortese, shallots and thyme, glazed with cream and butter).

Additionally Alfredo's offers chicken; lamb chops; loin of lamb; filet mignon; smoked pheasant; scaloppini of veal; or a veal chop. Every day there is a fresh special pasta selection. You can also have hickory smoked sea scallops or ricotta stuffed tortellini with tiger prawns and roasted spicy red pepper sauce. Your biggest problem at Alfredo's may be choosing.

The dessert I chose was a Frangelica souffle. It was wonderful. White chocolate, Grand Marnier, peach melba with raspberry creme anglaise, and other dessert souffles are available, depending on the chef's selection. Souffles need to be ordered as you are ordering your meal. Pastries are prepared daily. The service is friendly. Alfredo's also presents a Champagne Sunday Brunch from 10:00 a.m. to 2:00 p.m.

The Westin has begun to offer patio dining overlooking Gore Creek just outside of Alfredo's during the day. Hamburgers and prawns are among the selections for this location.

Alfredo's accepts Visa, MasterCard, American Express, Diner's Club, Choice, and Carte Blanche. Younger children can have a half order of fettuccine alfredo.

ALPENROSE TEA ROOM AND RESTAURANT $$$$
100 East Meadow Drive
in Vail Village Inn Plaza
476-3194

A grand variety of European pastries greets guests at the entry to Tea Room Alpenrose. Make sure to save room. This is a great restaurant to have on your list.

Warm rolls and a fresh salad come with your meal. Appetizers include smoked trout; steak tartare; shrimp cocktail; fettuccine florentine; jumbo cold shrimp; and coquilles St. Jacques, a blend of scallops and shrimp.

Entrees are mostly veal dishes: paillard of veal; veal marsala; Mozart schnitte; and veal Oscar, among others. I had the paillard of veal with scallops, shrimp and crab. It tasted as intriguing as it sounds. Also, I once was lucky enough to be at the Alpenrose when they served a rib eye of veal as a special; it was spectacular. Other choices include chicken and roast pork. They also offer fresh seafood including salmon and prawns. Specialties for the gourmet include osso buco; pepper steak a la francaise; and saltimbocca. I can vouch for the pepper steak a la Francaise, as I enjoyed it thoroughly. Vegetables at Alpenrose are crisp and their presentation is beautiful.

During the winter, Alpenrose is also open for lunch with a wide variety of hot and cold entrees. They also offer chef specialty entrees for lunch.

I personally find it enjoyable during the summer when Alpenrose is open for breakfast. A patio breakfast at the Alpenrose can be the perfect start to an enjoyable day in Vail. Patio lunch is also available in the summer.

Since you pass by the confiserie-patisserie on the way into the restaurant, you have no choice but to be bedazzled at the selection of pastries. The Napoleons are a special treat. The danishes are excellent. In addition to the pastries, they serve European iced chocolate and European iced coffee.

Tea Room Alpenrose accepts Visa, MasterCard, American Express, and Discover Card.

AMBROSIA $$$$
Village Inn Plaza just behind Vail Travel
Vail Village
476-1964

Ambrosia can be a little difficult to find. Once you find it tucked in behind the Vail Village Travel Agency, you will definitely want to come back. The interior architecture is magnificent. One room has a vaulted Gothic ceiling and the other room has a beautiful wood coffered ceiling panels. The detailing is excellent.

Ambrosia has a long standing tradition of serving the highest quality Continental cuisine. The restaurant has been around for approximately a quarter of a century. The regular customers keep coming back. The atmosphere is elegant but relaxing. The wait staff is knowledgeable and congenial.

Frog legs are a popular appetizer, well seasoned and sauteed in lemon butter until tender and delicious. Other appetizers include oysters; salmon; escargot; mussels; and shrimp. Beef steak tartare is also available.

Entrees include elk steak with a fruity black currant sauce or a creamy pepper sauce. The scallops are served in a curry cream sauce with chutney. I have had the Salmon Suchet which was great. It consisted of fresh poached salmon with a white wine sauce and dill. I've had the grilled boneless lamb loin on a bed of seasoned spinach with rosemary mustard sauce and was very pleased. I have also enjoyed their rib eye of beef. They have seven different ways of preparing veal; if you are a veal lover, you can come here every night of the week without being bored. Other beef; fowl; lamb; and seafood dishes are on the menu.

For dessert I enjoyed an excellent Austrian apple strudel which came a la mode. I have also eaten their wonderful Ice Palatschinken. If you cannot pronounce this, just ask for their crepe dessert. It is one great dessert, consisting of a crepe filled with french vanilla ice cream covered with chocolate sauce or raspberry syrup and whipped cream. And if you are good, they will cover one half with the chocolate and the other half with the raspberry sauce. Other desserts include a poached pear with vanilla sauce laced with chocolate syrup or a poached pear with homemade raspberry sauce. They also serve an incredible lemon custard with raspberries and raspberry sauce; this is a very delicate dish. Homemade cheesecake is available. It is worth your while to inquire after the cheesecakes, as each day there is a different variety. Other desserts include orange creme caramel and chocolate mousse.

Ambrosia accepts Visa, MasterCard, and American Express.

ANDERSON'S CABIN $$$$$$
Arrowhead Ski Mountain
926-3029

Anderson's Cabin at Arrowhead Ski Area offers a cozy getaway. It is an almost 100 year old cabin that has been renovated. Now it is a private dining retreat in Bachelor's Gulch. Both lunch and dinner are served here.

For lunch, visitors ski through virgin powder and beautiful aspen groves to reach the cabin. Lunch includes hot soup, excellent fresh bread, and flank steak. Dinner guests are taken to Anderson's Cabin by snocat from the base of Arrowhead Mountain.

Inside there is a warm wood stove and chandeliers glowing with real oil lamps. There is no electricity here. Smoked salmon starts you off. Then you have a choice of beef tenderloin; rack of lamb; veal chops; broiled salmon; or grilled elk steaks.

Desserts are fresh fruit pies or cobblers a la mode.

AUSTRIA HAUS "STUEBERL" $$$
Sonnenalp Hotel
476-5656

Elegance is the word for the Austria Haus "Stueberl." This is Sonnenalp's smallest and most charming restaurant. The restaurant will offer a freshly prepared specialty menu from the alpine regions of Europe -- regional specialties and old world favorites.

Enjoy breakfast as well as dinner.

Austria Haus accepts MasterCard and Visa.

BART AND YETI'S $$
Lionshead Mall
476-2754

Bart and Yeti were two dogs, presently residing in doggie heaven. The restaurant named in their honor is an excellent lunch spot, especially for hamburgers and fries or onion rings. I have enjoyed their chicken sandwich with plum sauce, called Purple Passion. Chili dishes, Irish stew, soup and salad round out the menu. A daily lunch special is often advertised in *The Vail Daily*.

For the hearty appetite, Bart and Yeti's offers BBQ pork ribs; london broil; and chicken fried steak after 5 p.m.

The restaurant has convenient location on the Lionshead Mall and a wonderful terrace. On sunny days many ski instructors bring their classes here to eat, relax and soak in the rays. The service is very, very quick, designed to get you back on the slopes ASAP. But location and service aren't everything: Bart and Yeti's served their millionth meal during 1991. With a million meals to the restaurant's credit, it must be providing a good deal.

Desserts include apple, blueberry and cherry pie, served a la mode if you choose, with vanilla ice cream.

Bart & Yeti's accepts Visa and Mastercard.

BEANO'S CABIN $$$$$
On the Mountain
Beaver Creek
949-9090
949-5750

How about this? Ride a sleigh pulled by a snocat through pine and aspen forests to Beano's Cabin where you will enjoy memorable gourmet dining. In the summer a horse drawn wagon carries you to this mountain retreat. Either way, it is a trip to be remembered. Arriving at the cabin you will find white linen tablecloths and gourmet food in the rustic cabin setting. Enjoy a six course dinner while listening to musical entertainment and watching a crackling fire.

Homemade bread, salads, and soups start you off. As for dinner, virtually all items are cooked over wood to give a mountain flavor. Wood-fired pizza is an appetizer. Entrees include swordfish with lobster green chile; rotisserie-roasted chicken; grilled tenderloin; grilled veal chop; grilled vegetables and corn ravioli; or roast loin of lamb with polenta.

Desserts are fresh baked daily. A popular dessert is chocolate bread pudding with bourbon whipped cream. Other desserts include ices and fresh fruit sorbets.

Beano's has a full bar and extensive wine list. Entertainment is provided by local singer Mac McCain. A children's menu is also available.

Beano's Cabin is open to the public six nights per week. Wednesdays are reserved for Beaver Creek Club members.

Make your plans through the Activities Desk at Beaver Creek, 949-9090, or by calling 949-5750. Beano's accepts Visa, MasterCard, Diner's Club, Carte Blanche, and American Express.

BEAVER TRAP TAVERN $$$
St. James Place
Beaver Creek
845-8930

The Beaver Trap Tavern describes itself as "A Neighborhood Bar In The World's Nicest Neighborhood." It is a little hard to find in the St. James Place condominium complex. Walk to the east end of Beaver Creek's Promenade. Look up a couple flights to see their sign.

Appetizers include chicken wings; onion rings; cajun popcorn shrimp; calamari; chips with salsa or guacamole; battered shrimp; buffalo wings; and 8" pizzas.

Entrees include N.Y. steak; T-bone steak; porterhouse steak; shrimp and scallops; pork tenderloin; blackened catfish; chicken breast with avocado; cajun shrimp; pasta primavera; plus fish and chips. I enjoyed a T-bone steak which came with cooked carrots and mashed potatoes.

The Beaver Trap Tavern also serves lunch and Sunday Brunch. They also provide boxed lunches.

Brunch offerings include a variety of egg dishes; french toast; Neptune crepes with shrimp and scallops; plus blueberry pancakes. You can have a complimentary champagne or mimosa.

Lunch offerings include tasty sandwiches: tuna; club; burgers; french dip; pastrami; alouette herb cheese steak sandwich; ham; and smoked turkey with Swiss cheese.

Desserts include cheesecake; carrot cake; chocolate cake; and apple pie. I enjoyed the carrot cake.

A Kids' Menu offers peanut butter and jelly; grilled cheese; chicken nuggets; or fish and chips. The reasonable $3 price includes a soft drink and an ice cream sundae. Beaver Trap Tavern features magic shows on Saturday nights.

The Beaver Trap Tavern accepts Visa, Mastercard, and American Express. The restaurant will also provide room service to St. James Place.

BLACK DIAMOND BAR AND GRILL $$$$
Beaver Creek Lodge
845-9800 ext 751

The Black Diamond Bar and Grill is a beautiful restaurant in a beautiful hotel. Free valet parking is available. The restaurant features Continental and American cuisine. Food is prepared in an open air bistro style kitchen.

Excellent rolls come with your meal. Soups and salads are a la carte. The Caesar salad is said to be excellent. Appetizers include escargot; scallops; mushrooms; steak tartare; and jumbo shrimp.

I sampled a few entrees, all of which are excellent. The filet mignon was the biggest piece of filet mignon I have ever eaten; it was done to my liking, rare all the way through. The fresh salmon was excellent. It comes grilled, steamed, or blackened, served with the chef's daily sauce. The boneless breast of duck was served sauteed in a pink peppercorn sauce, intriguing and enjoyable.

Other entrees include chicken dishes such as cajun chicken New Orleans; scampi; excellent pasta such as pasta pescadore with shrimp, salmon, and scallops; prime sirloin steak; prime rib; veal medallions; and either rack of lamb or grilled lamb chops.

Desserts include cream caramel; cheesecake; mousse; cherry pie; gold brick sundae; and a chocolate covered cheesecake. The gold brick sundae was quite good, although I am used to a little more chocolate on top. I thoroughly enjoyed the chocolate covered cheesecake.

Breakfast and lunch are also served at the Black Diamond Bar and Grill. Egg and omelette specials are on the breakfast menu. For lunch they serve a number of quality sandwiches. Or enjoy a Swedish seafood platter with salmon, shrimp, and scallops. In the late afternoon Black Diamond Bar and Grill serves wonderful milkshakes.

Black Diamond Bar and Grill accepts all major credit cards.

BLANO'S PIZZA COMPANY $
100 East Meadow Drive
Vail
476-6677

Blano's offers pizzas and subs. They have scenic seating upstairs as well as an outdoor patio. They have the Ford Park and Dobson Ice Arena concessions. Delivery and catering are available.

BLU'S $$$
    Next to Gore Creek
    Downstairs from the Children's Fountain
    Vail Village
    476-3113

Blu's prides itself on serving exceptional food at modest prices. In addition to the price/food ratio, Blu's has a desirable location overlooking Gore Creek. Only a lovely green grass lawn separates the restaurant from Gore Creek. This is a wonderful place, especially in the summer. When Blu's takes out its entire front wall, the restaurant acquires a lovely terrace feeling.

Blu's, a locals favorite, has a huge menu; it hardly seems possible that they can prepare so much food each day.

Blu's is open for breakfast, lunch, and dinner. Breakfast highlights are Belgian waffles and a wide selection of egg offerings. For lunch they have sandwiches; seafood dishes; crepes; and pastas. Their lunch specials are salmon; hash O'Brien with poached eggs; curried lamb; and chicken pot pie.

Dinner specials include breast of chicken Southwest; pepper seared tenderloin of beef; cheese and mushroom ravioli; and rack of lamb with roasted shallots.

I have personally enjoyed a number of meals at Blu's. The Barbary duck roasted with caramelized pecans, black currants, and cherries was excellent. I loved their grilled salmon with fresh tarragon, capers and light cream; the salmon was as fresh as could be, and not overcooked. Blackened tuna with oriental slaw and wasabi soy sauce is an excellent choice. I have enjoyed a breast of chicken sauteed with almonds and assorted vegetables. Another offering at Blu's is a chicken breast stuffed with marinated feta cheese, glazed with pepper jelly. Blu's bacon and cheeseburger with pan fries at $4.95 is an excellent value. I especially enjoy their Greek salad for a light dinner or a great lunch.

Other interesting items include Detroit steak sandwich; smoked ribeye; black pepper fettuccine with scallops and blue cheese sauce; plus beer battered catfish. There is a whole host of great sounding dishes here, but I will mention just one more. And that is "kick ass California chicken relleno", a whole poblano pepper poached with jack cheese, wrapped in a chicken breast and flour tortilla, covered with sauce camerone. Just think, you can have your "ass kicked" for only $11.75. So give it a go.

Desserts include several varieties of cheesecake plus daily specials. Blu's accepts Visa, MasterCard, and Diner's Club.

BOOCO'S STATION $$$
Main Street
Minturn
827-4224

Booco's Station may just offer the best BBQ ribs in the Rockies. They cook their ribs slowly with wood smoke right in house. Hickory, which gives the meat a strong flavor, is blended with apple wood to soften the flavor. Three types of BBQ sauce are served at Booco's. Brisket is another choice. Coleslaw; french fries; beans; and corn bread come with your meal.

If you don't hanker for ribs or brisket, you can have trout; smoked salmon; halibut; catfish; or a fish special of the day. Booco's often has several fish specials. The half smoked salmon is a specialty; it is smoked lightly and then grilled with herbs and tomatoes. Booco's also offers chicken fried steak; smoked turkey; pizza; smoked prime rib; and New York steak, smoked or grilled.

Of course, you may want some excellent appetizers to precede your meal. Try onion rings; smoked trout with horseradish cream; individual pan pizza; smoked chicken wings; or popcorn shrimp with chipotle mayonnaise.

I enjoyed the chocolate devil's food cake for dessert. They also serve fruit pies.

Booco's Station is just the sort of place people expect to see when they come out West. In keeping with the old, rustic feel, the interior of Booco's Station is mostly exposed wood with wooden floors and huge exposed wooden beams. The restaurant derived its name from William Woodruff Booco, a homesteader. Indeed, the town of Minturn was originally named after the late Mr. Booco. His great grandson still frequents Booco's. People from all over the county have dug up old mining, skiing and railroad relics which have been donated to Booco's.

You should expect to meet a lot of pigs when you go to Booco's, as the owners have become attached to the pig logo. The wait staff's uniform includes a pig bolo tie, and pigs can be found in nearly every corner of the restaurant. There is even a Pigs Nose brand of scotch, imported from Scotland. Incidentally, Booco's Station has a huge mirrored bar, enjoyed by many locals.

Despite this rustic atmosphere, Booco's has introduced jazz to the BBQ world. Jazz groups entertain on Fridays and Saturdays. Programs have included the Mark Miller Band, Justin Illusion Band, and the Chuck Lamb Quartet. Country swing dancing is the highlight on Wednesday evenings. And there is a big screen TV for the sports people.

Booco's accepts MasterCard and Visa. A children's menu is available for the "piglets" with hot dogs; hamburgers; and smoked chicken. Booco's offers catering and banquets.

THE BRASS PARROT $$

Avon Center
Avon
949-7770

The Brass Parrot is located in the Avon Center on the southwest corner of Avon Road and West Beaver Creek Blvd. The Brass Parrot entrance can be found off the mall on the first floor. It may be a little hard to find but worth it. It is definitely a locals place. The Brass Parrot has a big bar with two televisions. The dining room has one television. In good weather, dine on their outdoor patio.

Appetizers include potato skins; onion rings; and cheddar fries. Salads are excellent. If you are having an entree a salad comes with the meal.

Entrees include pepper chicken; prime rib (in various sizes); scampi; fish and chips; fresh catch of the day; and spaghetti. They also serve burritos and taco salad. Burgers are available as are "make your own" sandwiches with a variety of cold cuts to choose from. I had the prime rib. It was spectacular, especially when compared with the higher priced cuts offered in Vail. The meal came with a roll, excellent squash, and wonderful mashed potatoes.

Desserts include strawberry sundae; hot fudge sundae; pies; cobblers; and cheesecake. I had a blackberry cobbler a la mode. It was terrific.

The Brass Parrot accepts Visa and MasterCard. There is a children's menu with spaghetti; grilled cheese sandwiches; and chicken wings.

THE BRISTOL AT ARROWHEAD $$$$

926-2111

The Bristol at Arrowhead is a beautiful restaurant in a gorgeous location. It is part of the clubhouse for Country Club of the Rockies at Arrowhead.

In the winter horse-drawn sleigh rides are available before dinner.

Appetizers include steak tartare; tuna sashimi; lobster quesadilla with pineapple salsa; baked oysters; and avocado pancakes with crabmeat and chipolte salsa. I enjoyed the avocado pancakes, a unique dish. Excellent sourdough bread comes with your meal. Soups and salads are a la carte.

Entrees include cajun-style blackened salmon with peach-mint chutney; Florida snapper; roast half duckling; grilled veal chop topped with roquefort butter and deep-fried enoki mushroom; double cut pork chop; roast rack of lamb coated with dijon mustard, served with an orange-mint hollandaise; a couple of chicken offerings; four cheese and chive ravioli topped with shrimp; jumbo prawns, curried with a sweet ginger sauce; grilled filet mignon; and anaheim chile stuffed filet mignon, grilled and topped with ancho chile butter. I decided on the roast duckling, an excellent choice. The duckling was set on a date puree and topped with an orange cumin sauce. The taste was wonderful. The meat was moist with hardly any fat.

Desserts include a sour cream apple pie and a creme caramel as the basic offerings. They also have an array of fantastic sounding desserts which rotate from time to time. I had the sour cream apple pie a la mode and loved it. Other desserts tend to be combinations of cake, mousse, chocolate, and nuts. They all sounded wonderful.

Lunches are also available at the Bristol. Calamari; enchiladas; beef fajitas; club sandwiches; chicken salad; and grilled fresh tuna on linguine, among other choices, are on the lunch menu.

The Bristol accepts Visa, MasterCard, and American Express.

THE BULLY RANCH $$
Bavaria House
Sonnenalp Hotel
476-5656

The Bully Ranch offers an authentic and fun Western concept. Enjoy the informal atmosphere plus good Western style cooking. The Bully Ranch accepts Visa and MasterCard.

C.J. CAPER'S $$$
Day's Inn
North Frontage Road in West Vail
476-5306

C.J. Caper's is an enjoyable restaurant. It is especially enjoyable if you have a number of kids under 10 years of age. If so, the children's menu contains a number of items for $1.99.

C.J. Caper's provides you with complete meals. Appetizers include Vietnamese spring rolls; baked brie; onion rings; quesadillas; calamari; paté; and roasted corn guacamole. Further, they have baked bean and sirloin chili. They also serve Fremch onion soup and a soup du jour.

Entrees include pecan chicken with chutney; New York strip steak; prime rib; BBQ baby back ribs; Thai shrimp; and a fresh catch of the day. Pasta dishes are also available. Additionally, they serve Mexican favorites such as fajitas and burritos. Another interesting dinner on the menu is raspberry peppercorn duck.

I enjoyed a rare New York strip steak. An oriental salmon, the fresh catch of the day, was spectacular. I have also enjoyed their chicken breast pasta.

Vegetables served with the entree are fresh and plentiful.

Desserts include raspberry cinnamon bread pudding; banana torte; macadamia torte; sinful chocolate cake; coffee ice cream balls rolled in a chocolate batter; brownie a la mode; and apple crisp. The raspberry cinnamon bread pudding is a real winner. The banana torte was wonderful.

The children's menu at $1.99 includes macaroni and cheese; hamburgers; grilled cheese sandwiches; pizza; and peanut butter and jelly sandwiches

C.J. Caper's also offers an extensive carry out menu. Portions can be family sized or geared to a large group. Casseroles, soups, salads, breads, and their wonderful desserts are available.

Breakfast, brunch, and lunch menus are available. Kids' meals are $1.99.

C.J. Caper's accepts American Express, Visa, MasterCard, and Diner's Club.

THE CAFE $$
Westin Hotel
Cascade Village
476-7111

The Cafe is a good place to get a quick meal. The fare is on the simple side and meant to be so. It is located in the lower lobby of the Westin. In the summer with the French doors open, guests enjoy poolside and creekside dining.

Appetizers include steak soup; red chile; nachos; baked brie; and quesadillas with numerous types of fillings. Cobb salad; turkey salad; chicken tenders; and fruit salad are also available. I enjoyed my fruit plate.

The Cafe features a number of sandwiches. These include hamburgers; tuna salad; BBQ chicken; turkey; ham; and rare roast beef with swiss cheese or brie. I have personally had the hamburger and rare roast beef, finding each delicious.

For those looking for an entree, the Cafe serves a 10 oz. New York strip; an 8 oz. filet mignon; trout; and chicken breast.

Desserts include cheesecake; "intense" brownie; and "serious" carrot cake. I enjoyed each one a la mode (at separate meals).

The Cafe is open for breakfast (great french toast), as well as for lunch dinner.

The Cafe accepts American Express, Visa, MasterCard, Diner's Club, Discover Card, and other major credit cards.

CAFE COLORADO $$$
Evergreen Lodge
Vail
476-7810

Cafe Colorado, situated on the ground floor of the Evergreen Lodge (just off the South Frontage Road), is an excellent place for a quiet dinner. If you want noise, you can just head over to the Altitude Club at 250 South, right after dinner for some swinging entertainment.

Cafe Colorado's appetizers include chicken tenders; shitake alfredo, consisting of sauteed shitake mushrooms in a light cream sauce over pasta; seafood puff pastry with shrimp, scallions and sun-dried tomatoes; or a gourmet 6" pizza with your choice of toppings. Rolls and soup or salad come with your entree.

The entrees include mesquite chicken; medallions of pork tenderloin topped with dry roasted peanut bread crumbs and mango chutney sauce; a grilled New York strip steak, 10 oz. cut lean with peppercorn sauce; or a grilled beef tenderloin with proscuitto ham demi glace sauce. I thoroughly enjoyed the pork tenderloin with mango chutney. It was a unique treat. I have also enjoyed the mesquite chicken with creole sauce.

Cafe Colorado also offers pasta including pasta with shrimp and scallops or a pasta primavera. Seafood dishes include trout and scampi. There are daily specials.

Desserts are prepared daily. Cheesecake; pecan pie; peach torte; cream brule; and a chocolate topped chocolate brownie are among the offerings. I had the latter a la mode and enjoyed it.

Cafe Colorado accepts Visa, MasterCard, American Express, and Discover Card.

CASSIDY'S HOLE IN THE WALL $$

Avon
949-9449

Cassidy's Hole in the Wall reopened in 1992 as a Western saloon, restaurant, and dance hall. Locals love it. Cassidy's is an entertaining place. On the first floor you are in the heart of the action. On the second floor you can relax while still being part of the scene. Watch the newspapers for information about live bands and dancing. Country swing is popular at Cassidy's. Live bands entertain every Friday, Saturday, and Sunday.

The bars on either floor dominate the spaces; they are very accessible. The food is good basic bar food.

The menu is huge but moderately priced. Southwestern dinners on the menu include stuffed sopaipillas; succulent chicken breast smothered with chili con queso and diced green onion; charbroiled chicken breast topped with Santa Fe salsa; blue corn enchiladas; tostada grande; and, would you believe, smoked quail.

The menu also includes old-fashioned hamburgers with home-cut fries; baby back ribs, drenched with tangy BBQ sauce; and a double-decker BLT. The Big Bob Burger, an entire pound of USDA choice ground beef, is certainly a challenge. The Bob Burger is named after Avon's world famous Bob Bridge. Salads are also popular. Steaks, chicken fried steak, and pan-fried trout are also on the menu.

Desserts include an apple sopaipilla which comes a la mode; it is delicious. An avalanche pie (huge jamocha ice cream pie combined with caramel, fudge, and marshmallows) is available for the daring.

Cassidy's accepts American Express, Visa, MasterCard, and Discover Cards.

The management wants guests to know that while a multitude of trophy game heads are part of the interior design, all these trophies were taken before 1940.

CHAMPIONS TAVERN AND RESTAURANT $$

Edwards Business Center
Edwards
926-2444

Champion's Tavern and Restaurant is three miles west of Avon on U.S. 6. If you take I-70 West to the Edwards exit, make a left on U.S. 6; watch for Champion's on your right.

Champion's Tavern and Restaurant is a local place with local spirit. It serves quality food together with live entertainment and dancing. There are two pool tables as well.

Appetizers include chicken wings; nachos; onion rings; potato skins; and chicken fingers.

Entrees include prime rib; bratwurst; chicken fried steak; sirloin steak; N.Y. strip steak; and BBQ ribs. Chicken comes teriyaki; cajun; parmigiana; or cordon bleu. Fish items include orange roughy and halibut.

Champion's offers half pound burgers; reuben sandwiches; and open face prime rib sandwiches.

There is a children's menu and summer night dinner specials. Desserts include vanilla ice cream; caramel and hot fudge sundaes; brownie sundaes; fresh fruit pie; and N.Y. cheesecake.

I can personally vouch that the prime rib is great. It comes with salad; bread; baked potato; and a vegetable medley. I also enjoyed the brownie sundae.

Champion's accepts Visa and MasterCard.

CHANTICLER $$$$

Vail Spa Building
Lionshead
476-1441

The beautiful Chanticler is located opposite the Radisson Resort in Lionshead. To park under the Vail Spa building, approach from South

Frontage Road. The Chanticler is formally depicted, charming country French. There are two separate wonderful dining rooms, the L'Auberge Room with soft white walls and the Hunt Room with mahogany paneling. A glass and mahogany bar near the entrance is a wonderful design.

Chanticler prides itself as being one of the very best restaurants in Vail. Chanticler did receive the honor from Esquire as the "Best Classic Restaurant" in Vail. Their menus are developed from scratch, and they use only the freshest ingredients.

Homemade breads are served. My favorite was baked with a tomato, oregano flavor. Salads are also excellent. They are served with either a raspberry, walnut or a champagne herb dressing.

Appetizers include oysters Rockefeller and escargot with artichoke hearts. Other appetizers include mushrooms en croute; mussels provencale; pheasant paté; or Norwegian smoked salmon.

I have focused on seafood dishes at the Chanticler. Their tuna was quite good although I felt it was a little overdone. The waitress assured me that if I had said something immediately, this would have been corrected. The salmon was great, especially the salmon in filo. Sauteed scallops in filo with a citrus beurre blanc were absolutely spectacular. The presentation in a wonderful medley of julienned vegetables was a sight to behold. I have also enjoyed lobster tails and jumbo prawns at the Chanticler. Broiled orange roughy in citrus butter is another favorite. Seafood pastas and seafood salads are delightful entrees.

Poultry dishes available include roasted fresh duck served with a luscious orange Grand Marnier sauce and a tender roasted breast of fresh pheasant with a truffle cream sauce. I enjoyed the pheasant, especially. Another favorite is baked chicken breast stuffed with lobster, boursin, and scallions, served with a creamy lobster sauce.

A featured beef dinner is the tournedos au poivre, peppered tenderloin, sauteed and topped with a brandied wild mushroom sauce. New York steak with shallot butter is available. Oven roasted rack of lamb with dijon mustard and seasoned bread crumb crust in a fresh mint glaze; veal chop with morel mushrooms; and oven roasted loin of caribou are tempting entree choices.

Desserts included flan; cheesecake; ice cream crepe covered with chocolate sauce; and a white chocolate, raspberry tart. Favorites include a creme brule or a macadamia, mocha mousse torte. Especially wonderful is the apple crisp a la mode. Chanticler's signature dessert is a Grand Marnier souffle.

The Chanticler accepts Visa, MasterCard, Discover Card, Diner's Club, and American Express.

CHART HOUSE $$$$
Lionshead Mall
476-1525

The Chart House offers an excellent view of Vail Mountain through huge picture windows.

The restaurant features an excellent salad bar. Two different kinds of bread are served warm. One is their unique dark version squaw bread;" the other is sourdough. They have also created a delicious, award winning New England clam chowder. I preferred the salad bar and squaw bread.

The Chart House features wonderful prime rib roast beef. You have a choice of a regular cut, a big cut, or a huge "Callahan" cut. Their menu includes a daily selection of fresh fish. I enjoyed an excellent fresh salmon.

Other seafood and beef dishes are enjoyable. Seafood offerings on the regular menu include scallops; swordfish; shrimp; and lobster tail. Beef dinners on the menu include sirloin steak; New York strip steak; filet mignon; and teriyaki beef kabob.

Desserts include mud pie; chocolate mousse; and sundaes. If you order the mud pie, you may need a partner. The size is incredible. Allegedly there is at least a pint of coffee ice cream in every serving.

The Chart House accepts Visa, MasterCard, and American Express. The Chart House organization is here to stay; the original opened 30 years ago in Aspen. A children's menu is available.

THE CHEESE SHOP $
Crossroads Shopping Center
476-1482

The Cheese Shop has cheese, for sure. They also have crackers; paté; salmon; caviar; salads; sandwiches; coffees; chocolates; nuts; and dried fruits.

"Entrees to go" (with baskets to borrow) make a great mountain picnic.

CHICAGO PIZZA $
Wal-Mart Center
Avon
949-4210
476-7000 (Vail Deliveries)

Chicago Pizza serves authentic Chicago pizza which I enjoyed. Additionally, they offer broasted chicken from 2 pieces to 21 pieces. They will probably even sell you 42 pieces.

Pastas on the menu include spaghetti with red marinara sauce plus meatballs or Italian sausage; fettuccine alfredo; or fettuccine with white clam sauce. Try their homemade lasagna. Meatball or Italian sausage sandwiches are also available.

Chicago Pizza combines their own free delivery with free delivery of movies from Mammoth Video (in Vail only).

CHILI WILLY'S $$
Main Street in Minturn
827-5887

Chili Willy's is a definite misnomer. The place should be called "fantastic fajitas;" they are fantastic. The Mexican/Southwestern ("Tex/Mex") food is served in a wonderful, friendly atmosphere. You feel you are in the old West except for the multitude of license plates which cover the interior walls.

Back to the fajitas as they are Chili Willy's famous house specialty. You have your choice of beef, chicken, or pork strips, even a combination of two or three. The meat is marinated, grilled, and served with grilled onions on a sizzling skillet. Add lettuce, cheese, guacamole, or sour cream from a side dish. Place your choices in a hot tortilla. Then enjoy.

In addition to fajitas, Chili Willy's serves burritos; tacos; blue corn enchiladas; chile rellenos; tostadas; flautas; chimichangas; and chili. Try them all and become an expert on Tex/Mex favorites. Chili Willy's also serves Western-style baby back ribs or a T-bone Mexicana.

Of course they have yellow corn tortilla chips which are fried fresh each day. Their salsa is made from the freshest red tomatoes, jalapeños, chiles, onions and spices. Indulge yourself within reason, as your entree will certainly be a lot to eat.

Margaritas are available in several flavors such as pina colada, watermelon, peach, strawberry, kiwi, raspberry and strawberry-banana. What a combo! They even come without alcohol, as "flavoritas," for the kids.

Salads and vegetarian entrees are available.

For dessert I had a chocolate chip cookie a la mode that was topped off with chocolate sauce and whipped cream. Sopaipilla baskets are also available. These are a pastry item sprinkled with cinnamon and sugar. They are served with honey for dipping. The chimichanga dessert tortilla is stuffed with cherry or apple filling, topped with ice cream and fluffy whipped cream.

Chili Willy's accepts Visa and MasterCard. A children's menu is available.

CHINA GARDEN $$
Avon Center
Avon
949-4986

The China Garden Restaurant offers fine Mandarin and Szechuan cuisine. The Avon Center is a building located on the southwest corner of Avon Road and West Beaver Creek Blvd.

Appetizers include eggrolls; fried prawns; BBQ pork; BBQ spare ribs; and Chinese chicken salad.

House favorites include special duck; sizzling scallops and beef; velvet chicken and scallops; Hunan beef; sizzling lobster and steak; volcano shrimp and pineapple duck. The menu contains a host of other offerings from poultry to pork to beef to lamb to seafood. They also have vegetarian meals. I was especially pleased with my choice of a pineapple duck. The duck and pineapple pieces are simmered together and presented in a pineapple shell. I was content.

China Garden Restaurant accepts Visa and MasterCard. Take out is available.

CLANCY'S $$

In Cascade Village
Next to the Westin Hotel
476-3886

Clancy's is a great place as long you don't have too much against Chicago. This is a Windy City Irish pub, for sure. I love it, even though I grew up in Detroit when Bobby Lane was a better quarterback than Johnny Lujak. Probably some of you don't remember it quite this way, if you remember it at all. Well back to Clancy's. Clancy's is a friendly, locals hang out because the food is good and reasonably priced. Additionally, there are television screens for sports and games in the back room.

Appetizers include spiral spuds; onion rings; chicken fingers; and chicken wings. You can have a Caesar salad to which you can add grilled chicken or grilled steak.

Sandwiches include a Vienna quarter-pound all beef frank; a half-pound hand packed hamburger; or grilled chicken. You can enjoy a 12 oz. NY strip or a 16 oz. T-bone steak. I have tried them all and been satisfied.

Great pizzas are also available, made with mozzarella, cheddar and parmesan. They come in 8" and 12" sizes.

Desserts include apple pie; tollhouse cookie pie; or a wonderful hot fudge sundae.

Clancy's accepts Visa, MasterCard, and American Express.

CLEAVER'S DELICATESSEN $

Lionshead Mall
476-6084

What a great, convenient store to have on the Lionshead Mall. Find a friendly atmosphere here. Cleaver's specialty is mountain subs, which include everything from vegetarian to double-diamond roast beef submarine sandwiches. The menu also offers bratwurst; hot dogs; gyros; and pizza. Their grilled cheese and reuben sandwiches are tasty. Bagels and cream cheese together with a hot cup of coffee will gets your morning off to a great start. Muffins; cookies; and cinnamon rolls are tempting. Homemade fudge is more than tempting; it is simply exquisite.

Cleaver's will lend you a backpack to carry a mountain lunch which they prepare.

Cleaver's respects ecological and environmental issues. They serve dolphin-safe tuna and have a recycling program.

Ice cream bars; popsicles; carrot cake; and wonderful fudge are here to tempt your appetite. To rehydrate yourself after skiing grab a bottle of orange juice; apple juice; or Gatorade. Cleaver's accepts Visa and MasterCard.

COLUMBINE $
Red Cliff
827-4223

If you want to eat luscious food up in the mountains where the locals eat, head for the Columbine in Red Cliff. You will get great Mexican food at reasonable prices. Red Cliff is a picturesque place. My Colorado Mountain College painting class frequents Red Cliff for the views.

The New Mexican homestyle menu includes enchiladas; tacos; burritos; fajitas; and nachos.

The owner, Diana Cisneros, is a wonderful and generous lady who serves wonderful food. Red Cliff can be reached by bike or ski tour as well as by car. Indeed, a Shrine Pass experience will lead you right past the Columbine. So go for it.

COLUMBINE BAKERY $
Opposite City Market
Avon
949-1400

The Columbine Bakery in Avon is a great spot for breakfast, lunch, or an early dinner. They are only open until 6:30 p.m.

Breakfasts are simple. They include eggs; orange juice; danishes; croissants; and muffins. If you wish, enjoy a side of bacon; ham; or steak.

For lunch Columbine Bakery offers a variety of meals including chili; soup; quiches; Polynesian chicken; and beef borguignon. Their sandwiches include tuna salad; egg salad; corned beef; bacon, lettuce and tomato with avocado; turkey and swiss cheese; ham and swiss cheese; and Philly steak. My favorite is a puff pastry turnover with ground beef inside.

Desserts are excellent. The bakery offers a great variety. And, guess what? A free bakery dessert comes with your already low priced lunch. This is fantastic. Be sure to check it out. Take out is available.

The Columbine Bakery will accept Visa and MasterCard, but only if your bill comes to over $15.00, which is hard to do.

COVERED BRIDGE CAFE $$
Beaver Creek Promenade
949-1306
845-5762

The Covered Bridge Cafe in Beaver Creek, located at the west end of the Beaver Creek Promenade is an enjoyable, "fun" place to eat.

Appetizers include nachos; chicken nachos; fried cheese; potato skins; onion rings; and onion soup.

Covered Bridge Cafe serves a number of sandwich items. These include tuna salad; chicken breast; turkey; and BLT. Additionally, they have burgers galore, including cheese; mushroom; smokin' hickory; and guacamole varieties.

The CBCafe also has a number of salad offerings: chef's salad; Italian chicken salad; Caesar salad; chicken fajita salad; and two other chicken salad varieties.

A kids' menu which includes hamburger; grilled cheese; fried chicken fingers; and PBJ.

Desserts include fried peaches; hot upside down pie a la mode; and milk shakes.

Covered Bridge Cafe accepts Visa, MasterCard, American Express, and Discover Card. Take out and delivery is available.

COYOTE CAFE $
Village Hall
Beaver Creek
949-5001

Coyote Cafe is a casual place located in the perfect place to catch Beaver Creek's aprés ski crowd. Heading down the stairs from the ski area, you will see Coyote Cafe at the base of the steps.

Coyote Cafe provides Southwestern food like tacos, burritos, and fajitas, but also serves pizzas. Additionally, they have regular American sandwiches. They may or may not have desserts. Check with the waitress.

The Coyote Cafe has TV. screens. It also has music. It is a great aprés ski place to go; you can also get a quick lunch here; finally try Coyote Cafe for the nightlife atmosphere.

CROOKED HEARTH TAVERN $$$
Hyatt Regency
Beaver Creek
949-1234, ext. 2260

The Crooked Hearth Tavern is more casual than the Patina Grill. The Tavern offers excellent sandwiches for lunch. It is a great place for après ski. The dinner menu includes prime rib; goulashes; beef bourguignon; cheese fondue; excellent salads; and specialty pizzas. Entertainment is offered for après ski and in the evening.

CUCINA RUSTICA ITALIANA $$$$
In the Lodge at Vail
476-5011

Cucina Rustica Italiana's menu consists of superb rustic Italian cuisine which is served in a relaxed alpine setting.

Their offerings are unique and extensive. For instance take their Insalata Contadina: baby lettuce, toasted pinenuts, roasted tomato, vinaigrette, croutons and parmesan. Or else you can try their octopus salad with potatoes. You will be served tasty bread with superb olive oil in which to dip your bread.

Entrees include beef carpaccio with truffled olive oil and parmesan cheese; fresh salmon marinated in oranges; grilled sea bass with Portofino BBQ sauce; or cured beef with arugula and grapefruit. Other entrees include lamb chops with pinenuts and mint; grilled veal loin chop with garlic and rosemary; paillard of beef with lemon, parmesan, and olive oil; swordfish steak with capers, lemon, and oregano; prawns with garlic; salmon; trout with balsamic vinegar; roast monkfish with capers and basil; braised lamb leg with potato pancakes. The list could go on. I personally have enjoyed their quail.

Pasta offerings include macaroni in Italian blue cheese and red endive or risotto with fontina cheese and truffle essence. I thoroughly enjoyed a veal conneli con pesto. Another interesting dish is potato dumplings with tomatoes, basil and mozzarella cheese.

The Italian chefs who provide this authentic variety of offerings come from the Splendido Hotel in Portofino, a "sister hotel" to the Lodge at Vail.

Desserts are fantastic. I thoroughly enjoyed their bread pudding. A fresh daily selection of pastries is prepared daily.

During the ski season, Cucina Rustica Italiana has a truly amazing lunch buffet for those who wish to lunch with great food in elegant surroundings. It is just steps from the Vista Bahn. Noteworthy, a number of the higher level private ski instructors bring their clients here for lunch. The offerings include meats, salads, pastas, cheeses, dried fruits and more. You can get in and out quickly and thoroughly satisfied.

Cucina Rustica accepts MasterCard, Visa, and American Express.

CYRANO'S $$$

At the Top of Bridge Street
Vail Village
476-5551

Cyrano's is one of the "where it's at" aprés ski bar and restaurants. It is located close to the bottom of the Vista Bahn Express Lift. You can ski right up to its back balcony. The huge bar space downstairs is one of the places people go to see and be seen, especially with the idea of meeting the "right one," at least for the evening. It's a crowded scene, reminiscent of the party scene in Breakfast at Tiffany's (for those of us who remember).

Cyrano's provides a dance floor and plenty of disco music. Enjoy their front deck on Bridge St. or a rear deck facing Mill Creek and Vail Mountain. You cannot ask for much more than creekside dining with spectacular mountain views plus a hot, hot, hot dance club.

Cyrano's focuses on a Pacific Grill theme. Their menu has a wide range of choices. I have been very pleased with the salmon; the mahi-mahi; and the striped bass. I can certainly recommend ordering from the seafood specials. The shrimp tempura is accompanied by a sake and soy dipping sauce.

Other entrees include prawns; lamb; filet mignon; prime rib; plum duckling; lemon chicken; teriyaki chicken breast; grilled buffalo sausage; and a vegetable pasta. The plum duckling has been very popular. A number of people have loved the sauteed chicken breast with sliced avocado and macadamia nuts in a lime cream sauce. Another interesting item is Thai seafood curry with coconut milk and saffron.

Appetizers are tasty. I had beef carpaccio and loved it. Other appetizers include crab egg roll; California roll; chicken satay; Vietnamese spring roll; mussels; fried calamari; and artichoke.

Desserts include a Maui brownie (preferably a la mode); black bottom banana cream pie; Key lime cheesecake; mud pie; and banana split. Cyrano's features Ben & Jerry's ice cream. I personally loved the banana cream pie a la mode.

Cyrano's also offers breakfast with omelettes of all kinds. Their french toast with cream cheese inside is wonderful. For lunch they have sandwiches; fajitas; and pasta dishes. Salads are also available.

Cyrano's accepts Visa, MasterCard, and American Express. They have a children's menu. While there is music and dancing downstairs at the bar level, you are well insulated from these sounds upstairs in the dining room.

DJ McCADAM'S DINER $
Concert Hall Plaza
Lionshead Mall
476-2336

I do not want to write about DJ McCadam's. I am so addicted to their blintzes. Even thinking about DJs gets my hunger reflex going. But DJs is more than a blintz place. It also has great french toast and numerous egg dishes. Pasta frittatas combine linguine and eggs with spinach and bacon; chicken; or garden vegetables. Indeed, DJ McCadam's was voted the best breakfast spot in Colorado by the Underground Gourmet.

DJ McCadam's has been around for more than a decade. It appeals to locals with its diner atmosphere. Pictures of diners adorn the walls. You sit belly up to the food bar; all of the cooking is done where you can see it.

Mexican food is a must here; remember to come hungry. The breakfast burrito is huge and delicious. You can choose a chicken burrito; quesadilla con pollo; or tostada grande (a vegetarian favorite).

Italian food is also available. Try pasta primavera; linguine with clam sauce; or spaghetti and meatballs.

Don't forget the fruit smoothies. They are spectacular. And maybe you can save room for a dessert crepe. Give it a try. By the way, they also have dinner crepes. An amazing amount of delightful food comes out of this wonderful diner.

The prices are great. They do not accept credit cards. During ski season, at least, they stay open 24 hours.

THE DAILY GRIND $
Bridge Street
Vail Village
476-5856

Want a great place for coffee and conversation? This is it. The Daily Grind serves up coffees and pastries for the lounger. They have espresso, cappuccino, and four daily specials. Coffee beans, ground or whole, can be taken home from the Daily Grind's extensive inventory.

Bakery items include fruit filled croissants and danishes, as well as muffins, bagels, and great cookies.

The Daily Grind also offers deli sandwiches: turkey; roast beef; ham and brie; or chicken salad. Soups; chili; focaccia pizzas; quiches; and salads are on the menu for lunch, aprés ski, or late night.

This has become a wonderful locals spot to be and to be seen. Poetry readings are scheduled regularly. Backgammon tables and plenty of newspapers help to make The Daily Grind a mellow place to relax and converse.

The Daily Grind accepts Visa and MasterCard. Catering is available.

DAIRY QUEEN $
West Vail
476-4414

Dairy Queen is located off of North Frontage Road between Safeway and Gart Brothers.

DOMINO'S $
Vail
476-0330
Avon
949-3230

Domino's delivers pizzas. In inclement weather they drive safely and cancel their time guarantee.

DOUBLE DIAMOND DELI $
Hyatt Regency
Beaver Creek
479-9786

This is an excellent deli which serves light breakfasts and generous sandwiches for lunch. Bavarian desserts taste great. It is conveniently located for guests at the Hyatt.

American Express, Visa, MasterCard, Discover Card, Diner's Club, and Carte Blanche are among the credit cards accepted here.

EAGLE-VAIL CAFE $
On the North Side of U.S. 6
Eagle-Vail
949-6393

This hidden little restaurant is a treat. Great food at low prices brings locals to the restaurant in droves. The Eagle-Vail Cafe also offers gas; the gas pump is out front of the entry door.

Eagle-Vail Cafe offers tasty breakfasts at a reasonable prices. Their lunches are solid meals. They serve hamburgers; steaks; brats; turkey; prime rib; and other sandwiches. I had the prime rib sandwich; it was a real meal with excellent prime rib and crisp vegetables plus french fries on the side.

The homemade pastry shelf offers a great selection at reasonable prices. You have to see it to believe it. The eclairs; custard cake; and danishes are exquisite.

The Eagle-Vail Cafe is not open for dinner. The Cafe accepts Visa and MasterCard.

EAGLEWOOD $$$$
Vail Athletic Club
325 East Meadow Drive
476-6836

Eaglewood is an elegant dining setting offering fresh American cuisine. The dining room is well designed, comfortable and includes a beautiful fireplace for a cozy, intimate feeling.

Appetizers include buffalo carpaccio; Maryland crab cake; green chile; lobster chili; black bean soup; and home made fettuccine with julienne vegetables in a dijon cream sauce.

Entrees include rainbow trout in parchment; pork ribeye with a molasses glaze; Long Island duckling; Boston cod; breast of chicken in pastry; grilled salmon filet; fettuccine pasta; grilled chicken with ricotta ravioli; artichoke and asiago pizza; grilled angus filet; pepper steak; roast rack of lamb; and California sea bass. The grilled yellow fin tuna was quite good served with an aged parmesan crust. I thoroughly enjoyed the potato crusted salmon which consisted of a Norwegian salmon filet which was marinated with lemon and parsley, roasted in a crust of thinly sliced potatoes, served with Mediterranean style salsa and tarragon aioli.

Luscious desserts are presented on a dessert cart. I loved the chocolate pie with many layers of different chocolates plus macadamia nuts. Other desserts include sour cream apple pie, homemade ice cream, and a cheesecake made with goat milk.

Children's portions are available. Eaglewood accepts American Express, MasterCard and Visa. Eaglewood features piano music on weekends.

FIESTA'S $$
Edwards Plaza Building
Edwards
926-3048

Fiesta's is a New Mexican Cafe and Cantina in Edwards operated by the Marquez sisters. Their Mexican recipes are generations old. Every entree is homemade. It is definitely a locals place.

The menu is extensive. Dishes include chicken enchiladas with jalapeño sauce; carne avocado burritos; blue corn Santa Fe enchiladas; and chile rellenos. Combinations are also available. Crabmeat enchiladas and carnitas are also served. Carnitas is the original name for fajitas, according to the Marquez sisters. Sopaipillas are smothered in Fiesta's award winning green chile. A favorite is the Del Mar enchilada; blue corn enchiladas are filled with seafood and smothered in white jalapeño sauce.

Desserts include fried ice cream; sopaipillas; apple chimichanga; and flan in caramel sauce.

On weekends breakfast is available. Fiesta's offers breakfast burritos; huevos Marquez; omelettes; hot cakes; or biscuits and gravy.

You can eat in or take out at Fiesta's. Fiesta's accepts Visa and MasterCard.

FONDUE STUBE $$$
Chateau Vail
Holiday Inn
476-5631

The Fondue Stube serves tasty fondue. You can select from a menu of cheese, beef, seafood and chicken fondues. I have enjoyed the lobster and the beef fondues. Sauces include cocktail; coconut curry; teriyaki; and bernaise.

The dessert fondue choices are either chocolate or walnut caramel. You dip fruit into the warm sauce. It can be addicting. The chocolate fondue is excellent, but may be a little bitter for young children.

The Fondue Stube accepts MasterCard, Visa, American Express, and Diner's Club.

FRENCH DELI (LES DELICES DE FRANCE) $
Lionshead Mall, Opposite the Gondola
476-1044

There is a line; there isn't a line. It all happens so fast at this great little restaurant, the French Deli.

It's open for breakfast and lunch. Give it a try. Breakfast items include egg dishes, french toast, continental with bread and fruit, or lox and bagel.

For lunch enjoy soup of the day; chili; or salads. Sandwiches available include ham; roast beef; salami; turkey; pastrami; and corn beef. Additionally, they serve tuna salad or chicken salad. Specialities include paté, brie, and roast chicken. Sample the pastries which change daily.

The highest priced item on the menu is $7.95 (and that is for the smoked salmon). So, show up and enjoy this friendly little place. And remember if there is a line, it will not last. Catering is available.

G.T.'S DINER AND MALT SHOP $
St. James Place
Beaver Creek
845-7130

G.T.'s Diner and Malt Shop is a fun place with a 50s look that is located at the east end of the Beaver Creek Promenade. Look up a couple of flights and you will see the sign.

I had a coffee malt which was excellent. Numerous other flavors of shakes and malts are offered. Cones and sundaes are also on the menu.

G.T.'s serves breakfast offerings which include omelettes, french toast, and pancakes.

G.T.'s also offers pizzas and sandwiches. Sandwiches include Philly cheese steak; pastrami; burgers; hot roast beef; meat loaf; chicken; ham; BLT; club; egg salad; tuna salad; plus peanut butter and jelly.

G.T.'s Diner and Malt Shop accepts Visa and MasterCard

THE GALLERY $$
Radisson Hotel
Vail
476-4444

The Gallery is a convenient place to eat. Appetizers include buffalo wings; potato skins; nachos; and spinach quesadilla. Numerous salad offerings are available. Try chicken Caesar salad; salmon cobb salad; taco salad; or sirloin steak salad.

Specialties are fajitas; seafood fettuccine; Texas chili; cheese pizza; roasted herb chicken; and pepper steak.

Enjoy your choice of a variety of sandwiches and burgers: grilled chicken; Philly cheese steak; southwest club with chicken, bacon, jack cheese, and guacamole; Italian burger; bacon burger; and cheeseburger.

For dessert try a brownie sundae; Ben & Jerry's ice cream; or fried ice cream rolled in nuts and cinnamon, which is served in a sweetened tortilla shell with hot fudge.

The Gallery accepts Visa, MasterCard, and American Express.

GAMBETTA'S PIZZA AND PANE $$
Gateway Plaza
476-7550

Gambetta's Pizza and Pane is an authentic Italian restaurant and pizzeria open for lunch and dinner. The pricing is very reasonable, especially if you have adolescents on board. It has a casual atmosphere in the beautiful

Vail Gateway Arcade. You do get an hour and a half of free underground parking. All the pizzas and pasta are homemade.

Every Italian basic is available: meatball or sausage parmigiana; eggplant parmigiana; sausage with green penne; chicken breast; spaghetti; lasagna; ravioli; baked ziti; manicotti; rigatoni; fettuccine. Also, they have shrimp marinara; chicken parmigiana; chicken marsala; snails; and calamari. A dinner salad comes with your entree as well as excellent bread with oil. I thoroughly enjoyed linguine with a medley of shrimp, clams, and mussels.

And then of course there are pizzas. Pizza can be had focaccia (bread with tomatoes and spices, but no cheese); Neopolitan (thin crust); and Sicilian (thick crust). Additional pizza toppings include sausage; pepperoni; beef; salami; Canadian bacon; green peppers; onions; jalapeños; tomato; black olives; spinach; anchovies; and mushrooms. Are you bored with ordinary pizza? There is a Sante Fe pizza with chicken, BBQ sauce and Bermuda onions. Basilico pizza includes fresh basil, fresh plum tomato, fresh garlic with a side of marinara sauce. Gambetta's indeed serves exceptional pizzas.

A full complement of salads is available, including Greek salad with feta cheese and olives. They also offer a seafood pasta salad with semolina pasta, shrimp, white fish and vegetables.

The kids' menu has either spaghetti, rigatoni, or ravioli. Desserts include spumoni and cheesecake. The cannoli is excellent.

Gambetta's accepts Visa and MasterCard.

GASHOUSE RESTAURANT AND BAR $$$
Edwards
926-2896
926-3613

The Gashouse Restaurant and Bar is four miles west of Beaver Creek in Edwards. It has a log cabin look and a real locals atmosphere. If you want to get out of the super new into the genuine old, head for the Gashouse. It used to be a gas station. Then it became the Gashouse Bar. Now it has developed into an excellent eating place. The log cabin decor includes trophy heads and license plates.

Appetizers include Rocky Mountain oysters; nachos; chips and chili; chicken wings (buffalo wings); crab cakes; and shrimp to be peeled and eaten.

The Gashouse advertises itself as the home of the $7.95 steak dinner. Indeed it has a variety of steaks at numerous prices on its menu. Baby back ribs are a house specialty. Chicken dishes are served as well. Excellent fish items are always on the menu. They also serve pasta marinara and cajun shrimp. I had snow crab legs and loved them. Other fish specials that night were salmon; swordfish; and mahi-mahi. Excellent mixed vegetables and rice come with the entree.

On Tuesday and Wednesday evenings the Gashouse goes Mexican. They serve enchiladas; burritos; tacos; and tostadas. Some nights they feature an open microphone for anyone to use.

Desserts include apple pie; pecan pie; and Kentucky Derby pie. I had the latter a la mode. The pie was a mixture of chocolate and caramel, sweet and powerful. I was glad I ordered the ice cream to go with it.

The Gashouse accepts Visa and MasterCard.

GENO'S ITALIAN SANDWICHES $
Avon
949-0529

If you hanker for the Vienna Beef Stand ambience of Chicago, head for Geno's. They serve the kind of Vienna beef sandwiches that you can get "only at a wedding." They use the best ingredients, some direct from Chicago.

In addition to the Vienna beef sandwiches, Geno's offers Vienna beef hot dogs; Italian sausage; homemade meatballs; and BBQ beef.

GOLDEN EAGLE INN $$$$
Village Hall, Beaver Creek
949-1940

The Golden Eagle Inn is a comfortable restaurant on the Promenade in Beaver Creek. It is well decorated. Numerous rooms help to give the restaurant an intimate atmosphere.

Bread, butter, a salad or soup of the day comes with each entree. Appetizers include baked lobster and brie in filo or sesame crusted loin of elk. Shrimp cocktail and grilled shrimp with minted relish are also available.

There is a wide variety of entrees. Seafood dishes include trout; tuna; salmon; scampi with penne pasta; and a seafood stew. I had the baked sole with lobster and brie. It was served with a light lemon, tomato and caper cream sauce. It was heavenly. I have also enjoyed their roast duckling with port wine shallot sauce, slow roasted with fruits and herbs, then finished with a coating of honey and pecans -- wonderful.

Chicken; sweetbreads; and a variety of steaks, including filet mignon and pepper steak, are available. Additionally, roast rack of Colorado lamb and roast loin of elk are on the menu. The wild game medley includes combinations of elk, grilled quail, and a daily game selection. Other poultry dishes include smoked cornish game hen and grilled pheasant breast.

For a pasta meal try chicken breast with linguine; scampi over black bean fettuccine; or grilled salmon and eggplant on fresh egg fettuccine.

Desserts include flan; crepe with fruit compote; devils food cake layered with raspberries; chocolate terrin; and cheesecake. I chose the puffed profiterole, filled with ice cream and covered with a great chocolate sauce. What a delight!

The restaurant is also open for lunch and is within easy walking distance of the Beaver Creek slopes. Lunch includes burgers, reuben, and pastas. Salads; enchiladas; and quesadillas are also on the menu. Consider having a late dinner after attending a concert at Beaver Creek.

The Golden Eagle Inn accepts American Express, Visa, and MasterCard.

GONDOLA CAFE $$$
Lionshead Mall
476-2665

The Gondola Cafe specializes in fondues and crepes. Appetizers include cheese dishes and onion soup.

Crepes contain chicken; beef; and ratatouille.

Fondues feature a selected blend of European cheeses; succulent breast of chicken; tender sirloin chunks; or a combination of the chicken and sirloin.

Other specialties are fettuccine primavera; fettuccine alfredo; cheese ravioli; Italian lasagna; breast of chicken; and fillet of beef.

Desserts include chocolate fondue served with a tray of assorted fruits; ice cream filled crepe covered with sauce caramel, chocolate, pecans and whipped cream; ice cream crepe covered with a whole banana, pecans and whipped cream; or mud pie.

Since the Gondola Cafe is near the Lionshead base, they serve hearty breakfasts and lunches. Breakfast choices are Belgian waffles; pancakes; eggs; or oatmeal. Lunches include quiche or baked brie with sliced apple and french bread plus numerous sandwiches.

It is a friendly place and often not as crowded as other places in Lionshead Mall. So give it a try, take your time and enjoy it.

The Gondola Cafe accepts Visa, MasterCard, and American Express

GONDO'S $
Under the Gondola
Lionshead
479-9929

Gondo's is named after an African water hole. It is a place to also "water up" for those who need to replenish their liquids after a day on the mountain skiing, biking or hiking.

The spinach pizza is a winner. Fresh spinach is sauteed in olive oil with fresh garlic, parsley, and black olives. The calzones are terrific. Chili is also a highlight entree. Since the prices are low, it is a locals place. A couple of televisions are tuned to sports channels.

Gondo's accepts Visa and MasterCard

HAAGEN-DAZS $
Crossroads Shopping Center
476-4136

Haagen-Dazs opens at 8:00 a.m. and offers more than just great ice cream. They offer wonderful yogurts. Enjoy a variety of coffee blends. Muffins; coffee cake; bundt cake; breads; brownies; and cookies are also available. Getting back to ice cream, check out their ice cream pies and cakes.

Haagen-Dazs is located next to a bus stop. So you can warm up here or cool off here, depending on the season, while waiting for a bus.

Haagen-Dazs accepts Visa and MasterCard.

HI HO'S PARLOUR $
Main Street in Minturn
827-5609

Check out Hi Ho's Parlour in Minturn. It is a real old-fashioned soda fountain. They serve lunch, pastries, coffee house items, and booze. It is a real locals hangout.

Hi Ho's offers various ice cream sundaes, all decadent treats. Pastries, too, are excellent.

If you are hungry for a real meal try the chili bowl, a scooped out sourdough bread filled with fantastic chili. Hi Ho's offers a number of sandwiches.

Hi Ho's Parlour accepts Visa and MasterCard.

HONG KONG CAFE $
Vail Village
476-1818

The Hong Kong Cafe, steps from the Vista Bahn chairlift, is a great place for lunch or aprés ski. Despite the name, Hong Kong Cafe is not a Chinese restaurant. They do offer Chinese appetizers during aprés ski and into the night.

They serve burgers; brats; hot dogs; teriyaki chicken; fish and chips.

Check the papers for live entertainment. Hong Kong Cafe accepts American Express, Visa, and MasterCard.

HUBCAP BREWERY AND KITCHEN $$
Crossroads Shopping Center
476-5757

The Hubcap Brewery and Kitchen is the first brewery of Vail. Almost everybody in town wishes they had thought of this enterprise because it is definitely a winner. With their own brewery system, casual atmosphere and fine food, the Hubcap has become a must place to go for many locals. Clearly the younger set loves it here as do many others.

Hubcap's appetizer menu includes calamari; peel 'n' eat shrimp; quesadillas; spicy fries; chicken wings; mussels; artichokes; soft pretzels; and wontons (with shrimp and cream cheese). They also serve homemade soups and good salads.

Hubcap entree favorites are herbed rotisserie chicken; grilled mahi-mahi; pot pies; burgers; fish and chips; fresh seafood catch of the day; N.Y. strip steak; vegetarian platter; plus BBQ ribs and chicken. Sandwiches include bratwurst; grilled chicken; hot roast beef; hot turkey; BLT with avocado; french dip; tuna salad; grilled cheese; and Italian sausage. Their burgers and sandwiches are served with french fries. I personally think their meatloaf and mashies is a great meal. I also enjoyed a N.Y. steak sandwich smothered with onions, peppers, mushrooms, and swiss cheese served on a baguette.

The Hubcap describes its desserts as decadent, sinful, gooey and naughty. If this is what you've been waiting for, give it a go. I chose a tasty chocolate, peanut butter cheesecake. Other choices included seven layer chocolate cake; carrot cake; frozen mint ice cream pie; and several varieties of Ben & Jerry's ice cream flavors.

The Hubcap accepts Visa and MasterCard. The kids' menu includes burgers; meatloaf and mashies; hot dogs; and spaghetti.

THE IMPERIAL FEZ AT VAIL   **$$$$**
    Vail Run Resort
    North Frontage Road
    Vail
    476-1948

A. Rafih Benjelloun is your host at this exciting Moroccan restaurant. Here you will take your shoes off before entering the dining area. Also, you will sit at low tables without chairs. You will be expected to eat with your fingers which are washed before you eat and after you finish; the rose scented water is poured over your hands in a lovely ritual. You are given a towel to be placed over your left shoulder; this is for cleansing your fingers during the meal. This is authentic Moroccan food, decor and ambiance. If part of coming to Vail for you is to get away from it all, come to the Imperial Fez.

Be hungry when you arrive at the Imperial Fez. The menu is generally preset although you do choose an entree. Before the entree you are given a bowl of soup which you eat with bread or sip it up from the bowl. The soup is excellent as are the vegetable dishes.

B'Stella is the next course which is often the best remembered by guests. It contains cornish hen which is cut up in an excellent pastry dish and topped with powdered sugar.

Entree choices include lamb; beef; fish; prawns; pheasant; cornish hen; and duck. I have tried lamb, red snapper, and prawns. My favorite is the duckling with honey and almonds. Vegetarian choices are available.

Rafih insists that it is healthy to eat all of this great food. He points out that Moroccans only use ingredients that promote health. Fresh vegetables, herbs and spices are utilized. He believes that the olive oil lowers high-density cholesterol levels. He also asserts that it lubricates the throat and vocal cords. Rafih aims for psychological satisfaction, also. He encourages people to pamper themselves, and Rafih pampers his guests.

Most nights belly dancing is the entertainment. The dancer is talented and comical. Occasionally a band plays Moroccan music. Come to the Imperial Fez to have a great time out on the town.

The Imperial Fez accepts Visa and Mastercard.

IRON HORSE RESTAURANT AND PIZZA $
Christie Lodge
Avon
949-0290

Iron Horse Restaurant and Pizza gives you nothing fancy. A locals place; it is also very convenient for people staying at the Christie Lodge, with its entrance off the inner atrium.

Pizza is a major feature of the Iron Horse; they do deliver.

Appetizers include potato skins; onion rings; chicken wings; and chicken fingers.

Entrees include steak; chicken fried steak; veal parmesan; chicken parmesan; spaghetti; lasagna; and shrimp stuffed with crab. They also serve hamburgers and meatball sandwiches. I had the Iron Horse burger, a hamburger covered with pizza sauce.

The children's menu includes steak; chicken fingers; spaghetti; and hamburgers.

Desserts include cheesecake; ice cream; brownies; and the Iron Mountain, a brownie topped with ice cream and other delicious items.

Iron Horse Restaurant and Pizza accepts Visa and MasterCard.

THE JACKALOPE $$
West Vail Mall
476-4314

So you want to eat where the locals eat? Well, the Jackalope is where locals eat and drink. At the Jackalope there is a real sense of local spirit and enthusiasm. There are multiple big screen televisions to keep you up to the moment on sporting activities. Pool tables are available and well used. Watch the newspapers for live music and dancing here.

They have good Mexican food at a reasonable price; or else, the locals would not eat here. They have fajitas (beef, chicken or vegetarian); tacos; burritos; quesadillas; chile rellenos; and more. For a great meal try their beef burrito with green chile sauce; ask for a second dab of sour cream on the side as you may need it. The cheese and onion enchilada is wonderful. Hamburgers; Philly steak sandwiches; steak dinners; and shrimp are also on the menu.

Breakfast is available in addition to their lunch and dinner menus. If you want to wake up to huevos rancheros, head on over to the Jackalope.

Desserts include pecan pie and Key lime pie. Naturally sopaipillas are also available. I have tried and enjoyed them all.

If you eat where the locals eat, you have to know what a jackalope is -- a jack rabbit with antlers instead of long ears. The jackalopes were threatened with extinction it seemed; however, a small colony of these wonderful, lucky critters was discovered about 10 miles south of Vail. Be on the lookout for them. It could make your day if you sight one bouncing around at the side of the trail. A number of sightings have occurred on Lost Boy in the Game Creek Bowl. Good luck to you.

The Jackalope accepts Visa and MasterCard.

JUNE CREEK GRILL $$$
    Singletree Golf Course Clubhouse
    Edwards
    926-3528

The June Creek Grill is beautifully located in the heart of the Singletree Golf Course with an excellent view of Arrowhead from picture windows. It is cozy and comfortable inside, and the food is intriguing.

The house salad is wonderful, believe me. Appetizers include oysters; shrimp; artichoke; calamari; and pizza. The calamari are softly fried and very tender.

Entrees include chicken thighs; a half mesquite smoked chicken; venison loin; Atlantic salmon; scallops; pork chops; and rib eye. I had a special rib eye with a pizza cheese topping and pasta on the side; it was creative and intriguing. June Creek Grill usually has several specials to complement the basic menu.

Desserts sound appealing. I can guarantee you that the Maui macadamia banana cream pie is spectacular. Other dessert offerings are toasted pound cake with vanilla ice cream or pumpkin gingerbread with warm butterscotch and fresh cream.

June Creek Grill accepts Visa and MasterCard. Lunch is also available.

K.B. RANCH CO. $$$

Lion Square Lodge, Lionshead
476-1937

If you are a steak and salad eater, K.B. Ranch Co. is the place for you. They have a 50 item salad bar. With a name like K.B. Ranch Co. they ought to have steak, and they do. Enjoy beautiful views of Vail Mountain out huge picture windows while you dine.

The 50 item salad bar is included with all full dinners. It includes homemade specialties like Caesar salad, homemade breads, shrimp, ravioli and black beans. All the vegetables are fresh.

Side dishes do cost extra; but you may not need them with the exquisite salad bar at your service. Furthermore, K.B. Ranch usually offers special prices in the off-season, and locals love it; but you do not have to be a local to enjoy the special prices. Just check out the back page of the *Vail Daily*. If the ad is upside down, don't worry.

K.B. Ranch's steaks include 12 oz. New York strip; filet mignon; top sirloin; and peppered sirloin. Colorado's finest double lamb chops are also on the menu. I have personally enjoyed each of these entrees.

Seafood dishes are on the menu including salmon and trout. Additionally, they have fresh fish specials daily. I have enjoyed their chicken and duck.

Desserts include apple crumb pie; mud pie; and other ice cream desserts. The mud pie is topped off with sliced walnuts, quite delicious.

K.B. Ranch Co. may be a little hard to find, even though they say it is right next to the Lionshead Gondola. It is; but not where most people think. Ask for directions. Remember it is in the Lion Square Lodge.

K.B. Ranch Co. accepts Visa and MasterCard. There is a children's menu with chicken or cheese ravioli.

KK'S BBQ $

Wolcott
"Center of the Universe"

It's outdoors in Wolcott, at the corner where you turn north heading for 4 Eagle Ranch, State Bridge Lodge, or Steamboat Springs. KK's serves fantastic BBQ ribs at reasonable prices. You cannot ask for more.

LANCELOT INN RESTAURANT $$$$
Next to the Children's Fountain
Vail Village
476-5828

Lancelot is the place to go if you enjoy prime rib. They make no bones about it. Prime rib is their specialty. The prime rib comes with salad; good hot rolls; and a baked potato. It makes great sense (at least to me) to order the King Arthur cut, which is big. This way you can have lunch for the next day in your "people bag" as you leave the restaurant.

The Lancelot does serve smaller cuts of prime rib as well as New York sirloin or pepper steak. The Lancelot has special slow cooking ovens for the roast beef and a special seasoning known only to the chef. It is so secret that not even the kitchen staff knows.

The menu has expanded. Diners come in to have fresh trout; lobster tail; or other seafood dishes. Additionally, the menu includes lamb; mesquite smoked chicken; pork ribs; or BBQ beef ribs. If you are into trying one of these other entrees, it may help you to know that the chef is a fishing addict; try the trout.

Appetizers include lox, shrimp cocktail, and herring.

For dessert I recommend the old fashioned apple strudel which comes hot and a la mode. They also serve cheesecake; peach melba; Jamaican hot fudge sundae; and chocolate mousse. I can personally vouch for the strudel and the mousse.

While you enter Lancelot from the children's fountain area, you go downstairs to dine at the level of the Gore Creek restaurants and shops. If you are lucky enough to get a window seat you can look out at Gore Creek. In nice weather you may eat outdoors on the terrace. The Lancelot has been recently remodeled to a brighter and lighter look, contemporary to the '90s

The Lancelot understands children's taste preferences.

The Lancelot accepts American Express, Visa, and MasterCard.

LA TOUR $$$$
121 East Meadow Drive
across from Crossroads
476-4403

La Tour presents cuisine francaise in an elegant manner. The reputation of Walter and Marie-Claire Moritz is well known in the Vail Valley. Now their location is even easier to find. A brand new glockenspiel adds identity to the restaurant, chiming hourly and playing songs.

Bread comes with the meal; an excellent salad is a la carte. Appetizers include shrimp; steak tartare; caviar; or lobster bisque among others.

Entrees include several veal recipes; sweet breads; several chicken recipes; and duckling with either orange or pepper sauce. Other entrees include pheasant; quail; venison; lamb medallions and lamb chops. Filet steak can be served with peppercorn sauce or sauce bernaise. Fish dishes include Dover sole; poached or grilled salmon; Colorado trout; and two different mixtures of shrimp and scallops.

I personally vouch for the duck with pepper sauce; the pheasant breast with smoked mushrooms; and the sauteed lamb medallions, bordelaise. Each of these entrees made it to the "wonderful" level. The meals come with varied and excellent vegetables, always well presented.

Desserts include fantastic sundaes; chocolate mousse; or cream caramel.

La Tour accepts major credit cards or personal checks with proper identification.

THE LEFT BANK $$$$$
In the Sitzmark Lodge
Vail Village
476-3696

Owner chef Luc Meyer together with his wife Liz bring 30 years of experience in creative cuisine to the table. The setting is formal yet comfortable. If you get one of the window seats you can enjoy a good view of Gore Creek.

When I first dined here it seemed easiest to pick my meal from their specialty list. This was an excellent choice for me, but I expect so are the other choices. I had La Soupe des Tomates en Surprise to start. This is a bowl of tomato soup with a puff pastry topping. It was an enjoyable surprise. On another occasion I had the potato leek soup.

For my entree I had Le Saumon a l'Oseille. The salmon was covered with a wonderful cream sauce. The entree was accompanied by crisp, fresh, and delicate vegetables. I especially enjoyed their thinly cut squash. On another occasion I had a seafood pasta. The scallops and shrimp were very fresh and the pasta itself was excellent.

Other entrees include chicken; veal liver; veal loin, sweet breads; duck breast; beef tournedos; elk; trout; striped bass; swordfish; and poached shrimp.

For dessert the house specialty is a La Tarte Chaude aux Peches et son Sorbet. The pastry chef covers thinly sliced peaches with an apricot glaze. The tart is served with an excellent sorbet topping and fresh whipped cream on the side. On another occasion I had the pecan brittle ice cream with a caramel sauce. Oh my, it was great. Other desserts include creme brule; mousse au chocolat; fresh berries; pecan pie; and la tarte au citron. With 24 hours notice you can have a souffle Rothschild, which has a zesty lemon flavor.

Take note the Left Bank accepts no credit cards. They will accept a personal check or traveler's checks.

LEGENDS $$$$
In the Poste Montane
Right off the Plaza in Beaver Creek
949-5540

Legends is an elegant looking restaurant in the Post Montane at Beaver Creek. It has an interesting menu and is a thoroughly enjoyable place to eat. For an appetizer I had a quesadilla with chorizo, sirloin and cilantro. It was tasty. Combined with an excellent hot bread, this took the edge off that ravenous post-ski hunger. Other appetizers include oysters; New Zealand cockles; escargot; Caesar salad; and clam chowder.

For an entree, I had a walnut crusted sea bass with banana and ginger sauce. It was a wonderful surprising mixture of tastes. Other fresh fish items on the menu include yellowfin tuna; mahi-mahi; salmon; sea scallops; and ruby rainbow trout. I enjoyed a taste of salmon; it was fresh and done to perfection. Crab legs are also available. A San Francisco style cioppino with shrimp, clams, white fish, crab and scallops in a spicy broth is another one of their specialties.

Steaks; chicken; and hamburgers are available. Pastas come with chicken and shrimp or with scallops, shrimp, salmon and crab. A vegetable pasta is available.

Desserts include rhubarb custard; mud pie; and raspberry hazelnut cheesecake. The mud pie is excellent.

There is a children's menu including items such as macaroni; chicken; and hamburger.

Legends accepts American Express, MasterCard, and Visa.

LIONSHEAD BAR AND GRILL $$
Concert Hall Plaza
476-3060

The easy-going atmosphere of a neighborhood bar and grill makes Lionshead Bar and Grill a favorite après ski establishment. Open for breakfast, lunch and dinner, its prices are reasonable. The TV screens tuned to sporting events add to the fun.

I love their breakfast waffles. You can have them plain; with pecans; or with fresh fruit. They also serve eggs; huevos rancheros; and buttermilk biscuits with country sausage gravy.

Mexican dishes make for a great meal including sizzling fajitas or chile rellenos. Burritos; enchiladas; and tacos grande are also available. Plus they serve mounds of nachos. Macho nachos can be a meal for two.

Grilled items include their "steak burgers extraordinaire;" southern style chicken fried steak; pastrami reuben; beef; chicken; and pork. The guacamole hamburger steak is excellent. The burgers are all 1/2 pounders, a full meal with french fries on the side. Soups, chili and salads are on the menu. They also offer a few chicken dishes.

Desserts include cheesecake and assorted homemade pies.

With plentiful food at reasonable prices, you will find locals. Lionshead Bar and Grill accepts Visa and MasterCard. Take out is available.

THE LORD GORE RESTAURANT $$$$
Manor Vail Lodge
Gold Peak
476-5651

Legend has it that Lord Gore of the Manor Gore on the east coast of Ireland journeyed to the U.S. and then into the unknown wilds of the Rocky Mountains on a hunting expedition in the 1850s. His trip has been described as the costliest, longest, and most astonishing expedition ever. Wagons carried cases of fine foods; choice wines and liquors; plus fine china, linens and silverware. This legend lives on today at the Lord Gore Restaurant.

The Lord Gore Restaurant offers a fantastic view of the Golden Peak section of Vail Mountain. The interior design is elegant with beautiful dark paneling behind you and great window views before you. The chairs are large and comfortable. There is also a wonderful terrace in front of the restaurant for sunny weather.

Caesar salads and steak tartare are available. Soup, salads and bread are enjoyable. Appetizers include escargot and wild mushrooms; calamari with curry coriander sauce; smoked buffalo; corn fried oysters with tomato tequila salsa and chipolte cream; smoked Norwegian salmon; and shrimp cocktail.

The Lord Gore Restaurant's menu offers filet mignon; filet mignon with three pepper sauce; rack of Colorado lamb; wild game; paillard of veal; veal forestiere; duck breast with apricot chambard glaze; chateaubriand; scampi Mediterranean; fresh ruby red trout; seafood fettuccine; and fresh salmon. Daily fish specials are available. I have had the duck and the filet mignon with three pepper sauce. Both items were cooked to my liking.

Desserts include New York style cheesecake; fresh fruit; pecan pie; and apple strudel.

A children's menu is available. Breakfast, lunch, and Sunday brunch are also served.

Manor Vail accepts Visa, MasterCard, American Express, Diner's Club, and Discover Card.

LOS AMIGOS $$
    Top of Bridge Street
    Vail Village
    476-5847

Los Amigos is a popular aprés ski bar and restaurant located in the Golden Peak House. Its back deck is on the slopes, near the base of the Vista Bahn lift; you can ski to it. From the Bridge Street side the restaurant is reached via a circular ramp, a feature the children love.

I had the enchilada especiale with chicken which was hot, hot, hot. But they kept my water glass full. Chile rellenos is a specialty of the house. Key lime pie is a dessert feature as well as apple crisp. I enjoyed the pie.

Judy and Shirkie Evans are the owners and they are on site. Shirkie is responsible for the northern Mexican food served here. Each of his recipes is made from scratch. Shirkie Evans also manages the BBQ menu at the 4 Eagle Ranch.

Children are welcome here. The atmosphere is lively. Los Amigos accepts Visa and MasterCard.

LOST ARMADILLO $
    Benchmark Plaza
    Avon
    949-7099

The Lost Armadillo is a light and airy Mexican restaurant. It is a fun place to be casual.

Appetizers include nachos; nachos with guacamole; chicken wings; firehouse chili; and flautas.

Entrees include fajitas; tacos; burritos; chile rellenos; and quesadillas. They also serve burgers and steaks. I had the steak Mexicana. It was enjoyable.

Dessert offerings are simple. I had a tasty apple pie a la mode. Sorbet is also available.

L'OSTELLO $$$$$
    705 West Lionshead Circle
    476-2050

Well, if newspaper reviews can make a restaurant, this should be it. L'Ostello is loved at the five star level by *The Denver Post*, *The Rocky Mountain News* and the *1991 Gabby Gourmet Restaurant Guide*. Between these reviews and my experience, this is a five star restaurant.

Some items on the menu may change, but there will always be a "scarlet-

cooked roast rack of lamb, crusted in a bouquet of herbs and set on a saucing that is at once heady in aroma and deep in flavor." While these enticing words were written by Bill St. John of *The Rocky Mountain News,* I concur. Indeed, the lamb is so great that it is often difficult to choose another entree. The tender lamb is served with a pastry of ripe goat cheese in a filo crust.

Other entrees include a thick veal chop; a crabmeat ravioli that draws critics' raves; grilled dry angus sirloin; seared yellow fin tuna; crispy striped bass; seared salmon; or salmon simply steamed. I tried the striped bass and thoroughly enjoyed it. I've had the fettuccine with duck served hunter style and loved it. I had another duck dish, a daily special, which was absolutely the best prepared duck meals I have ever tasted.

Lets go back to appetizers. Dinner begins with a wonderful warm homemade bread with chive butter or olive oil dip. Appetizers include curried prawns; fried spinach gnocchi; sauteed sweetbreads; and grilled marinated tuna.

Desserts are a specialty of the house. They include a smooth creme brule with a thin, caramelized coating; a magnificent chocolate mousse cake with fresh raspberries and raspberry sauce; plus deep-fried bananas with bourbon gelato and rich chocolate sauce.

Right outside the main L'Ostello Restaurant is a comfortable sitting area around the central fireplace. You can drink from the bar and listen to fine jazz; you can also eat here.

There is an early children's menu from 5:30 to 6:30. L'Ostello accepts American Express, Visa and MasterCard.

LOUIE'S $$$$
Wall Street
Vail Village
476-9008

Appetizers include calamari; shrimp on angel hair pasta; sauteed sea scallops; wild mushroom pie; crabmeat; cervichi; blackened prawns in pesto cream sauce; plus artichokes and cheese. Salads and soups are available a la carte. The crab and lobster bisque is excellent.

For entrees I have had both the grilled salmon and the prawns. Both meals were excellent with fresh fish. I have also been delighted by the honey thyme pheasant, a boned half pheasant marinated in hard cider, served with a honey apple thyme sauce. Louie's offers daily fish specials.

Louie's serves steak, including a cajun New York strip; veal medallions with shitake mushroom sauce; venison; and lamb dishes. Roasted duck or grilled chicken breast are also available. Chicken breast stuffed with crabmeat and asparagus has proven to be a winner. Louie's also offers Italian dishes: lasagna or fettuccine prima primavera con pollo. Alternatively, they feature linguine with lobster, chicken, and mushrooms in a lobster cream sauce. Scampi; flounder; and tuna are other options.

Desserts are varied. I have enjoyed their chocolate cake and cheesecake.

There is a children's menu. This includes 1/2 price on the pasta meals. Louie's accepts American Express, Visa, and MasterCard.

In the spirit of Satchmo, you are entertained with live jazz, Wednesday through Sunday, 10:00 p.m. till closing time.

LUDWIG'S RESTAURANT $$$$
Sonnenalp Hotel, Bavaria Haus
(across from InterFaith Chapel)
476-5656

Ludwig's Restaurant, named after former King Ludwig of Bavaria, focuses on Continental cuisine with a fusion of Nouvelle American. Dine in a beautiful room with attractive Bavarian wooden beams and ceiling trim. Sit back, relax, and let the wait staff take care of you.

Excellent bread and crisp salad start you off. A favorite salad is wilted spinach salad with wild mushrooms. Appetizers include seafood in a light saffron sauce; escargot in puff pastry; or Special Oysters Southwestern. For this latter dish the oysters are slightly warmed with lime and cilantro sauce. Lobster bisque; cajun seafood gumbo; and a chef's daily cauldron special are on the menu.

Venison; quail; beef; pork and grilled lamb chops have their place on the menu. Salmon in filo is a specialty of the house. A fresh Oregon salmon is wrapped in a filo pastry and baked; it comes served with a champagne scallop sauce. You can also have salmon grilled with papaya cream sauce or baked Oregon salmon with tomato and an opal basil sauce.

Smoked duck breast with raspberries is a favorite of mine. The duck is smoked with a special mixture of woods resulting in a wonderful flavor. The sweetness of the raspberries creates an intriguing combination.

Pasta dishes such as mostaccioli with winter vegetables are excellent. Or you can dine on fettuccine with fresh ricotta.

Desserts include Bavarian cream pie; Mile High Meringue with chocolate sauce; and blackberry torte. Desserts are baked fresh daily in the Sonnenalp bake shop.

Daily breakfasts and Sunday brunches are served. Breakfast entrees are great; however, the buffet is so healthy you may choose to go with it.

Ludwig's provides terrace service in summer.

The Sonnenalp accepts Visa and MasterCard. Children can select from the Bully Ranch menu while sitting with the family in Ludwig's. The Bully Ranch is another Sonnenalp restaurant which is informal and less expensive.

LUIGI'S $

Radisson Hotel
476-4444

Luigi's offers Italian pizzas and pasta. A choice appetizer is their Italian skins, potato skins stuffed with Italian sausage, green onion, and topped with melted cheese.

Pasta meals include spaghetti with either meatballs or Italian sausage; bake ziti topped with mozzarella cheese; fettuccine; and cheese ravioli.

Dine on entrees like pasta shells stuffed with ricotta cheese combined with meatballs or Italian sausage; chicken alfredo; or veal parmesan. Choose an Italian submarine or a Luigi burger.

Ice cream is a winner in Luigi's dessert selection. In addition to spumoni, the menu features a fudge brownie sundae; Kahlua and ice cream shake; fried ice cream; plus Ben & Jerry's ice cream and sorbet.

Luigi's accepts Visa, MasterCard, and American Express.

MAY PALACE $$$

Next to the Children's Fountain
Vail Village
476-1657

The May Palace offers good food enhanced by a wonderful view down Vail Valley and overlooking Gore Creek. In the summer they have Vail's only outdoor bar on their spacious deck. The May Palace specializes in Szechuan, but also serves Mandarin and Cantonese dishes.

May Palace has a wide variety menu of Chinese offerings. I have personally had a number of entrees and have been impressed with the high quality and the speed of delivery.

For appetizers I have sampled the egg rolls, fried dumplings, and fried wanton. I especially enjoyed the egg rolls.

For entrees I have enjoyed the sizzling beef and scallops meal; the Kung Pao chicken; the House Special duck; the deluxe moo-shu; Mongolian beef and Treasures of the Sea. The beef and scallops were served with mushrooms, broccoli, and bamboo shoots. The Kung Pao chicken came with peanuts, green onions, and red peppers. It was hot. The House Special duck was smothered in a sauce with Chinese greens, bamboo shoots, broccoli, and mushrooms. With the deluxe moo-shu, you get chicken, beef, and pork to put into your pancakes. The pancakes were very fresh. The Mongolian beef was excellent. Treasures of the Sea includes shrimp, scallops, crabmeat, and abalone combined with Chinese greens and snow peas. Each meal was good and hearty. You can select from a wide variety of choices.

Lunch is available. With May Palace's speedy service, it can be a good

place to eat lunch while skiing Vail Mountain. Take out service is offered.
May Palace accepts Visa and MasterCard.

McDONALD'S $

West Vail
476-1966

McDonald's can be found to the west of Safeway and Gart Brothers off of the North Frontage Road.

MICHAEL'S AMERICAN BISTRO $$$$

In the Gateway Plaza
476-5353

Enjoy new creative American Cuisine in a unique dining atmosphere. Michael's has the top floor view overlooking the atrium in the new Gateway Plaza. Note the grand vista across Vail Valley from inside the restaurant or from their outdoor deck.

Michael's grilled fare includes roast duckling with honey cumin and grilled cherrywood smoked salmon. I have had both of these entrees and found them excellent. But look at this. The roast duckling was served with a side of tacos filled with quinoa. The salmon had polenta topped with brie and succotash on the side. What a delightful surprise. This is creative. I have also enjoyed their pepper steak cooked medium rare, as ordered. The T-bone steak, served with heaps of garlic mashed potatoes was wonderful.

Another time I ordered chicken molé with a slice of fried banana on the side, very original and intriguing.

Other menu items include tuna pepper steak with ginger served with garlic mashed potatoes and fried onion rings; duck breast with orange mustard seed chutney; roast rack of lamb; and elk tenderloin. Steak, veal and scallops are also available. The grilled veal loin is finished with a wild mushroom and madeira sauce. The sea scallops are covered with a pistachio crust and prepared with curried apples. The scallops were fresh. I also enjoyed linguine with grilled shrimp and scallops.

Try the gourmet pizzas -- wow! Their pizza recipes include one with tomato, roasted garlic, fresh mozzarella, oregano and basil and another with spicy shrimp and roasted onion sauce. I especially enjoyed a gourmet pizza with smoked duck sausage and peach ginger barbecue sauce.

What is more, you can see the food being cooked by sitting at the food bar. There is a lovely open kitchen. Many of the delicacies are smoked over woods of cherry, alder, mesquite or hickory.

Lunches are worthwhile here. I had a pepper tuna (medium rare) over spinach and Oriental noodles dish which is about the best light lunch meal I

159

have ever enjoyed. In fact, I have enjoyed it a number of times. Their cherrywood smoked salmon was an excellent lunchtime experience. The hamburger was a quality offering served with corn relish and spicy waffle fried potatoes. Other meals include Caesar salad; smoked Gulf prawn quesadilla; chicken; and steak. They have a wonderful breast of duckling. Also, look for the gourmet pizzas at lunchtime. And they do have a children's lunch menu.

Desserts at Michael's are excellent. I had a chocolate paté with raspberry and pistachio sauce and enjoyed it. I have also eaten their delectable apple strudel a la mode. Other desserts include Irish cream cheesecake; a three layer chocolate cake; and homemade ice creams or sorbets. If they offer you a brownie with raspberry puree plus espresso, chocolate chip ice cream, take it; I'm sure you will be glad. Their mud pie is great. Finally and especially, order a "chocolate bag" which they fill with homemade ice cream or a strawberry milkshake. This is a dessert to be savored. They also serve chocolate bags filled with hazelnut and white chocolate mousse. As you can see, your predicament is choosing.

Michael's takes American Express, Visa, MasterCard, and all Major Credit Card.

MINTURN COUNTRY CLUB $$
   Minturn
   827-4114

Minturn Country Club offers beef, poultry, and seafood dishes (such as shrimp and shark) which you cook over a communal charcoal grill. The scene around the grill is casual and relaxed. Enjoy it. A garden fresh 23 item salad bar comes with your entree.

You go to their "Butcher Shop" area after you have been seated. You view and choose your own cut of steak, fish, shrimp, or chicken. The charcoal grill is next to the "Butcher Shop," as is the salad bar. The prime rib is already cooked by the restaurant. I have enjoyed eating at the Minturn Country Club on several occasions. The food is always fresh and wonderful. In my opinion the roast beef is especially marvelous.

Side dishes including corn-on-the-cob, huge baked potatoes, and great BBQ beans are a la carte. Minturn Country Club offers fruit pies for dessert.

As for the name, Minturn Country Club asserts, "The only thing missing is the golf course."

Minturn Country Club accepts Visa and MasterCard.

MINTURANO PASTA PALACE $$
Main St.
Minturn
827-9204

Minturano Pasta Palace offers you an Italian pasta feast at reasonable prices.

Appetizers include antipasto; dinner salad; garlic bread; soup; 8" pizza; and the big ball (a mixture of sausage and beef).

They offer numerous sauces including marinara; vongole (clam); pesto; Bologonese; quatro fromaggio; and puttenesco. Pastas include linguine; fettuccine; spaghetti; capellini; penne; and fusilli.

Additionally, Minturano Pasta Palace serves meat lasagna; eggplant lasagna; broccoli ziti; chicken parmesan; and steak Laurita.

I have personally have enjoyed both the calamari marinara over linguine and the steak Laurita. The steak Laurita came with marinara sauce, polenta, and a huge fried onion.

Desserts include spumoni; gelatoi; and cannoli with chocolate sauce and crushed pistachios.

Minturano Pasta Palace offers 1/2 price children's specials with the pasta dishes. They accept Visa and MasterCard.

MIRABELLE $$$$
At the Base of Beaver Creek Mountain
949-7728

Mirabelle is owned by Luc and Liz Meyer, the owners of the celebrated Left Bank in Vail Village. Don't look for this excellent French restaurant at the ski area. It is located just above the east security gate; it is not up at the ski area.

Appetizers include puff pastry with onions and salmon or snails in puff pastry. Oysters and scallops are also available.

Entrees include trout; shrimp; salmon; swordfish; lobster; chicken breast; duck breast; elk; sweet breads; rack of lamb; veal; rib eye of beef; and pork chop. The veal is exceptional. I had an entree which included beef and veal. I found the veal to be marvelous.

For dessert, be sure to try the pear tartlet. You must order this as you are ordering your entree. Other desserts include cheesecake; lemon cream pie; chocolate truffle cake; and macadamia nut cake.

Mirabelle does not accept credit cards. They do accept personal checks and traveler's checks.

MONTAUK $$$
Lionshead Mall
476-2601

Montauk is a wonderful seafood restaurant with a light and airy atmosphere. A variety of fresh fish and seafood tempt your palate. While waiting, you can doodle or color on butcher paper tablecloth. Kids love this.

Sourdough bread with sweet butter precedes the meal. Montauk has a raw bar with oysters, clams, and shellfish. For appetizers Montauk specializes in fried calamari with spicy tomato sauce. Other excellent appetizers include peel & eat shrimp; roast duck salad; and vine ripe tomato salad.

Choose from a variety of seafood specials. I have enjoyed Hawaiian opah; seared rare tuna; Florida grouper; Alaskan bass; snow crab; jumbo grilled scallops; and Maine lobster. A very interesting and excellent dish is the blackened snapper over a tortilla combined with sweet and sour cabbage, tomato salsa, and tequila lime butter. I have loved them all. The fish at Montauk has always been very fresh. Other seafood dishes include yellow fin tuna; sterling salmon; pan fried rainbow trout; swordfish; halibut; New England bass; mahi-mahi; marlin; and prawns.

Your fish dish comes with a wonderful sauce. Each evening you have the choice of one of four sauces. The sauces are rotated. They have included cantaloupe relish; tomato herb butter; spicy peanut; or avocado salsa. Others include dijon cream; sweet and sour ginger berry; orange mint vinaigrette; red pepper basil cream; tequila lime butter; red pepper cream; and soy ginger vinaigrette. My favorite is their orange mustard sauce.

Steak and chicken are available for those who seek an alternative.

The desserts are fantastic. I had a wonderful fruit shortcake. The chocolate tureen with raspberry sauce was great fun. The sand pie is excellent; the portions are huge and probably should be shared. Sand pie is similar to mud pie, but uses chocolate chip ice cream with a caramel sauce and whipped cream topping. Other desserts include Key lime pie; pecan pie; cheesecake; and flourless chocolate cake. There are daily pastry specials.

A children's menu features fish sticks; hamburger; or a grilled cheese sandwich. The Montauk accepts American Express, MasterCard, and Visa.

MR. NATURAL JUICE BAR $
West Vail Mall
476-7205

This unusual store in Vail may be part of the wave of the future. Here you can get freshly squeezed juices from organically grown fruits and vegetables. The organic products used here are cultivated at a significant distance from pesticides or growth enhancing chemicals. When ready, the produce is washed in Mr. Natural's purified water. It certainly is interesting to have this organic store on the same block as McDonalds, Dairy Queen, and Subway. Mr. Natural's also offers vegetarian deli items, granola and yogurt. What the heck, give health a try.

NOZAWA $$$
Days Inn, West Vail
476-9355

You will have to search out Nozawa; but if you like sushi or Japanese cooked foods, it will be worth it. It is located in the Days Inn in West Vail off the North Frontage Road.

Nozawa's decor is simple and enjoyable. There is a six seat sushi bar. Nozawa serves raw fish delicacies including tuna, salmon, and shrimp. They also serve sushi rolls: a combination of rice, salmon, crab, avocado, and seaweed. The sushi chef is experienced and likable. His sharp knife moves oh, so quickly as he prepares the delights. There always seems to be a friendly atmosphere around the sushi bar.

Nozawa offers cooked Japanese cuisine as well as the sushi. Appetizers include eggrolls; skewered grilled chicken; and grilled thinly sliced steak.

For an entree, I had the sukiyaki and loved it. Other Japanese entrees include shrimp tempura; steak teriyaki; and chicken teriyaki.

Nozawa accepts Visa, MasterCard, and American Express.

OPINIONS $$$
Homestead Court Club
Homestead Drive, Edwards
926-2136

Opiñions is a lovely restaurant with great views. Excellent bread is served. Appetizers include herb and cheese toast; grilled bass; salmon pinwheels; carpaccio of venison; and a pesto pizza with fresh vegetables and smoked provolone. I enjoyed the wafer thin slices of New Zealand Red Deer.

Opiñions has great pastas: smoked game hen with linguica and linguine; baked penne with gorgonzola, ricotta, parmesan and feta cheese; angel hair with fresh salmon and scallops. The tasty smoked game hen pasta was done to my liking, combining smoked chicken, spicy Portuguese sausage, sweet red peppers, garlic and fresh oregano, with linguine and linguica. Opiñions also offers several fish dishes: grilled halibut; cajun catfish; and North Atlantic salmon. Filet mignon; herb roasted chicken; sauteed medallions of red deer; and double thick pork chop are other offerings.

I enjoyed chocolate fudge pie for dessert. Other choices include strawberry shortcake; baked apple crisp; N.Y. cheesecake; frozen pineapple souffle; dark chocolate mousse; and Haagen Dazs ice creams. The waitress recommended the apple crisp and the mousse.

There is a children's menu with burgers; spaghetti; roasted chicken; and pizza. And they have an entertainment room for the kids while adults can watch big screen TV in the bar. Opiñions accepts Visa and MasterCard.

ORE HOUSE $$$
Under the Clock Tower
Vail Village
476-5100

The Ore House claims to be Vail's original steak house. Under the Clock Tower its location is easy to spot and convenient. A deck provides some of Vail's best "people watching."

Appetizers include popcorn shrimp and baby back pork ribs. Dinner salad and fresh baked bread come with your dinner entree.

Steaks and prime rib are excellent. Rocky Mountain trout was flavorful. I also enjoyed a delicate salmon. Other entrees include Colorado rack of lamb; baby back pork ribs; yellow fin tuna; Alaskan king crab; and rock lobster tail. They have several ways of preparing chicken specialties. They also serve a vegetarian plate.

I have enjoyed their Key lime pie and their mud pie. Cheesecake is also available.

The Ore House accepts Visa, MasterCard, American Express, and Diner's Club.

Aprés ski starts at 3:30 p.m.

PADDY'S SPORTS BAR AND GRILL $$
Eagle-Vail Business Center
on north side of Highway 6
949-6093

Paddy's is in Eagle-Vail and it is definitely local. Crowded anytime, it is really crowded when a major sports event is on television. The big bar has lots of televisions. A small restaurant has one television and plentiful good food. A small patio is enjoyable in good weather.

Paddy's serves breakfast, lunch, and dinner. For breakfast they serve eggs and omelettes. They also offer pancakes and a breakfast bar. Breakfast is served only on Saturday and Sunday.

For lunch, they have sandwiches; 1/2 pound burgers; Mexican dishes; prime rib sandwich; cajun chicken breast; broiled tuna steak sandwich; spaghetti; fresh fish and chips.

Appetizers include potato skins; hot chicken wings; temperate wings;

and zucchini fingers.

Entrees include prime rib; top sirloin; eggplant parmesan; linguine pescadore; Italian shrimp; chicken ricotta; chicken parmesan; vegetable primavera; lasagna; sausage and chicken ziti; red snapper and chips. I enjoyed the eggplant parmesan. I, among others, watch the newspapers for their fantastic lobster specials. They start serving at 4 p.m. and can be out of lobsters by 5 p.m. I've seen it happen. Get there early.

Desserts include Key lime cheesecake; apple pie; hot fudge brownie sundae; and Snicker's pie. The cheesecake was creamy and the brownie sundae was tasty.

A new game room at Paddy's lets parents enjoy dinner or a drink while their kids have fun. A family oriented restaurant complements the family oriented menu. Children enjoy either the kiddie room or the game room. These rooms are separate from the bar and restaurant. The game room contains a video arcade and sporting events: shuffleboard; a golf putting game; basketball hoops; and air hockey.

Paddy's accepts American Express, Visa, MasterCard, and Diner's Club. There is a $2.95 children's menu including such items as 1/4 lb. cheeseburger; linguine with meatball; grilled cheese; chicken tenders; plus fish and chips.

PALMOS CAPPUCCINO AND SPIRITS $$$
Vail Gateway Plaza
476-0646

Palmos Cappuccino and Spirits has a beautiful design and considers itself "Vail's Premier Cappuccino & Espresso Bar." In addition to espresso, cappuccino, and spirits, Palmos offers delicious pastries. In the afternoon and evening they serve Scandinavian gravlox appetizers.

Palmos accepts Visa, MasterCard and American Express.

PATINA RISTORANTE ITALIANO $$$$
In the Hyatt-Regency at Beaver Creek
845-2842

This beautiful dining room, set in simple dark woods, achieves an elegance diners enjoy. Take in the tremendous view of Beaver Creek Mountain. In good weather you can dine on the patio, a wonderful setting for an Italian eating experience. Their menu is a cornucopia of Tuscan cuisine.

To begin you receive excellent bread with olive oil. Appetizers include eggplant; calamari; octopus; shrimp; beef carpaccio; and antipasto. Soups and salads are a la carte.

Seafood entrees include fresh grilled scampi served with garlic on a bed of spinach; pan fried trout; salmon with grapefruit; and swordfish. Their swordfish is a big seller; it is grilled in virgin olive oil and topped with a blend of tomato, garlic, capers, and black olives. The trout was enjoyable. Patina Ristorante also offers prime rib; veal chop; lamb chop; elk with wild berry compote; duck with candied pecans; breast of chicken; grilled beef tenderloin; and the scaloppini of the day.

In addition to the above entrees, Patina Grill offers a variety of pastas and pizzas cooked in a wood-burning stone oven. You can have pizzas with goat cheese; shitake mushrooms; salmon; or shrimp. The pastas are wonderful. They serve an excellent linguine with shrimp, scallops, and mussels. Additionally, they have a pheasant filled tortellini. I suggest the lobster ravioli, served in a cream sauce with crab meat and scallops.

Patina Grill offers a variety of Health Mark foods with specially prepared low-fat and cholesterol reduced menu items. Margarine can replace butter if you wish. They also have and are developing a Cuisine Naturelle. Scallops and pasta in marinara sauce; lamb chop with couscous; white albacore tuna; and whole wheat pizza are on this menu. To continue the health theme, have a side of spinach salad and a fruit plate dessert.

For children twelve and under, smaller portions are half price.

Desserts are special pastries baked fresh daily. These delights include chocolate cake; cheesecake; apple pie a la mode; and tira misu. This last dish is hard to describe but incredible. It is a creamy mixture combined with delicate lady fingers topped with rich chocolate. Make a couple extra bump runs tomorrow to work off the calories. Or come back to the Patina and stick to the Cuisine Naturelle the following night.

Patina Ristorante Italiano accepts all major credit cards. They are open for breakfast (starting at 7 a.m.) and lunch, as well as dinner. There is a Sunday Bellini Brunch, featuring a concoction of peach juice and champagne.

Peter Grewe entertains guests with his special blend of instrumental piano in the lobby.

PAZZO'S PIZZERIA $

East Meadow Drive
Village Center
Across from Crossroads
476-9026

Pazzo's Pizzeria offers breakfast, lunch and dinner seven days a week. You can dine in or take out. The locals do.

Breakfast includes omelettes and egg dishes plus their famous breakfast burrito. Waffles; french toast; muffins; and granola are offered as well.

In addition to the numerous pizza offerings (with twenty one topping choices), Pazzo's serves pasta: spaghetti; ravioli; lasagna; rigatoni; and manicotti. They also serve a number of calzone dishes which they call

Pazzones.

Fruit smoothies round out the menu. Spumoni is available for dessert.

PEPI'S RESTAURANT $$$$
Vail Village
476-5626

Pepi's Restaurant, located in the Gasthof Gramshammer, is situated at Vail's most prestigious intersection. Weather permitting, the restaurant opens its terrace, extending dining to the corner of Bridge Street and Gore Creek Drive. The Austrian setting greets the passerby.

Inside the restaurant, there are two dining rooms: the main dining room and the Antler's Room with different menus. The Antler's Room menu focuses on game dishes. Also, all the dinners for two are served in this room. The main dining room offers European fare with a German accent.

Pepi's appetizers include the unexpected rattlesnake (when they can catch it); shrimp; escargot; nova salmon; steak tartare; salmon mousse; duck paté and caviar. I enjoyed a lobster bisque. Breads are good while salads are crisp and creative.

Entrees available are New York steak; pepper steak; roast duckling; five different types of veal; lamb; pork; and chicken. Enjoy fish and seafood dishes: trout; salmon; scampi; and tuna. Game specialties include elk; boar; antelope; buffalo; pheasant; caribou; venison; and ox. Gourmet dinners for two include rack of lamb; chateaubriand; roast duckling flambe; Dover sole; and rack of venison.

A vegetable platter and pasta primavera are also available.

The food is well presented and the vegetables are garden fresh. I have ordered both the roast duckling and the New York steak. I was thoroughly delighted with each meal.

For dessert try apple strudel a la mode or heisse liebe which consists of hot raspberries over vanilla ice cream. Each was wonderful. Numerous other desserts are available including hazelnut torte; Black Forest torte; white chocolate mousse with a touch of Jamaican rum; linzer torte; New York cheesecake; Coupe Romanoff (marinated strawberries with Grand Marnier over vanilla ice cream); sacher torte; and cream custard with caramel sauce.

Lunch is available, served inside or outside on the sunny patio. Bratwurst is a favorite for lunch. I have enjoyed both the veal and the pork varieties. Blintzes, covered with raspberry sauce, are delicious. I recommend pushing most of the sauce off to the side in order to let the wonderful flavor of the blintz filling come through. Other lunch offerings include salmon; Nova; trout; steak tartare; wurst salad; and wiener schnitzel. Salads; pastas; and hamburgers are also available.

Sunday evening features an Austrian buffet.

Pepi's Bar next door offers après ski and evening entertainment. Sheika's, a night club discotheque, is located beneath the lounge.

Pepi's Restaurant accepts Visa, MasterCard, American Express, Diner's Club, and Carte Blanche.

PIZZA BAKERY $
Lionshead Mall
476-1633

The Pizza Bakery delivers a hot pizza in three minutes. This is a great place to grab a pizza and get back on Vail Mountain, or you can linger on the lovely deck, overlooking the mountain.

While pizza is their specialty, they also have pasta. You can even have buckets of pasta at reasonable prices. Pizza Bakery also serves tacos; BLT.; cheeseburgers and BBQ.

They will deliver. You may notice their delivery bike zooming around Lionshead Mall.

PIZZA EXPRESS OF VAIL $
West Vail Mall
476-2300

Pizza, gyros, pita sandwiches, salads, and calzones are on the menu. Free delivery is available.

PIZZA EXPRESS, PASTA PUB $$
Benchmark Plaza
Avon
845-7744

Pizza Express, Pasta Pub specializes in pizza. They have a wide variety of toppings. The basic cheese pizza is excellent. They feature a Western BBQ pizza and a California pizza, among others. They also serve chicken tetrazzini; spaghetti; shrimp scampi; chicken cacciatore; and prime rib.

They do not serve desserts. They accept Visa, MasterCard, and American Express.

PIZZA HUT OF AVON $
Nottingham Road
Avon
949-0158

Pizza Hut has delivery available.

POPPYSEEDS BAKERY AND CAFE $
North Frontage Road
West Vail Mall
476-5297

Poppyseeds began as a donut shop, but it has sure grown. Now it is "Vail's definitive bakery." It offers numerous types of oven fresh pastries, including wonderful donuts and muffins. They bake their own breads, ready for you to take home. Additionally, they make their own Gore Range Granola for you to take with you. Poppyseeds specializes in coffee, including espresso and cappuccino.

Poppyseeds also has soups and delicious sandwiches. You can have as much soup as you like. The soups vary on a daily basis but there is always chili. I tried the salami -- a great sandwich.

I love both their bundt cake and carrot cake as dessert items. Their decadent strawberry chocolate brioche is addicting.

Poppyseeds is also in the dinner business. Their "Take Home Dinners" include veggie lasagna; veggie burritos; baked pasta dishes; veggie or beef chili; multi-course dinners; and awesome desserts.

The new owners are expanding the operation slowly. They want to keep it a locals place and not turn it into an expensive patisserie.

RACQUET CLUB RESTAURANT $$$
East Vail
476-4700

Tucked away in residential East Vail is a great restaurant with a beautifully designed interior space in a wonderful environment. It is a short five mile drive from Vail Village. There is plenty of free parking. Also, the East Vail bus stops right outside.

The Racquet Club is a warm and friendly place. In the winter, warm your bones at the cheery fireplace. Upstairs visit the Old Muddy Bar. A number of menu items can be served in the Old Muddy, where you'll frequently find a sporting event on the televisions.

At the Racquet Club Restaurant appetizers include squid; sashimi; carpaccio; wild mushrooms; and smoked trout. Soups and salads are a la carte. They include gazpacho; crab and corn chowder; and Caesar salad.

The Racquet Club has a wide variety of entrees. They serve grilled breast of chicken; grilled shrimp; pan seared salmon; marinated leg of lamb; and pan seared veal chop. I had the grilled shrimp which was marinated in cilantro, garlic, olive oil, and lime. The shrimp were served with a fine angel hair pasta. Side orders, such as mashed potatoes or shoestring potatoes, are a la carte.

Desserts include fresh fruit cobblers; seasonal berries; cappuccino chocolate chip gelato; peach champagne sorbet; and a variety of daily specials. I enjoyed a chilled orange mousse in a chocolate shell.

The Racquet Club Restaurant also serve lunch meals which include salmon; lamb; burgers; and salads.

The Racquet Club accepts Visa, MasterCard, and American Express. They do offer a children's menu.

RED LION $$
Top of Bridge Street
Vail Village
476-7676

The Red Lion is a conveniently located restaurant at the top of Bridge Street. A favorite après ski place, the Red Lion frequently has live entertainment. Televisions with your favorite sporting event are arranged around the bar. With a setting like this you will find locals hanging out.

The Red Lion has good food at reasonable prices. Starters include nachos, a mountain of crisp yellow and blue corn tortilla chips covered with chili, melted cheese, green onions, diced tomatoes, jalapeño and black olives. With an appetizer like this, who needs an entree? Or would you prefer doo-dahs?" Doo-dahs are chicken wings, which the locals love. You can have them with a spicy sauce, the classic style; but you can also have them spicy sweet in a Polynesian sauce or barbecued in a smoky Western sauce.

Hamburgers and hot dogs are great. They have ten different hamburgers on the menu, all starting with a half pound of hand-pattied USDA choice ground beef, charbroiled to order. As for steak, the twelve ounce Kansas City strip is spectacular. Fries and onion rings are mouth watering.

Mexican dishes include blue corn enchiladas with either seasoned beef or chicken; a Mexican burger with cheese, jalapeño pepper and guacamole; or a Red Cliff burger topped with green chiles, cheese, jalapeños and salsa on the side. They also serve a taco salad or a chicken fajita salad.

Numerous BBQ items are also available. I have eaten the beef brisket; the BBQ chicken; and the spare ribs. All were enjoyable.

Fish dishes are available. They include charbroiled swordfish with jalapeño butter; fresh tuna steak, charbroiled with lemon-pepper butter; and cajun catfish lightly brushed with cajun mustard and garlic butter.

Desserts include the ice cream covered avalanche brownie or gold brick sundae. I've had both and enjoyed them.

The Red Lion is a friendly place. In the summers they take out the windows. Then the Red Lion virtually becomes a part of the street scene on Bridge Street; just what the architect ordered.

Lunch and dinner are served continuously starting at 11:00 a.m. seven days per week. American Express, Visa and MasterCard are accepted. In the off season watch for specials in the newspapers.

RENO CAFE AND BAR $
Red Cliff
827-8995

Reno Cafe and Bar is located high up in the mountains above Vail on U.S. 24. It is a locals place that seriously welcomes those passing through. It is run by the Salazar family. Try their burritos and sopaipillas. Have fun, but make sure there is a sober driver to get you back down the mountain. Also, look around while you are there. Red Cliff is a picturesque place, frequented by local artists.

RESTAURANT PICASSO $$$$$
Cordillera Lodge
926-2200

Restaurant Picasso and Cordillera offer European elegance and Rocky Mountain splendor. I went up in the autumn, a great time to see the splendor of golden aspen in the setting sun. The meal was wonderful, to say the least.

I had the fixed *menu de gustation,* an offering Restaurant Picasso varies weekly. Executive Chef Fabrice Beaudoin prepares an amazingly well balanced medley of flavors. An intriguing mixture of sweet and bitter tastes lead to a grand sensory delight. It was obvious that a great deal of thought and culinary experience went into the meal and its presentation.

Come to Restaurant Picasso hungry. Hard rolls and butter along with a bit proscuitto will arrive quickly to assuage that hunger. A quail and asparagus salad signaled the beginning of a great meal. The mushrooms and quail thighs were a wonderful combination; the lettuce and asparagus provided an excellent backdrop.

Then the sauteed sea scallops with Belgium endive and orange were served. The endive and orange blended perfectly; the scallops were luscious and large. My entree was a roasted lamb tenderloin in a crust of thyme accompanied by Provencale ratatouille. The ratatouille was excellent. The lamb was rare and wonderful.

For dessert my waiter presented a chocolate sorbet with a bitter orange coulis. The combination was fantastic; my only (very, very mild) complaint was that I would have enjoyed more orange or less chocolate because it was the combination that was so delicious. Three exquisite small pastries come with the bill, an enjoyable sweetness.

The *menu de gustation* can come with a different wine to complement each course, but you need not order the wine.

A number of exciting offerings characterize the regular appetizer menu:

roasted goat cheese with mixed greens; smoked and fresh salmon mixture; cauliflower soup with fresh mussels; yellow corn and wild mushrooms risotto; plus marinated shrimp with tomato and ginger sauce.

Menu entrees included sauteed sea scallops; salmon, cooked on one side; sauteed pheasant with green cabbage; sauteed beef tenderloin with bordelaise sauce and potato cake; lamb with sweet potato puree; and veal medallions with fresh pasta.

Children do not generally come to Restaurant Picasso. The restaurant accepts Visa, MasterCard, American Express, and "practically every credit card."

How do you get there? From either Vail or Avon head West on I-70 until you reach Edwards (the next exit after Avon). Make a left turn off the highway; then make the next right turn onto Route 6. This right turn will be marked by a green and white sign stating Nordic Center, Cordillera. Proceed west on Route 6 past the Edwards Building Center, Lake Creek Road, and the trailer park. You will then make a left turn onto Squaw Creek Road. The same Nordic Center, Cordillera sign will help guide you. Proceed straight up this road without making the right turn that might beckon and confuse you. When you come to an old schoolhouse on your left, painted red and white, get ready to make a left turn onto Cordillera Way. Once again a sign or two will help you find the way. You will come to a security gate. Tell the guard you are going to Restaurant Picasso. The guard will give you a sign to place in your windshield and tell you that the Cordillera Clubhouse in which Restaurant Picasso lies about two miles further up the road. Follow the road until you find the parking area to the right of the road; Cordillera's Clubhouse is on the left. Arrive early so you can look around this special place.

RUSSELL'S $$$$
228 Bridge St.
Just Across the Covered Bridge in Vail Village
476-6700

Russell's focuses on steak and ribs. They claim to be Vail's only licensed certified angus beef restaurant. Sounds impressive; and the beef is impressive. The prime rib entree that I had was really quite excellent, done rare as I had asked. On another occasion I had a delectable 20 oz. porterhouse steak which was also done rare to my taste. Peppercorn steak; New York filet; steak teriyaki; and Russell's kabob are also on the menu.

Breads and salads are quite good. Appetizers include scallops in garlic butter; baby back ribs; smoked salmon; and shrimp cocktail.

Seafood items are also on the dinner menu. Alaskan king crab legs; scallop fettuccine; and Rocky Mountain trout are on the regular menu.

Russell's also has seafood specials, focusing on the freshest fish available that day.

Russell's signature side dish is scalloped potatoes au gratin. This includes four different cheeses, onions and cream.

Desserts include cheesecake; mud pie; apple pie a la mode; and various other ice cream dishes. I had the cheesecake; it was New York quality. The apple pie a la mode was extraordinary, totally filling in its own right; you can think about sharing desserts.

There is a friendly hang loose attitude at Russell's. They have a children's menu from 5:30 to 6:30.

Russell's accepts American Express, Visa, and MasterCard.

THE SALOON $$$
Minturn
827-5954

The Saloon is a favorite for tourists and locals alike. Plan on getting your fill here -- they serve huge helpings of Tex/Mex food. The setting is like a grand bar inside a grand barn. It can get rowdy. Come early or you will wait a long time.

The Saloon serves fajitas; burritos; tostadas; enchiladas (chicken or seafood); and chile rellenos. Quail is also a house specialty. The Saloon also serves plenty of steaks; BBQ chicken; BBQ ribs; and duck. I ordered a chicken meal; the whole chicken was served. What a surprise!

There is a great picture of John Wayne on the wall. Hearsay indicates that the Saloon motto is: "If John Wayne didn't drink it, we don't serve it!"

Desserts include apple pie and turtle pie.

The Saloon accepts American Express, Visa, and MasterCard.

SEASONS AT THE GREEN $$$
Vail Golf Course Clubhouse
476-8057

Wonderful food in a great golf course setting with a mountain background make Seasons at the Green a feast for the eyes as well as the palate.

The decor of this restaurant is beautiful to say the least. A grayed out pink tone to the walls works well with the pinkish light. There is plenty of space for their open plan design. Most of all the decor does not detract from the absolutely magnificent views to be seen through the big picture windows. When the leaves are changing colors in the fall (although slightly out of season for the ski set or the families with kids who need to be in school) is a wonderful time to eat at Seasons at the Green. Diners will be surrounded by summer green and autumn gold.

In the winter, try a horse-drawn sleigh ride which couples and families love. Call ahead for the sleigh ride/dinner package. Vail's outdoor skating rink is also located here, and the clubhouse serves as a Nordic Ski Center for trails marked out on the Vail Golf Course. You can check these opportunities out before dining.

Appetizers include nachos with quesadilla dip; hot chicken wings (buffalo wings); duck filled roasted green chiles; quesadillas layered with chicken, mango and brie; BBQ shrimp and bacon skewers; dungeness crab cakes; and a crisp vegetable medley. Rolls with butter or olive oil come with your entree order, but a salad does not. Salads available include lamb and arugula; chicken and orange with avocado; or Caesar with dungeness crab. There are several varieties of soup as well, including black bean or eggplant with green chiles.

It may be hard to think about entrees after all the appetizers. Nevertheless, there are great entrees to sink your teeth into. These include venison with sausage; London broil; New York steak with green chile sauce plus escalloped tortillas; petite filet with tiger prawns; lamb kabob; chicken breast cilantro; citrus BBQ chicken breast; cajun chicken; roasted pheasant with red currant sauce; and crisp duck with sun-dried cherry port sauce. I had the duck, and I loved it. Another time I had the grilled N.Y. steak with green chile sauce which was great; however, I found the escalloped tortillas to be a little dry for my taste.

If you are partial to seafood, Seasons At The Green can accommodate. Their menu includes seafood tacos in filo with avocado; blackened yellow fin tuna with chile aioli on a bed of wilted spinach; poached salmon; and jumbo prawns with cornmeal cakes.

If you lean toward pasta, take a look at the ravioli offerings which include black bean and scallion; smoked chicken; herbed shrimp and scallop; or buffalo in egg pasta. If you are hankering for a sandwich, Seasons At The Green offers burgers; crabmelt on sourdough; open turkey breast; and chicken or beef fajitas. Furthermore, they have salad entrees which include chicken pasta salad; warm fajita salad; and turkey salad in jumbo shells.

Desserts include fresh fruit tostadas; lemon tequila mousse with lemon zucchini cookie; poached pear with cream anglaise; hot apple strudel; warm berries with Grand Marnier and french vanilla; and midnight chocolate torte. I thoroughly enjoyed the rich chocolate torte.

Lunch is available throughout the week. A number of items off the dinner menu are also available at lunch. Other offerings include blackened pasta with crab; Monte Cristo sandwich; and jumbo prawns. Champagne brunches are featured on the weekend. There is a children's menu including fish fingers; burgers; spaghetti; chicken fingers; grilled cheese sandwich; pizza; or ravioli. Great french fries come with some children's dishes.

Seasons At The Green accepts Visa; MasterCard; and American Express.

SHOGUN $$$$
Mountain Haus
Northeast of Covered Bridge
Vail Village
479-9000

Enjoy Japanese food in Vail. Sushi is a favorite here. Shogun also serves authentic Japanese entrees. It is a wonderful place to eat.

The Seafood Delight (variety of seafood items) is tasty, especially the scallops. If you are new to Japanese food, the Chicken Katsu would be a great place to start. While the dish is definitely Japanese, it is similar enough to "good old fried chicken" that it will be pleasing even to the younger generation. It is a chicken filet coated with Japanese bread crumbs and deep fried. I have also enjoyed their chicken teriyaki. Shrimp tempura was another tasty dish. Teriyaki beef; charcoal grilled Norwegian salmon; jumbo sea scallops; jumbo tiger shrimp; and whole Maine lobster are other choices. The signature dinner at Shogun is the Shogun Nabe, a lobster combined with a variety of other seafood items. Sukiyaki and shabu shabu are enjoyable Japanese beef dishes. Miso soup or salad; garden fresh vegetables; and steamed rice accompany each entree order.

Appetizers at Shogun feature bean curd; chicken; scallops; shrimp; octopus; and sashimi.

Then, of course, there is sushi, a treat for sushi addicts. Sushi consists of varieties of raw fish, cut into fine servings. A sushi bar sitting can provide great entertainment as well as delicate tastes for the palate. Give it a try. You can choose from tuna; salmon; squid; crab; halibut; shrimp; eel; mackerel; abalone; scallops; and red snapper among others. I have found Shogun's sushi to be excellent on a number of occasions. A lovely aquarium situated behind the sushi bar makes for a wonderful view.

Enjoy a chocolate sundae with a Japanese twist. Your ice cream comes tempurized, that is deep fried with chocolate poured over the pastry. What a great surprise. The problem is this dessert can be just as addicting as the sushi. Oh well, there are worse fates; you just have to ski twice as hard tomorrow to balance out the calories. Cheesecake and sherbert are other dessert choices.

You can have lunch at Shogun. Chicken teriyaki; beef teriyaki; and a California roll with shrimp tempura are on the lunch menu.

Shogun accepts Visa, MasterCard, American Express, and Discover Card.

SHRINE MOUNTAIN INN $$$$
Shrine Pass Road
Vail Pass
476-6548

Want to have dinner above it all? Try the Shrine Mountain Inn, located 11,209 feet above sea level, open summer only. Dine in a rustic cabin atmosphere with a tremendous view of the Gore Range.

The dinner menu changes regularly. Usually three special dishes are served each night. The evening I ate there, they were serving paella; veal chop stuffed with spinach; and grilled salmon with shitake mushrooms. I had the paella with pork, chicken, terrizo sausage, shrimp, mussels, and clams served over Spanish rice. It was excellent. The meal came with sweet potato soup, a leafy salad, and wonderful rolls. The dessert was chocolate mousse which was a little sweet.

From what I overheard, everyone was enjoying the atmosphere and the food. The staff was congenial.

Lunches are also served at the Shrine Mountain Inn. Burgers; pasta; and tuna are among the items on the menu.

Best make reservations for an evening meal. They are not necessary for lunch.

Shrine Mountain Inn accepts Visa and MasterCard.

SIAMESE ORCHID $$$$
In the Gateway Plaza
476-9417

Siamese Orchid is a great hit, serving Thai food in an elegant setting. Another advantage: free valet parking during the ski season.

The menu is vast, and I do mean vast, with an array of curries, beef, pork, chicken and seafood. The menu also features vegetarian dishes. Thai cuisine is complex. Cooks use more than 20 sauces to complement the entrees. The sauces are a combination of Chinese, Malaysian an Southeast Asian flavors. The blending leads to exotic and unique flavors. The sauces are made from scratch, taking hours and even days to prepare. The recipes have been handed down for generations.

The entrees can be prepared mild, medium or hot and spicy. If you choose anything other than mild; be prepared!

Appetizers include wonderful spring rolls with homemade plum sauce; char-broiled beef, pork or chicken marinated in Thai spices, and then served with peanut sauce and cucumber dip; shrimp sauteed in spicy lemon dressing; or lemon flavored soup with coconut milk, ginger and chicken.

Entrees include a peanut curry with spinach, stir fried with chicken;

crispy whole fish flavored with a spicy sauce; duck stir fried with cashew. This is only a sampling. When the restaurant is not too busy, the kitchen staff will make a special effort to vary the entree to your liking.

Remember to have fried bananas before you leave; or try one of their coconut desserts.

Siamese Orchid accepts American Express, MasterCard and Visa. It is open for lunch as well as dinner.

SUBWAY $

Lionshead Mall
479-9727
West Vail
476-3827
Avon
949-1312

Three Subway locations in the Vail Valley serve fast and hearty sandwiches.

SUNSET GRILL $$

Holiday Inn (Chateau Vail)
On South Frontage Rd., just West of four way stop
476-5631

The Sunset Grill at the Holiday Inn (Chateau Vail) offers an all American meal selection at all American prices. It is a nice place to eat, nothing fancy. If you get there while there is still light (especially sunset light) you will be pleased by their west facing wall of greenhouse type windows.

Appetizers include shrimp; potato skins; and calamari. They have a special tomato based seafood specialty, Seven Seas Soup. French onion soup and a soup du jour are available. I enjoyed the calamari.

Salads, sandwiches, and burgers are also available on the dinner menu.

Entrees include three different types of steak; bratwurst; wiener schnitzel; pork chop; shrimp brochette; chicken parmesan; jumbo shrimp; and a couple of fettuccine dishes. I enjoyed the charbroiled half roasted chicken, basted with teriyaki. All entrees are served with a house salad plus vegetables and potatoes.

Desserts include flan; cheesecake; apple pie; and pecan pie. I enjoyed the pecan pie.

Breakfast and lunch are also served at the Sunset Grill with the same all American theme. During daytime you get the fabulous view of Vail Mountain.

The Sunset Grill accepts American Express, Visa, and MasterCard.

Miki's Lounge adjoins the restaurant, frequently offering live piano entertainment. There is a lovely fireplace here.

SWEET BASIL $$$$
One block west of the Children's Fountain
Vail Village
476-0125

Sweet Basil is an award winning restaurant in the heart of Vail Village. *Esquire* rated Sweet Basil as the "best new American cuisine." This is a high spirited place with a lively bistro atmosphere. *The Denver Post* and *The Rocky Mountain News* have each given excellent reviews of Sweet Basil.

Sweet Basil has a wide range of entree choices. One favorite is the rack of lamb. I enjoyed this entree, rating it with the best lamb dishes I have ever eaten. I was also thrilled with a seared rare tuna, to which I give high praise. I loved a braised sea bass with sweet peppers, onions, fennel, and saffron. Other entrees include a grilled salmon filet with Chinese black bean sauce, shitakes and leeks or a roast chicken breast with red curry potato puree. Or choose grilled double pork chop with apple smoked bacon, shitake, potato pancake and smoked tomato cream. As you can see, Sweet Basil's menu is creative.

Appetizers include crispy lasagna with chicken confit and wild mushrooms; shrimp spring roll; fried rock shrimp salad with potato chips, smoked red pepper sauce and chive oil; crispy soft shell crab; and seared tuna sashimi with red pepper angel hair pasta and wasabi cream. Or you can turn your attention to pizza. They serve pesto pizza with goat and parmesan cheese and a caramelized onion and rosemary pizza. Seafood pastas and rabbit pastas are available, as is a vegetarian pasta. There is no children's menu for dinner but children like pizza and pasta.

Lunch is available here; and there is a children's menu for lunch. I had a grilled leg of lamb sandwich which I enjoyed. A rare seared tuna sandwich; a soft shell crab sandwich; and a spinach enchilada were also available, as were burgers, salads, pastas and pizzas.

Desserts include the spectacular chocolate, caramel, macadamia tart with vanilla sauce. Another great dessert I enjoyed was peanut butter ice cream sandwich with caramel and chocolate sauce. Desserts include a plum apple crisp with cognac ice cream or cinnamon-ginger cream pie with chocolate sauce. Sweet Basil has homemade ice creams and sorbets.

The menus may vary; however, the rack of lamb and the spectacular chocolate, caramel, macadamia tart are almost always available.

Sweet Basil accepts Visa, MasterCard, and American Express.

SWISS CHALET $$$$
Sonnenalp Hotel
476-5656

The Swiss Chalet is a great place for fondue and authentic Swiss cuisine. They claim their Fondue Neuchatelois recipe comes from the French region of Switzerland. I enjoyed it. They also serve Raclette Valaisanne: a traditional raclette with the addition of beef tenderloin and veal sausages. You can also have beef fondue or sea food fondue. Fondue bourguignon features beef tenderloin served with assorted fruits and dipping sauces.

Appetizers include sauteed forest mushrooms; crepes stuffed with cheese, bacon, and onions; duck breast on green field lettuce with balsamic raspberry vinegar; and game paté garnished with sauce cumberland and served with homebaked bread.

To start, sample either goulash or red onion soup. Another choice is their beef consomme with Austrian liver spaetzle.

Entrees include veal; beef; and venison specialties. A favorite is sauteed beef tenderloin in green peppercorn. The Swiss Chalet has a rainbow of ways to prepare veal. A seafood choice is sauteed shrimp, scallops, and clams with fresh linguine pasta in a delicate tarragon sauce. Another offering is poached Oregon salmon in a watercress sauce. Or try bratwurst and knackwurst with sauerkraut for a real Swiss meal.

There is a salad bar and breads are homemade daily.

The dessert specialties are amazing, freshly baked by a gifted pastry chef. Try famous Bavarian Cream Pie. They also serve a chocolate fondue with fresh fruit. Pastries and tarts are baked fresh daily. Or choose from a variety of ice cream sundaes. The Coupe Pecan which includes ice cream with caramel topping, roasted pecans and fresh whipped cream sounds like the choice for my next visit.

The Swiss Chalet accepts Visa and MasterCard. It is open for breakfast and lunch as well as dinner.

SWISS HOT DOG COMPANY $
Lionshead Mall
476-2013

The Swiss Hot Dog Company features delicious bratwurst. The regular size contains two in a bun; however, you may prefer the triple to fill a mountain man hunger. Ernst Larese, the proprietor, enjoys speaking "English" with his patrons. Larese uses his own recipe of meats and spices for the brats. There are no preservatives or colorings added to the sausages. The buns are french rolls from a local bakery. Vienna hot dogs are also served. Swiss Hot Dog Company has developed a regular following among the locals in Lionshead.

SZECHWAN LION $$$
304 Bridge St.
Vail Village
476-4303

For Chinese food, try Szechwan Lion, serving fine Mandarin and Szechwan cuisine for lunch and dinner daily. If your order totals $50.00 or more (easy with adolescents), the food will be delivered directly to your door.

House specialties include Peking lobster; a seafood medley; orange flavored spicy beef; crispy or imperial shrimp; house special duck; Hunan lamb; and teriyaki chicken. I have personally tried the house special duck which is simmered first in an exotic blend of spices, then smothered in a sauce with Chinese greens, bamboo shoots, broccoli and mushrooms. I have also eaten the mixture of shrimp, chicken and beef called Sizzling Three Ingredient Tastes. Both meals were enjoyable. Of course, Szechwan Lion has a host of regular offerings on their menu.

The Szechwan Lion is open for lunch. It is located near the bottom of the Vista Bahn.

The Szechwan Lion accepts American Express, Visa and MasterCard.

traMONTI $$$
Charter Condominiums
Beaver Creek
949-5552

traMonti is located just off the main lobby at the Charter. You are welcomed with a blazing, heart warming fire place. Behind the fireplace is a huge beautiful bar. Restaurant seating is off to the right, a spacious and pleasant setting. traMonti focuses on fine Italian cuisine.

The breads are excellent as is the oil for dipping. I had calamari fritti for an appetizer. This is the best prepared calamari that I have ever experienced in the Vail Valley, or anywhere, save Monterey. The calamari were fried but light, not at all oily. The spinach potato gnocchi is also excellent. Other appetizers include grilled shrimp; spicy Italian sausage; and carpaccio.

Soups and salads are also available. Additionally, traMonti specializes in pizza. The pizza with pesto, scallops, sun-dried tomatoes and feta cheese is excellent. Another pizza features spicy shrimp and goat cheese. Grilled peppers, zucchini and eggplant complement a smoked mozzarella pizza.

Pastas, all homemade, are excellent. traMonti offers a wide variety. You can order either an appetizer or an entree amount on most of the selections.

Entrees include fish; chicken; rabbit; and veal dishes. I had wonderful grilled lamb chops with roasted shallot, rosemary sauce and ratatouille. traMonti informs diners that all of their chicken, beef and veal dishes are made from the finest free-range natural products available.

Desserts are wonderful. I had cannoli. One was cherry flavored. I preferred the chocolate flavored one. Next time I will try their chocolate roll with hazelnuts and pistachio. They also serve espresso soaked lady fingers or rum soaked sponge cake. Sorbets are available. Naturally traMonti offers a full complement of after dinner coffee drinks.

traMonti features piano music with Brett Riggin playing on weekends. traMonti accepts American Express, Visa, and MasterCard.

TRAPPER'S CABIN $$$$$$
Beaver Creek Mountain
476-9090
949-9090

Trapper's Cabin on top of Beaver Creek Mountain is rustic -- but also magnificent and luxurious. The cabin is approximately 3,000 square feet. It has spectacular views of the Gore and Sawatch mountain ranges. The cabin itself sits at 9,500 ft. above sea level. When you dine at Trapper's, you also spend the night there.

A cabin keeper serves as host and bartender during the day. A chef prepares the meals and appetizers. The appetizer menu includes (are you ready for this?) rattlesnake; trout; and buffalo salami. The entree menu includes sauteed elk steaks with bourbon and wild mushroom sauce; sliced pheasant breasts (baked hunter-style); brandy duck breasts in blackberry sauce; or salmon grilled with a dill butter sauce.

Television, radio, and the telephone are absent from this retreat. Hiking, mountain biking and horsebackriding are popular activities. There is also an outdoor hot tub on the deck.

Luggage is checked in at the Park Plaza in Beaver Creek Village. From there the cabin keeper escorts the guests to the cabin.

TURNTABLE RESTAURANT $
Minturn
827-4164

Located by the railroad tracks this restaurant also has a miniature train circling around the walls of the restaurant. Open from 5 a.m. to 3 a.m., the Turntable is a casual place serving full breakfasts with great pancakes; burgers; sandwiches; Mexican specialties; chicken; and steaks. Fresh homemade desserts and soft ice cream are tasty treats.

A children's and a senior citizen's menu are available. The Turntable accepts Visa and MasterCard.

THE TYROLEAN INN $$$$
400 East Meadow Drive
Vail
476-2204

The Tyrolean Inn is an award winning restaurant; specifically the Inn won the prestigious Five Star Diamond Award, designating the Inn as one of the top 50 Continental restaurants in the country.

The Tyrolean Inn is a landmark building in Vail with its Bavarian architecture. The post and beam interior design includes antlers and trophies of the hunt. Service is gracious and friendly. The setting is elegant alpine. During the summer there is an outdoor patio with a great view of the mountains.

Appetizers include wild game paté made from wild boar, venison and buffalo; artichoke hearts smothered in snow crab and herbed cheese; or baked brie with hazelnuts.

Entrees at the Tyrolean are wonderful. I have had the mandarin orange pepper duck twice and found it to be an excellent dish both times; I understand it is a locals favorite. The duckling was served with a delightful mango chutney and pepper sauce. I have also had the pheasant Kroatzbeere. The pheasant was marinated in apple wine, then sauteed with blackberries, shallots and brandy. Another enjoyable meal was the scampi "papriche." The sauteed gulf shrimp were simmered in a garlic and fresh herb red pepper sauce, served on a bed of linguine with fresh oregano. The pepper steak Madagascar is an exceptional meal. It is sauteed with Madagascar green peppercorns, flamed in brandy and finished with sauce espagnole. Another favorite is Veal Hawaii. Strips of veal are combined with a pineapple, raisin and ginger sauce. The dish is topped off with toasted almonds.

The Tyrolean specializes in game dishes: venison sauerbraten; wild boar Budapest; elk forestiere; midnight sun caribou; and buffalo. You can order a medley of game dishes or you can have a game item together with a medley of seafood (salmon. shrimp and scallops). It is noteworthy that the owner Pepi Langeggar raises his own wild game. He bought a wild game ranch seven years ago where he has raised wild elk, deer, and sheep.

Other entrees include chicken; salmon; swordfish; beef tenderloin; Colorado lamb; and several types of veal.

Tasty bread and an eight vegetable salad come with the dinner.

The Tyrolean staff consists of professional people who are well trained. Mr. Langeggar states "We have to train people; it is a dignified profession, and not just a secondary job."

Desserts include apple strudel; linzer torte; white chocolate mousse (with a touch of amaretto flavoring); and chocolate paté with a raspberry sauce. They also serve a dessert which is one of my favorites in the Vail Valley, Vermont Cream Caramel (a delicate flan covered with an outrageously sumptuous syrup). Others insist you shouldn't leave Vail without having apple strudel topped with vanilla ice cream at the Tyrolean. What the heck, try them all.

The Tyrolean Inn accepts Visa, MasterCard, and American Express.

UP THE CREEK $$$

Overlooking Gore Creek
Downstairs from the Children's Fountain
Vail Village
476-8141

Up the Creek provides Vail's only streamside dining. Their terrace is a joy in the summer; you are practically on top of Gore Creek, enjoying the rushing waters. Indoors Up the Creek has a well-lighted greenhouse feeling. It is a casual and enjoyable place.

Every day handwritten chalkboards announce fish specials at Up the Creek. I advise you to check them over. These fish specials are excellent. Indeed, the appetizers are also mostly fish including: calamari; mussels; shrimp; herring; and salmon.

Trout; mahi-mahi; and catfish are on the regular menu. The trout is served with cashews and a cilantro lime butter sauce. The mahi-mahi is served with a jalapeño salsa.

Besides fish, I recommend the rack of Colorado lamb roasted in garlic, rosemary and dijon mustard crust. Steaks; pheasant breast; and chicken breast are also available. For a pasta try the cannelloni which are stuffed with ricotta cheese, spinach, seafood and spices.

The lunch menu has burgers; sandwiches; Italian pastas; and a fish special of the day. This is truly a unique setting for lunch, bathed in light.

Desserts include a tropical bread pudding that is marvelous. Also, the peanut butter ice cream pie is great fun. You can have cheesecake or apple pie. Try a fudge walnut tart or a sinful chocolate cake. Ben & Jerry's ice creams are featured.

There is a children's menu, and they like kids here. Up the Creek accepts American Express, Visa, and MasterCard.

THE UPTOWN GRILL $$$

Lionshead Mall
476-2727

"Santa Fe" is the label Uptown Grill applies to its spicy Southwestern fare. A family owns and runs the restaurant which may account for its friendly and personal service. The Uptown Grill, tucked in a Lionshead Mall corner, may be slightly difficult to find. But when you find it, you'll also discover culinary adventure.

I have enjoyed calamari as an excellent appetizer. Other choices have been grilled chile relleno; buffalo sausage; avocado red pepper quesadilla; and lamb sausage pizza.

For my main course I was delighted with the Szechuan duck tacos, a spicy dish. The duck served as an excellent backdrop for the extraordinary flavors. I loved the blue corn tortilla; request all three tacos in blue corn tortillas. I was also impressed with a tasty grilled salmon. The shrimp and pasta dish was good and spicy. Other interesting items include cornmeal crusted oysters on jicama cabbage salad; roasted stuffed prawns with blue corn polenta; grilled tequila marinated prawns; tamales of crab and shrimp on verde sauce; Szechuan grilled mahi tacos with ginger salsa; Navajo lamb tacos; and smoked chicken pesto linguine with cilantro pesto cream sauce.

Uptown Grill serves excellent pasta with offerings such as crab ravioli; black pepper fettuccine; and capellini with grilled shrimp.

For lunch I have had lobster and brie tacos and Navajo chicken tacos; both were extraordinary.

I have enjoyed their cheesecake for dessert. I loved their hot fudge sundae served in a cinnamon tortilla.

Uptown Grill does have some all American items, especially for lunch. You can get hamburgers and even pizza.

Uptown Grill accepts Visa and MasterCard. One note of caution: the menu is changeable but always creative.

VENDETTA'S $$$$
Bridge Street
Vail Village
476-5070

Vendetta's is a northern Italian restaurant. Its proximity to the heart of ski action means that its upstairs bar is often frequented by the aprés ski set.

Vendetta's specializes in veal. I have ordered both of their prime rib of veal entrees and found them to be wonderful. The first was a prime rib of veal filled with fontina cheese and prosciutto, dipped in egg batter, sauteed and topped with a brown veal sauce, chanterelles and fresh mushrooms. The other was a prime rib of veal seasoned, broiled and topped with chanterelles, mushrooms and sauce marsala. Vendetta's has five other veal recipes on the menu; you can surely find one suited to your taste with this plentiful variety.

Vendetta's also prides itself on its fish dishes. I have had the shrimp and scallop dish which is sauteed in white wine, butter, and garlic. This is served over angel hair pasta. There is also a linguine with salmon; a cioppino with steamed crab claws, lobster tail, scallops, shrimp, baby squid, mussels, and clams. They have daily seafood specials. Chicken; beef; and eggplant dishes are also on the menu.

All meals come with bread, salad, and vegetables.

As for desserts, I have had the chocolate cannoli and the creamy cheesecake; each was delightful.

Vendetta's accepts Visa, MasterCard, and American Express.

VILLAGE COFFEE MILL $
Beaver Creek Mall
949-0246

Specializing in gourmet coffee sales, this cafe-eatery also serves pasta salads; sandwiches; and homemade soups.

VILLAGER $$
Vail Village Inn
Vail
476-5622

The Villager Restaurant is beautifully detailed with Bavarian style wood paneling. Returning visitors may wonder if it is a Vail Village Inn Pancake House -- not anymore. While pancakes are available for breakfast, so are french toast; egg dishes; omelettes; and cereals.

Dinners have an Austrian American focus. Appetizers include shrimp cocktail; Atlantic smoked salmon; gravelox; steamed artichoke with curried mayonnaise; baked brie; and a grilled eggplant with red bell peppers.

Entrees sound fantastic. Ground veal and pork dumplings; roast pork with applesauce; Austrian meat dumplings with sauerkraut; roast veal with roast potatoes; roast leg of lamb; and veal liver with onions vary the daily features.

Regular entrees include free range chicken from their rotisserie; Santa Fe pork medallions; fresh grilled tuna steak; Colorado T-bone steak; rib eye steak; and filet of beef tenderloin.

There are pastas and pizzas on the menu as well. Villager fettuccine with delicate pasta, fresh basil, tomatoes, goat cheese and cream sounds like a hit. Their penne comes with Italian sausage while their pesto linguine comes with grilled chicken breast. Try a seafood pasta with shrimp and scallops or a pepperoni and mushroom pizza.

You can also dine on English grilled pork sausage or other European sausages. Cheese and beef fondues are available. Tender slices of veal and sauteed pork loin are on the men.

Lunch dishes focus on sausages; sandwiches; burgers; pizzas; and pastas. Aprés ski choices include the fondues; the smoked salmon; and the gravelox.

The Villager accepts Visa and MasterCard.

WANDERERS RESTAURANT $$$
950 Red Sandstone Rd.
At Potato Patch Club
476-1614

Wanderers Restaurant presents dishes from North and South America, Italy, India, and the Orient. Wanderers is located across Vail Valley from Vail Mountain. Take Red Sandstone Road to the north off of North Frontage Road. Watch for the signs for either the restaurant or the Potato Patch Club on the right side of the road. Potato Patch Club is an outdoor swim and tennis club; in winter there is ample free parking.

The restaurant is pleasant with a unique barrel vault running down the middle. Both the big windows and the huge deck provide great views of Vail Mountain. Along with the panoramic view comes a panorama of foods from around the globe.

Bread comes with honey butter; garlic butter; or olive oil.

Appetizers include calamari; spring roll; tostada; chicken satay; pizza; or samosa. I had the samosa which is like an Indian spring roll. It is a little more spicy.

Reading the entree menu is like traveling around the world: chicken molé; Szechuan stir-fry; oriental duck breast; Indian curries; cioppino; clam linguine; seafood risotto; veal marsala; and pasta primavera. Once I had the chicken molé with a chile and (unsweetened) dark chocolate sauce which was appealing. The real winner for me was the Indian Seafood Curry. Wanderers uses a recipe from northeast India with a Tandour touch. The meal is served with basmati rice and an exotic range of samblas. This was a terrific meal with a wide variety of tastes. American favorites are rib eye of beef and stuffed chicken breast.

Desserts include chocolate cake; turtle pie; fresh berries; cannoli; and cheesecake. I enjoyed the chocolate cake, but really loved the cheesecake with almonds.

Wanderers accepts Visa and MasterCard. Wanderers is available for parties and meetings. Groups will find its deck sufficient for sizable summer meetings. Party planners can choose a theme from "around the world."

WENDY'S OLD FASHIONED HAMBURGERS $
West Vail
476-4033

Having trouble finding Wendy's? It is the farthest west commercial building on North Frontage Road. In addition to regular offerings, this Wendy's has a salad bar and pasta bar.

WHISKEY CREEK $$$
Located in the Eagle-Vail Golf Course Clubhouse
949-4942

Whiskey Creek, located in the Eagle-Vail Golf Course Clubhouse offers real food with a great view. The restaurant prides itself on serving the "best steaks in the valley." However, they offer an excellent menu variety. The setting is country western and they play country western music, nice and soft.

Appetizers include sauteed mushrooms; buffalo carpaccio; chicken quesadilla; escargot; and calamari. They offer Rocky Mountain Oysters, the ranch variety.

Whiskey Creek offers numerous varieties of beef including pepper steak, filet mignon; New York strip; and a huge porterhouse. They also serve steak with crab or shrimp. Buffalo steak is available. Whisky Creek specializes in Dalhart chicken fried sirloin steak, with mashed potatoes and cream gravy.

Other entrees include liver and onions; teriyaki pork chops; BBQ ribs; honey lemon chicken; and duck l'orange. The duck was crisp and enjoyable.

Seafood meals include salmon; salmon with shredded crab; trout; and walleye pike. The salmon was fresh.

Excellent rolls and salads are served with all entrees. Desserts tend to be traditional such as pie a la mode or brownie a la mode.

There is a children's menu with offerings of chicken nuggets; hamburger; chicken fried steak; or BBQ ribs.

Sleigh rides on the Eagle Vail golf course can be arranged by calling ahead to the restaurant.

Whiskey Creek accepts Visa, MasterCard, and American Express.

THE WILDFLOWER $$$$$
in the Lodge
Vail Village
476-8111

The Wildflower is a five star restaurant where you can relax and be comfortable -- as long as you are not worried about the bill. Why worry? You might as well enjoy an elegant greenhouse atmosphere. The white walls set off baskets brimming with silk flowers in a panoply of colors. Feast your eyes on the impressive, close-up view of Vail Mountain.

Wildflower surprises diners with dishes they may have never have discovered before, such as dandelion greens with bacon or buckwheat blini with salmon tartare. Or you can try tuna and truffle tartare with waffled potatoes.

Another interesting dish is potato, wild mushroom and truffle lasagna. You can also sample grilled whole snapper with potato and eggplant curry; grilled duck breast with spinach pancakes; grilled Maine scallops; or grilled lamb loin. The sauteed monkfish with Chardonnay butter sauce was intriguing. I have also enjoyed their swordfish. Other seafood dishes available are trout; angler fish; sea bass; and lobster. Other meat dishes include veal, beef, pork and venison. The rack of lamb with home fries is excellent but expensive. The bread and salads are excellent.

Desserts include bread pudding, chocolate cake, apple strudel, chocolate ice cream with sauteed bananas, and strawberries sauteed in Zinfandel.

Wildflower accepts Visa, MasterCard, American Express, Diner's Club, and Carte Blanche.

WINDOWS $$$$
Radisson Hotel
476-4444

Windows is named for the picture windows providing a wonderful view of Vail Mountain. Windows is Vail's only rooftop restaurant.

The food is upscale to match the setting. The appetizer menu is luscious. Try grilled quail stuffed with duck sausage; poached salmon and asparagus; escargot with roasted garlic ravioli; smoked shrimp on a spicy peanut sauce; or buffalo tenderloin seared raw with three peppercorns sliced paper thin.

You can also enjoy wild turkey consomme; Caesar salad for two prepared at your table; or smoked pheasant salad.

Marvelous entrees include roasted pheasant; Colorado red meat trout; herb crusted veal chop with wild berries and apple walnut chutney; lobster tails; New York strip steak; Colorado rack of lamb; jumbo prawns stuffed with green onion and red pepper mousse; or a vegetable brochette. For variety try the medallion of buffalo tenderloin, double lamb chop, and roasted quail, each served with its own sauce.

If you have room for dessert and some extra time you can order a wild berry cobbler served with flaming Wild Turkey and Rainforest Crunch ice cream. It requires 30 minutes of baking time. Or choose a puff pastry filled with Grand Marnier cream, topped with flaming strawberry sauce. Another winner is white chocolate mousse and almond mousse dipped in chocolate nougat served on mandarin raspberry sauce.

Windows accepts Visa, MasterCard, and American Express.

THE ON-MOUNTAIN RESTAURANTS
For Breakfast And Lunch

COOK SHACK $$$
  Mid-Vail
  479-2030

    Cook Shack is a sit-down full-service restaurant with waiters and waitresses. The menu has a Southwest attitude. Reservations can be made and should be made.
    Appetizers include nachos; quesadillas; and onion soup. Salads include a shrimp salad; a cobb salad; and a spinach salad.
    The fajitas are fantastic. They come with tortillas, green and red peppers, guacamole and sour cream. Other items on the menu include pork and bean chili; pueblo chicken stew; or a tamale casserole.
    Cook Shack also serves club sandwiches; hamburgers and hot dogs. For the children they offer chicken nuggets and grilled cheese sandwiches.
    Desserts include ice cream; peach cobbler; and an unbelievable "mortal sin" creation. The amount of brownie, hot fudge, ice cream and whipped cream in this concoction should be against the law. Pick a partner or two and go for it. I understand that an occasional person takes on the whole "mortal sin" singlehandidly.
    Outside Cook Shack, a small terrace with lounge chairs is perfect for a rest during spring skiing. In the summer enjoy fajitas here.

DOG HAUS $$
  Avanti Express Center

    Located east of the Avanti Express Lift (Chairlift #2) the Dog Haus serves wonderful gourmet hot dogs , including fennel sausage and bockwurst, with a variety of mustards. Enjoy your hot dog on the picnic benches.

EAGLE'S NEST CAFETERIA $$
  Gondola Building
  Eagle's Nest

    A fantastic view of the Gore Range spread out before you enhances your enjoyment while eating, warming up, and resting. Restrooms are available as is a Complete Skier outlet for ski accessories.
    The cafeteria menu includes pasta dishes; lasagna; hamburgers; grilled chicken sandwiches; a salad bar; a potato bar; a taco bar; yogurt; fruit; and a variety of pastries. There is a deck floor above the restaurant level with indoor

189

tables as well as outdoor tables. For a more leisurely lunch with table service look into the Wine Stube. In the summer enjoy a Western BBQ.

GOLDEN PEAK RESTAURANT $$
Golden Peak
Vail Mountain

The Golden Peak Restaurant at the base of Golden Peak Center is an excellent place for breakfast. Lunch offerings include hamburgers; soups; sandwiches; and salads. Aprés ski is fun with great views to the east and west in the upstairs bar.

HI HO HOT DOGS $
Mountain Top/PHQ
Vail Mountain

Hi Ho Hot Dogs serves hot dogs; baked potatoes; chili; hot chocolate; and coffee on the deck outside Ski Patrol Head Quarters. You can eat at tables on the deck or head downstairs to the warming hut area. Restrooms are at the opposite side of Mountain Top/PHQ.

LOOK MA CAFETERIA $$
Mid-Vail
Vail Mountain

The cafeteria is located on the top floor serving pizza; hot dogs; bratwurst; cookies; and pastries. A Vail Beaver Creek Ski School Center offers private lessons and afternoon workshops.

The restrooms and a few telephones are located a half flight of stairs down.

McCOY'S BAR AND RESTAURANT $$
Base of Beaver Creek Mountain

McCoy's, operated by the Hyatt Regency, specializes in wonderful fruit filled pancakes. They also offer other breakfasts; excellent lunches; and fun aprés ski with hors d'oeuvres and entertainment.

MID-VAIL BUILDING
Top of Vista Bahn Express Lift
Base of Mountain Top Express Lift and Hunky Dory Lift
Vail Mountain

The Mid-Vail building houses Cook Shack Restaurant; Look Ma Cafeteria; Terrace Cafeteria; Terrace outdoor BBQ; restrooms; phones; Complete Skier for accessories; and a Vail/Beaver Creek Ski School Center for private lessons and afternoon workshops.

POPCORN WAGONS $
Vail Village
Lionshead
Beaver Creek

Located at the base areas, these delightful wagons are included in the On-Mountain section because they are open only for breakfast, lunch, and aprés ski. They offer much more than popcorn. Vienna hot dogs; gyros; sandwiches; bratwurst; sweet rolls; ice cream; cotton candy; soft drinks; hot chocolate; and coffee are among the offerings.

PRONTO'S PORCH $
On Flap Jack in Northwood Express Center
Near Northwoods Express Lift
Just below Pronto
Vail Mountain

Pronto's Porch is a small vending machine cabin which can come in very handy if you are hungry, dehydrated, cold, or just need a rest.

RAFTERS $$$
Spruce Saddle
Beaver Creek
949-6050

Rafters is the full-service sit-down restaurant for leisurely lunches at Spruce Saddle. It is located upstairs from the cafeteria. Views of the Gore Range and Vail Valley are spectacular. The menu tends toward Southwestern recipes. They also serve pasta; soups; and sandwiches.

RED TAIL CAMP $
Beaver Creek

Red Tail Camp is located at the base of Chairlifts #9, #10, and #11. Within the warming hut you will find fast food and restrooms. In the spring enjoy the outdoor BBQ.

SPRUCE SADDLE RESTAURANT $$
Beaver Creek

Spruce Saddle is the mid-mountain restaurant at Beaver Creek. An outdoor barbecue is operated in the spring. A Vail/Beaver Creek Ski School Center is located here for choosing private lessons or afternoon workshops.

TERRACE CAFETERIA $$
Mid-Vail
Vail Mountain

Hamburgers and other sandwiches as well as a salad bar are found on the Terrace level which features a huge outdoor deck. In mild weather enjoy an outdoor barbeque. The food looks great and tastes great. The menu includes grilled chicken; hamburgers; beans; potatoes; and corn on the cob. A 40-item salad bar pleases veggie fans.

A coffee bar serving pastries, espresso, cappuccino and standard coffees, allows skiers to catch a light breakfast or snack without standing in line.

Restrooms and a bank of eight phones are located on the Terrace level.

TRAIL'S END $
Gondola Building
Lionshead

Serving breakfast, lunch, and après ski, Trail's End is conveniently located in the Gondola building. Restrooms are downstairs where you can check baskets of clothing that you do not want to carry on the mountain. Vail's lost and found room is located here. Kids enjoy the video game room. A couple of pay telephones are located here, as is a Complete Skier outlet, offering accessories to enhance your skiing comfort.

Trail's End breakfast menu includes cereal; yogurt; croissants; pancakes; french toast; eggs and sausage. Its lunch menu includes sandwiches including a Philly steak sandwich, but no hamburgers. They offer a variety of filling luncheon specials.

Don Watson, a fantastic singer/guitarist entertainer, provides the après ski entertainment. He know how to work the crowd. There is plenty of beer and nachos. Take beer out on the deck in the spring (but no farther).

TWO ELK RESTAURANT $$$
Above China Bowl Center
and Tea Cup Bowl Center
Vail Mountain

Beautifully located at the top of Chairlift #14, overlooking China Bowl, the Gore Range and the Holy Cross Wilderness Area, the Two Elk Restaurant is a sight to behold. Its log architecture is magnificent. The smart move is to show up before 11:30 a.m. or after 2:30 p.m. Everyone loves this place.

Why is Two Elk so popular? Well, you can get burgers, hot dogs and corn dogs. But you can also find creative, fun fare. Follow the signs above different sections. If there are long lines, you may only have time to choose one section. There is a Pizza section; a Pasta section; a Grill section; a Salad section; a Potato section; a Cold Food section; a Liquids section; and a Dessert section.

My favorite is pizza with goat cheese topping. Other enjoyable pizzas are topped with sun-dried tomatoes; pine nuts; or spicy jalapeño. I've also enjoyed the pastas; the potatoes; the salads; and a grilled veggie sandwich.

Restrooms and telephones are located on each side of Two Elk. There is a Ski School Center on one side and a gift section on the other side.

Placards labeling the male vs. the female gender on the restroom doors are only vaguely different. So you may want to accompany your child to help.

WILDWOOD BAR AND GRILL $$
Wildwood Center
Top of Hunky Dory Lift (Chairlift #3)
and Game Creek Express Lift (Chairlift #7)
Vail Mountain

Wildwood Bar and Grill is outside and inside. It commands a grand view of Sun Up Bowl and allows you to avoid the lines at Two Elk and Mid-Vail.

Wildwood Bar and Grill serves up great smoked chicken from Booco's Station in Minturn. They also serve burgers and brats with sauerkraut.

Restroom facilities are available, although not the world's best.

THE WINE STUBE $$$
Gondola Building
Eagle's Nest
Vail Mountain
479-2034

A sit-down full-service restaurant with wait staff offers you the possibility of a relaxing lunch. Reservations can be made and during certain seasons may be necessary. The menu is interesting. Appetizers include smoked chicken pie; black and blue nachos; venison sausage; and lamb quesadillas.

Entrees include Southwest breast of chicken; cheese ravioli with grilled buffalo sausage; Southwest fajitas; fritatas with egg, potato and cheese. A number of sandwiches are available: chicken; turkey; lamb; and hamburgers. Salad items are on the menu.

For dessert try an apple cranberry crisp.

WOK 'N' ROLL EXPRESS $$
At the Base of China Bowl
Vail Mountain

You are hungry but you are skiing the Mongolia Bowls. The situation is hopeless. But, Wok 'N' Roll Express comes to the rescue with wonderful chicken yakitori barbequed on a skewer. Hamburgers are also a possibility. Of course, you will grab a Snickers.

RESTAURANTS BY LOCATION

HEART OF VAIL VILLAGE

Cucina Rustica Italiana (Italian)
Cyrano's (Eclectic)
Daily Grind (Coffee shop)
Hong Kong Cafe (Eclectic)
Lancelot Inn (Steak and seafood)
Left Bank (French)
Los Amigos (Mexican)
Louie's (Eclectic)
Ore House (Steak and seafood)
Pepi's Restaurant (German)
Red Lion (Eclectic)
Russell's (Steak and seafood)
Shogun (Japanese)
Sweet Basil (Eclectic)
Szechuan Lion (Chinese)
Vendetta's (Italian)
Wildflower Inn (Eclectic)

NEAR VAIL VILLAGE

Alpenrose Tearoom and Restaurant (Continental)
Ambrosia (Continental)
Austria Haus (Austrian American)
Blano's Pizza Company (Pizza)
Blu's (Eclectic)
Bully Ranch (Western)
Cafe Colorado (Eclectic)
The Cheese Shop (Sandwiches)
Eaglewood (Eclectic)
Fondue Stube (Eclectic)
Gambetta's Pizza and Pane (Italian)
Haagen Dazs (Ice cream and coffee)
La Tour (Continental)
Ludwig's (Continental)
May Palace (Chinese)
Michael's American Bristro (Eclectic)
Pazzo's Pizzeria (Pizza and breakfast)

Siamese Orchid (Thai)
Sunset Grill (Eclectic)
Swiss Chalet (Eclectic)
Tyrolean Inn (Continental)
Up the Creek (Eclectic)
Villager (Austrian American)

GOLDEN PEAK

Lord Gore Restaurant (Continental)

VAIL GOLF COURSE

Seasons At the Green (Eclectic)

LIONSHEAD

Alfie Packer's (Eclectic)
Bart and Yeti's (Eclectic)
Chanticler (Continental)
Chart House (Steak and seafood)
D.J. McAdam's Diner (Eclectic)
Cleaver's Deli (Sandwiches)
French Deli (Les Delices de France)(Sandwiches)
The Gallery (Eclectic)
Gondola Cafe (Eclectic)
Gondo's (Pizza)
K.B. Ranch Co. (Steak and seafood)
Lionshead Bar and Grill (Eclectic)
L'Ostello (Italian)
Luigi's (Italian)
Montauk (Seafood and steak)
Pizza Bakery (Pizza)
Subway (Fast food)
Swiss Hot Dog Company (Fast food)
Trail's End (Cafeteria)
Uptown Grill (Eclectic)
Windows (Continental)

CASCADE VILLAGE

Alfredo's (Italian)
The Cafe (Eclectic)
Clancy's (Pub)

NORTH SIDE OF VALLEY

Imperial Mataam Fez (Moroccan)
Wanderers (Eclectic)

WEST VAIL

C.J. Caper's (Eclectic)
Dairy Queen (Fast food)
Jackalope (Mexican)
McDonald's (Fast food)
Mr. Natural (Organic)
Nozawa (Japanese)
Pizza Express of Vail (Pizza)
Poppyseeds (Eclectic)
Subway (Fast food)
Wendy's (Fast food)

EAST VAIL

Vail Racquet Club (Eclectic)

VAIL PASS

Shrine Mountain Inn (Eclectic)

BEAVER CREEK

Beaver Trap Tavern (Eclectic)
Black Diamond Bar and Grill (Eclectic)
Clubhouse at Beaver Creek Golf Course
Covered Bridge Cafe (Eclectic)

Coyote Cafe (Eclectic)
Crooked Hearth Tavern (Eclectic)
Double Diamond Deli (Fast food)
G.T.'s Diner and Malt Shop (Eclectic)
Golden Eagle Inn (Eclectic)
Legends (Steak and seafood)
Mirabelle (French)
Patina Ristorante Italiano (Italian)
traMonti (Italian)
Village Coffee Mill (Coffeehouse)

AVON

Brass Parrot (Eclectic)
Cassidy's Hole in the Wall (Eclectic)
Chicago Pizza (Pizza)
China Garden (Chinese)
Columbine Bakery (Eclectic)
Domino's Pizza (Pizza)
Geno's Italian Sandwiches (Italian)
Iron Horse Pizza (Italian)
Lost Armadillo (Eclectic)
Pizza Express, Pasta Pub (Italian)
Pizza Hut (Pizza)
Subway (Fast food)

EAGLE-VAIL

Eagle-Vail Cafeteria (Unique)
Paddy's Sports Bar and Restaurant (Eclectic)
Whisky Creek (Steak and seafood)

MINTURN

Booco's Station (BBQ)
Chili Willy's (TexMex)
Hi Ho's Parlour (Old Fashioned Fountain)
Minturn Country Club (Steak and seafood)
Minturano Pasta Palace (Italian)
The Saloon (TexMex)

Turntable Restaurant (Eclectic)

RED CLIFF

Columbine (Mexican)
The Reno Cafe (Mexican)

EDWARDS

The Bristol at Arrowhead (Eclectic)
Champion's (Eclectic)
Fiesta's (New Mexican)
Gashouse (Eclectic)
June Creek Grill (Eclectic)
Opiñions (Eclectic)

CORDILLERA

Restaurant Picasso (Continental)

WOLCOTT AND NORTH

K.K.'s (BBQ)
4 Eagle Restaurant (BBQ)
State Bridge Lodge (Western)

MOUNTAIN RESTAURANTS

Anderson's Cabin (Eclectic)
Beano's Cabin (Eclectic)
Cook Shack (Eclectic)
Dog Haus (Fast food)
Eagle's Nest (Cafeteria)
Golden Peak Restaurant (Cafeteria)
Hi Ho Hot Dogs (Fast food)
Look Ma (Cafeteria)
McCoy's (Cafeteria)
Rafters (Eclectic)

Red Tail Camp (Fast food)
Spruce Saddle (Cafeteria)
Terrace (Cafeteria)
Trail's End (Cafeteria)
Trapper's Cabin (Eclectic)
Two Elk (Cafeteria)
Wildwood (Cafeteria)
Wine Stube (Eclectic)
Wok 'N' Roll Express (Eclectic)

RESTAURANTS BY SPECIALTY

CONTINENTAL

Alpenrose (Near Crossroads)
Ambrosia (Vail Village Inn Plaza)
Chanticler (Lionshead)
La Tour (Near Crossroads)
Lord Gore (Golden Peak)
Ludwig's (Sonnenalp Hotel)
Restaurant Picasso (Cordillera)
Tyrolean Inn (Near Vail Village)

ECLECTIC

Anderson Cabin (Arrowhead)
Beaver Trap Tavern (Beaver Creek)
Black Diamond Bar and Grill (Beaver Creek)
Blu's (Gore Creek, Vail Village)
Booco's Station (Minturn)
Bristol at Arrowhead (Arrowhead)
Cafe Colorado (Evergreen Hotel)
Crooked Hearth (Hyatt Regency at Beaver Creek)
Cyrano's (Vail Village)
Eaglewood (Near Vail Village)
Fondue Stube (Holiday Inn, Chateau Vail)
Golden Eagle Inn (Beaver Creek Promenade)
Gondola Cafe (Lionshead)
June Creek Grill (Singletree Golf Course, Edwards)
Louie's (Vail Village)

Michael's American Bistro (Gateway Building)
Opiñions (Homestead Club, Edwards)
Seasons At The Green (Vail Golf Course)
Shrine Mountain Inn (Vail Pass)
Sunset Grill (Holiday Inn, Chateau Vail)
Sweet Basil (Vail Village)
Swiss Chalet (Sonnenalp Hotel)
Up The Creek (Gore Creek, Vail Village)
Uptown Grill (Lionshead)
Vail Racquet Club Restaurant (East Vail)
Villager (Vail Village Inn)
Wanderers (Across Valley, Potato Patch Club)
Wildflower Inn (The Lodge, Vail Village)
Windows (Radisson, Lionshead)

FRENCH

Left Bank (Vail Village)
Mirabelle (Beaver Creek, East Gate)

GERMAN AND AUSTRIAN

Austria Haus (Sonnenalp Hotel)
Pepi's Restaurant (Vail Village)

ITALIAN

Alfredo's (Westin Hotel)
Cucina Rustica Italiana (The Lodge, Vail Village)
Gambetta's (Gateway Building)
L'Ostelle (Lionshead)
Minturano Pasta Palace (Minturn)
Patina Ristorante Italiano (Hyatt Regency at Beaver Creek)
traMonti (Charter Condominiums, Beaver Creek)
Vendetta's (Vail Village)

ORIENTAL

China Garden (Avon)

May Palace (Vail Village)
Nozawa (West Vail)
Shogun (Vail Village)
Szechuan Lion (Vail Village)

THAI

Siamese Orchid (Gateway Building)

MEXICAN

Chili Willy's (Minturn)
Columbine (Red Cliff)
Fiesta's (Edwards)
Los Amigos (Vail Village)
The Reno Cafe (Red Cliff)
The Saloon (Minturn)

MOROCCAN

The Imperial Mataam Fez (Across valley)

STEAKS AND SEAFOOD

Beano's Cabin (Beaver Creek Mountain)
Chart House (Lionshead)
K.B. Ranch Co. (Lionshead)
The Lancelot (Vail Village)
Legends (Poste Montane, Beaver Creek)
Minturn Country Club (Minturn)
Montauk (Lionshead)
Ore House (Vail Village)
Russell's (Vail Village)
Whiskey Creek (Eagle-Vail Golf Course)

PIZZA

Blano's Pizza Company (Vail Village Inn Plaza)

Chicago Pizza Factory (Avon)
Domino's Pizza (Across Valley and Avon)
Gambetta's Pizza and Pane (Gateway Building)
Gondo's (Lionshead)
Iron Horse (Avon)
Luigi's (Radisson)
Pazzo's Pizzeria (Near Crossroads)
Pizza Bakery (Lionshead)
Pizza Express of Vail (West Vail)
Pizza Express, Pasta Pub (Avon)
Pizza Hut (Avon)

CASUAL

Alfie Packer's (Lionshead)
Bart and Yeti's (Lionshead)
Brass Parrot (Avon)
Bully Ranch (Sonnenalp Hotel)
The Cafe (Westin Hotel)
Cassidy's Hole in the Wall (Avon)
Clancy's (Cascade Village)
Champion's Tavern (Edwards)
C.J. Capers (West Vail)
Covered Bridge Cafe (Beaver Creek)
Coyote Cafe (Beaver Creek)
D.J. McCadam's (Concert Hall Plaza, Lionshead)
Eagle-Vail Cafe (Eagle-Vail)
G.T. Diner and Malt Shop (Beaver Creek)
The Gallery (Radisson Hotel)
The Gashouse (Edwards)
Gondola Cafe (Lionshead)
Hong Kong Cafe (Vail Village)
Hubcap Brewery and Kitchen (Crossroads)
The Jackalope Cafe (West Vail)
Lionshead Bar and Grill (Concert Hall Plaza, Lionshead)
Lost Armadillo (Avon)
Paddy's (Eagle-Vail)
Red Lion (Vail Village)
Turntable Restaurant (Minturn)

COFFEE HOUSE/BISTRO

Daily Grind (Vail Village)
Village Coffee Mill (Beaver Creek)

SANDWICHES/ DELI/FAST FOOD

Cheese Shop At Vail (Crossroads)
Cleaver's Deli (Lionshead)
Columbine Bakery (Avon)
Dairy Queen (West Vail)
Double Diamond Delicatessan (Beaver Creek)
French Deli (Les Delices de France) (Lionshead)
Geno's (Avon)
Haagen Dazs (Crossroads)
Hi Ho's Parlour (Minturn)
McDonalds (West Vail)
Mr. Natural (West Vail)
Poppyseeds Bakery and Cafe (West Vail)
Subway (Lionshead, West Vail, Avon)
Swiss Hot Dog Company (Lionshead)
Wendy's (West Vail)

EXCITING ADVENTURES

Contents

Highlights

Vail Valley abounds with exciting adventurous activities in addition to alpine skiing, snowboarding, and telemarking. Residents of the Vail Valley live here as much for these other joys as for the alpine experiences. Ongoing seasonal activities are detailed below. Vail enjoys a host of activities that take place once a year, but last only for a few days. Among these are a bevy of races: kayak races; running races (up to a half marathon); mountain triathlon races; and World Cup mountain bicycle races. Field events include the lacrosse shoot outs and rugby tournaments. Exiting squash tournaments have been held at the Cascade Club. The Vail Eagles, Vail's tennis team, plays a late summer schedule (after Wimbledon and before Forest Hills). July 4th celebrations are ultra fantastic in Vail and especially at Nottingham Lake in Avon. The Jerry Ford Invitational Golf Tournament always draws big crowds. Gerald R. Ford Amphitheatre hosts many concerts in addition to Bravo! Colorado Music Festival and the Bolshoi Ballet. Tuesday nights, Hot Summer Nights musical events entertain with rock, country, and jazz. Both Vail and

Beaver Creek have wonderful weekend art festivals. Vail's festival is in July; Beaver Creek's festival is in August.

Also discussed in this section are support services, such as information providers and childcare. The Childcare section (or What to Do with Your Children When You Do Not Have Ski School) will provide parents ideas about how to provide kids fun time with peers while adults enjoy recreational activities. Après ski and nightlife are covered here, too. The following events, adventures and attractions are listed alphabetically.

A

ALPINE GARDENS

476-0103

One of Vail's loveliest summer attractions is Betty Ford Alpine Gardens, located in the Gerald R. Ford Park west of the Ford Amphitheater. The flowers, rocks, and flowing water make for a wonderful place to visit and relax. Enjoy the Mountain Perennial Garden, the Mountain Meditation Garden, and the Mountain Display Garden. Vail Alpine Garden, Inc. with many loyal volunteers has developed and maintained these beautiful gardens.

ART GALLERIES

CLAGGETT-REY GALLERY
Meadow Drive

COGSWELL GALLERY
Gore Creek Drive

GATEWAY GALLERY
Gateway Building

HARLEY PAINTINGS
Hey, that's me
Call 476-1521 for a viewing.

JILL VICKERS GALLERY
Gore Creek Drive

KNOX GALLERIES
 Vail Village Inn Plaza
 Beaver Creek Promenade

LIONSHEAD GALLERY
 Lionshead Circle

OLLA PODRIDA GALLERY
 Vail Village Inn Plaza

PORTRAITS BY ANDREA, INC.
 476-8890

VAIL FINE ARTS GALLERY
 Vail Village Crossroads Center

VAIL VALLEY ARTS COUNCIL
 Lionshead Parking Structure (east end)

WINDWOOD GALLERY
 Minturn

B

HOT AIR BALLOONS

Ballooning in the Central Rockies is exciting and invigorating; it is also calming and meditative. Choose your emotional mode for the morning and take off to a wonderful view of the Vail Valley. All balloon rides are scheduled for the morning when the air is calm in the Vail Valley. There is an inherent risk in being up in the sky, but lots of people go for it. If you plan to be the first couple to take wedding vows in a Vail Valley balloon, you are too late. One couple actually parachuted to the ground, hugging during the free fall phase, after a ceremony in the sky.

AERO VAIL
 476-7622
 (800)745-VAIL

Daily sunrise flights are available. Champagne is part of the experience.

BALLOON AMERICA
476-2473

Balloon America offers numerous flight lengths from 30 minutes up to two hours. They also have seats and seatbelts. First class flights include food and beverage service.

CAMELOT BALLOONS
476-4743

Camelot Balloons offers flights from one to three hours in length.

MOUNTAIN BALLOON ADVENTURES
476-2353

Mountain Balloon Adventures offers flights from 1 to 3 hours in length. A post-flight picnic celebrates the trek.

BICYCLING

Vail Valley provides excellent trails for bicycling. Remember all the rules about altitude; sun exposure; dehydration; head gear; and changeable weather. If you do not have your own bike, many are for rent in Vail or at Beaver Creek.

You can bike on Vail Mountain or Beaver Creek Mountain. There may be hikers or trucks on the same trails or terrain. Be careful. You can bike up the mountain or transport your bike on the Lionshead Gondola; the Vista Bahn Express Lift out of Vail Village; or the Centennial Express Lift from the base of Beaver Creek. Ride on the trails around the mountain or down the mountain. Trail Maps are available where you buy the tickets for the uphill rides and at the top. You can rent a bike at the top of the lifts and drop it off at the bottom of the mountain. Vail Associates also offers free 15 minute mountain cycling tip sessions three times a day; tours; lunch tours; and instruction tours. Call 479-4414, 479-4415, or 476-9090.

Vail Mountain has a practice area at the top of the Gondola, the Little Eagle Practice Area. Upper Fireweed is an intermediate ride which will take you from the Gondola over to Mid-Vail (the top of the Vista Bahn). Village Trail is an intermediate run from Mid-Vail back to the base of Vail Mountain. Lion Down is a more difficult way down to the base on the Lionshead side of the Mountain. Blackjack Loop and Kloser's Climb are difficult runs. Kloser's Climb takes you from the top of the Gondola to the top of Vail Mountain (Mountain Top/PHQ). Ride down Blackjack Loop to the base of Game Creek Bowl, easy enough; but you have to ascend a steep switchback trail to return to Eagle's Nest. Grand Traverse is under construction. Eventually it will be a 17 mile long trail for bikers or hikers that traverses around Vail Mountain providing an array of biking experiences.

Vail Mountain hosts World Cup Championship bike races. The racers do cross-country racing; downhill racing; and a competitive dual slalom course.

The biking business at Beaver Creek is brisk and booming. They are busy adding trails. Cinch and Dally are intermediate runs which begin at Spruce Saddle and lead to the base. Bachelor's Trail takes you to west from Spruce Saddle eventually leading to the road below Beaver Creek Village. You can bicycle up from Spruce Saddle on a difficult climb to PHQ (Patrol Headquarters). Without taking the Centennial Express Lift, you can ride the Western Hill Climb from the Village up to the top of Strawberry Park Lift (Chairlift #12); then you can climb higher to the top of the Larkspur Lift (Chairlift #11).

If you are a flatland biker, Vail Recreation District maintains a recreation path running east and west through Vail Valley. This path leads from Cascade Village (home of the Westin Hotel and the Cascade Club) through Vail Village and through Vail Golf Course, to East Vail. You can continue to the top of Vail Pass or consider going beyond to Copper Mountain; in fact, you can even get to Breckenridge on extensions of the bike trail. The ride from Vail to the top of Vail Pass is more difficult than the ride from Copper Mountain to the top of Vail Pass.

From Vail Pass summit you can bike the scenic unpaved Shrine Pass Road to Shrine Mountain Inn or all the way into Red Cliff. From Red Cliff take the highway down to Minturn. You will need to bike on I-70 East to return to Vail unless you have a car parked in Minturn (or Red Cliff).

You can ride a beautiful (but dusty) twenty six mile round trip tour via Red Sandstone Road to Piney River Ranch and Piney Lake. A more difficult trail to Lost Lake branches off as well from the main road.

Biking in either direction between West Vail (Exit 173) and the Minturn/Eagle-Vail Exit (Exit 171) requires biking on the I-70 freeway. Be careful; I recommend avoiding this section of highway by parking a car in Minturn.

This is just a short list of the most obvious bicycling adventures available. There are many more possibilities.

Bike guide tours are provided by:

PARAGON GUIDES
926-5299

PROSPECTOR MOUNTAIN BIKE TOURS
476-5968

Prospector Mountain Bike Tours offers weekend trips and custom trips.

RAFTMEISTER
476-RAFT
(800)247-0636

Raftmeister offers overnight hut tours.

SHERPA TOURS
476-3231
(800)543-4417

Day tours to six day vacations are available.

You should purchase *THE MOUNTAIN BIKING GUIDE TO VAIL, COLORADO* by Michael Murphy which goes into detail about a variety of bicycling tours from beginner to expert terrain.

THE BOBSLED

Vail Mountain off Lion's Way Catwalk
476-5601

My young daughter talked me into taking the bobsled ride on Vail Mountain; I tried every whichway to talk her out of the idea, but she persisted. So, we got in line, signed the liability waivers, put on our helmets, and we were off.

The bobsled course is about 3,000 feet long; the bobsled reaches speeds of about 45 miles per hour. It is definitely a thrill. Usually four people go down together on the sled. The bobsled follows a safe line down the course; however, it is difficult to feel safe as you zoom down without a driver. Your adrenalin starts pumping. The course has eleven curves, the highlight of the trip as you look at upcoming curves with a mixture of excitement and trepidation. Give it a try; I did, and I liked it. One thing is sure: it will be a memorable event.

The great thing about Vail's bobsled run is its accessibility. You can ski up to the start; and you can ski away from the bottom. How does this work so efficiently? Your skis are loaded onto a snowmobile at the top; the snowmobile brings your skis down to the bottom of the bobsled run. When the snowmobile comes back up, it brings up the bobsled that you have just ridden down for the new bobsled riders. A brilliant ergonomic set up.

The bobsled course start is located on Lion's Way Catwalk, near Avanti. You arrive by taking Cold Feet off of Avanti or by taking Lion's Way from Mid-Vail.

BRAVO! COLORADO MUSIC FESTIVAL

Bravo! Colorado Music Festival is one of the summertime happenings that makes Vail so appealing. The festival begins July 4 and lasts for three weeks. The festival features everything from full philharmonic orchestra concerts to intimate chamber music performances. The Gerald R. Ford Amphitheater is utilized as well as the Beaver Creek Chapel. Private homes and Vail lodges also provide space for congenial performances. The Colorado Symphony Orchestra and the Rochester Philharmonic participate in the Bravo series.

C

CARRIAGE RIDES

Carriage rides usually begin from Vail Village, where patient horses, drivers and dogs await passengers. These carriages add to the Tyrolean ambiance of Vail Village. To make special arrangements contact either Carriage Rides of Vail at 949-1008 or Rocky Mountain Carriage Company at 476-9422.

CHILDREN

(WHAT TO DO WITH CHILDREN WHEN YOU DON'T HAVE SKI SCHOOL)

BABY SITTING

Hyatt Regency Concierge
949-1234

Lodge at Vail Concierge
476-5011

Small World Play School (for children ages 3 months to 5 years)
Golden Peak 479-2044

Park Plaza at Beaver Creek Resort
949-2306

Vail Babysitting
827-5279

BEAVER CREEK CHILDREN'S THEATRE
949-9090

Beaver Creek Children's Theatre gives free performances on the Mall at Beaver Creek Resort. The Children's Performance Workshop Series for ages five to twelve introduces children to theatrical production.

BEAVER DAY CAMP (for ages 8 to 12 years)
949-2311

This programs offers fishing, archery, chairlift rides, adventure walks, nature crafts, theatre, and sports.

CAMP HYATT
949-1234

This program offers a wide variety of activities supervised by a credentialed staff.

FAMILY NIGHT OUT
476-9090
476-3941
949-9090

The Buckaroo Bonanza Bunch puts on a great play with J.B. Tucker "Showman" and his cast of stars. During the summer they play at Piney River Ranch. During the winter Family Night Out occurs on Thursdays at Trail's End in Lionshead. Dinner is included.

KID'S NIGHT OUT GOES WESTERN
476-9090
949-9090

During the winter Kid's Night Out Goes Western is without parents. Monday evenings the program is at Beaver Creek Children's Center. Thursday evenings the program is at Golden Peak Children's Center.

MARMOT DAY CAMP (for ages 5 to 7 years)
949-2311

Campers enjoy hiking, theatre, arts and crafts, plus field trips.

MATAWIN TEEPEE VILLAGE (for ages 5 to 12 years)
476-5601, ext. 4445

Matawin TeePee Village located on Beaver Creek Mountain offers campers an adventure back to the old West. Activities include fishing, archery, nature study, and overnight camping.

POTPOURRI DAY CAMP (for ages 2 1/2 to 5 and for ages 5 to 12)
479-2290
479-2292

The Potpourri Day Camp is run by the Vail Recreation District. There is also a Pre-Potpourri Day Camp for children between two and a half to five years of age.

Potpourri Day Camp features miniature golf; gymnastics; ice skating; archery; and visits to the Vail Nature Center. A Mountain Program adds excitement with outdoor experiences on the ski mountain. Potpourri Day Camp undertakes field trips to Denver and other nearby cities. In Denver they visit the planetarium, Water World, Elitch's Amusement Park, and similar activities. An overnight stay and evening hikes are available. Parents need to provide lunches for the daily sessions.

YOUTH SERVICES CENTER
479-2292

Located in the lower level of the Lionshead Parking Structure, Vail Youth Services Center provides a variety of activities for children of all ages. This service is provided by Vail Recreation District.

CROSS-COUNTRY SKIING

Beaver Creek Resort
949-5750, ext. 4313

Golden Peak
476-5601, ext. 4390

Vail Nordic Center at Vail Golf Course
479-2261

Cordillera
926-2200

U.S. Forest Service Trails
827-5715

Paragon Guides
949-4272

Vail Valley is an excellent location for cross-country skiing. There are numerous cross-country ski centers for lessons, relatively flat trails, and major tours. Guide services are available. You can arrange an overnight hut tour.

At Vail Mountain, the Cross-Country Ski Center is at Golden Peak. At Beaver Creek, the Cross-Country Ski Center is at McCoy Park which is actually up on the mountain; you ascend the Strawberry Park Lift (Chairlift #12) arriving at McCoy Park, with fantastic scenic views of the Vail Valley and the Gore Range. Information on McCoy Park under the Beaver Creek ski trails section of this book. Another cross-country ski center is located at the Vail Golf Course. The Vail Nordic Center has 10 miles of groomed track skiing. Lessons and clinics can be found here. A nordic ski shop is located in the clubhouse. Cordillera offers plenty of tracks for cross-country skiing. Cordillera, located five miles west of Beaver Creek Mountain, is a spectacular resort community.

Vail Pass and Shrine Pass are excellent ski tours. You can utilize Mary Ellen Gilliland's book, *THE VAIL HIKER AND SKI TOURING GUIDE*, for other exciting backcountry ski tours.

F

FISHING

AMERICAN ANGLER
476-1477
(800)327-1137

American Angler is located in Vail Village on Wall Street. American Angler is a complete tackle shop and guide service. They utilize the Gore Creek, Eagle River, and a private section of the South Platte River. Wading and floating opportunities are available. A fly casting school is offered.

GORE CREEK FLY FISHERMAN, INC.
476-3296

This is a shop and guide service. The shop is located in Vail Village on the lower level, looking out on Gore Creek. You can purchase whatever you need here for your fishing endeavors. Glen Lockay runs the shop and guide service with over two dozen guides to show you the way. A gourmet lunch is provided.

Gore Creek Fly Fisherman has private waters on the Eagle River. They have a free fly casting clinic each Saturday at 10:30 a.m. They offer fly-in, fly-out trips to the White and Green rivers. Overnight trips can be arranged.

VAIL ROD AND GUN CLUB
476-3939 (days)
926-3839 (evenings)

Vail Rod and Gun Club has 10 miles of exclusive private club waters on the Eagle and Roaring Fork Rivers. Rods and waders are included on all outings. They offer fly fishing schools, float fishing, half and full day wade-fishing.

Guides are all certified in First Aid and CPR. Lunches and beverages are provided.

Other listings for fishing guidance can be found in the GUIDES section.

4 EAGLE RANCH AND STABLES
On Highway 131, 4 miles North of Wolcott
926-3372

For the dude ranch/working ranch joys of the West come to the 4 Eagle Ranch and Stables. They say they will provide "the most fun you can have with your boots on."

4 Eagle offers horseback riding; hayrides; dinners; dinner parties; barn dancing and country swing dance instruction. They serve up chuckwagon breakfast, lunch, and dinner rides. Try a winter dinner sleigh ride. City slickers are welcome. For the artist, like me, it is a great place to draw or paint.

G

GOLF

Golf has become a major summertime sport in the Vail Valley. A number of courses are open with more on the way.

VAIL GOLF COURSE
Location: Just East of Vail Village

215

Holes: 18
Par: 71
Head Pro: Steve Satterstrom
Phone: 479-2260
Pro Shop: Full
Restaurant: Seasons At The Green

BEAVER CREEK GOLF COURSE
Location: Beaver Creek
Holes: 18
Par: 70
Designer: Robert Trent Jones II
Head Pro: Tom Clairy
Phone: 949-7123
Pro Shop: Full
Restaurant: Beaver Creek Clubhouse

SINGLETREE GOLF COURSE
Location: Near Edwards, seven miles West of Avon
Holes: 18
Par: 71
Designer: Jack Nicklaus
Head Pro: Mike Steiner
Phone: 949-4240
Restaurant: June Creek Restaurant

EAGLE-VAIL GOLF COURSE
Location: Eagle-Vail is between Vail and Avon. Take Exit 171. Go west on
    U.S. 6. Look for the entrance to Eagle-Vail on your left.
Holes: 18
Par: 72
Head Pro: Mike Fox
Phone: 949-5267
Restaurant: Whisky Creek Restaurant

WILLOW CREEK PAR 3
Location: Eagle-Vail
Holes: 9
Par: 27
Designer: Jan Niedziela
Head Pro: Mike Fox
Phone: 845-7273

COUNTRY CLUB OF THE ROCKIES (ARROWHEAD)
Location: West of Avon on U.S. 6
Holes: 18
Par: 72
Designer: Jack Nicklaus
Head Pro: Tom Apple
Phone: 926-3080

GROCERY MARKETS

VAIL MARKETS

EAST VAIL MARKET
Big Horn Road
East Vail

GENERAL STORE
Lionshead Mall

SAFEWAY
North Frontage Road
West Vail

7-ELEVEN
North Frontage Road
West Vail

VILLAGE MARKET
Crossroads Center

VAIL FOOD & DELI
Vail Road

AVON MARKETS

CITY MARKET
Beaver Creek Place

FOOD AND DELI
Eagle Vail Road

VILLAGE STORE
Avondale Lane

GUIDE SERVICES

EAGLE RIVER WHITEWATER/TIMBERLINE TOURS
P.O. BOX 3481
Vail, CO 81658
(303) 476-7487
(800) 339-RAFT
Rafting
  Colorado River
  Eagle River
  Arkansas River
Kayaking
Jetboating
Fishing
Hiking
Jeeping
Mountain biking

NOVA GUIDES, INC.
P.O. BOX 2018
Vail, CO 81658
(303) 949-4232
Snowmobiling
Snowcat Tours
Wildlife Tours
Rafting
  Colorado River
  Eagle River
  Arkansas River
Float Fishing
Shore Fishing
All terrain vehicles
Jeep tours

OUTBACK SKI GUIDES
(303) 926-3913
Exceptional ski tours

PARAGON GUIDES
P.O. BOX 350
Vail, CO 81658
(303) 949-4272
(303) 926-5299

Ski touring
Hut to hut in 10th Mountain Division trail system
Llama treking
Bike touring
Rock Climbing

PINEY RIVER RANCH
P.O. BOX 7
Vail, CO 81658
(303) 476-3941
Snowmobiling
    Lift-doo tours
        Ski half day and snowmobile half day
    Twilight dinner tours
Horseback Riding
Fishing and Boating
Hunting

RAFTMEISTER
P.O. BOX 1895
Vail, CO 81658
(303) 476-RAFT
(800) 274-0636
Rafting
    Colorado River
    Eagle River
    Arkansas River
Biking

TIMBERLINE TOURS
P.O. BOX 131
Vail, CO 81658
(303) 476-1414
(800) 831-1414
Snowmobiling
Rafting
    Colorado River
    Eagle River
    Arkansas River
Kayaking
Bicycle Tours
Fishing
    Float trips

Lake and stream fishing
Jeeping

VAIL/BEAVER CREEK CROSS COUNTRY SKI CENTER
458 B Vail Valley Dr.
Vail, CO 81657
(303) 476-5601, Ext. 4390
(303) 949-5750, Ext. 4313
Ski touring
Hut to hut in the 10th Mountain Division trail system

VAIL PACK COUNTRY OUTFITTERS
(303) 476-2793
(303) 827-5363
Hiking
Fishing
Mountain biking
Hunting
Cross-country ski tours
Snowshoe trips
Ice fishing

H

HEALTH CLUBS

CASCADE CLUB
Cascade Village
Near the Westin Hotel
476-7400

The Cascade Club is a major fitness center. I belong here because of the strong squash program with four squash courts. The two racquetball courts can be converted into squash courts when a major squash tourney is in town. The Cascade Club also offers indoor and outdoor tennis. Outdoors enjoy a swimming pool and hot tub. Upstairs you will find aerobics; steps; a running track; free weights; and weight machines. In the locker room areas are saunas; hot tubs; and steam rooms.

SHARON'S GYM
Eagle-Vail Business Center
845-9316

Sharon's Gym focuses on free weights. It is a favorite place for the locals who are serious with free weights.

THE SPA AT CORDILLERA
926-2200
949-7112

The Spa at Codillera has a 25-meter lap indoor swimming pool; and outdoor pool and hot tub; free weights; Lifecycles; Stairmaster; rowing machine; aerobic room with floating wood floor; treadmills; and weight machines.

They offer massage; hydrotherapy; and several types of body wrap. Body dry brushing and facials are available.

VAIL ATHLETIC CLUB
Near Vail Village
476-7960

Vail Athletic Club offers indoor swimming; weight room; and aerobics. They also have a unique climbing wall at the back of the aerobics area. Mountain climbing can be practiced here in relative safety, no matter what the weather is outside.

VAIL RACQUET CLUB
East Meadow Drive
East Vail
476-3267

Vail Racquet Club offers tennis courts, outdoor in the summer and indoor in the winter. They also have outdoor and indoor swimming. Racquet ball courts and a squash court are also available.

HELICOPTER SKIING

MAGIC MOUNTAIN HELI SKI
476-9539
668-5600
(800)HELISKI

If you are adventurous, give helicopter skiing a try. It will be an exciting memorable experience. According to Colorado Heli Ski U.S.A. Inc. skiers from ages five to 75 can enjoy the experience. They focus on having a great, great, great experience for everyone to get you to come back again and again and again. The folks here believe that intermediate skiers will be enthralled.

The guides are experienced. They have been skiing the backcountry for over fifteen years. Two rescue dogs go out on trips. The dogs go through a two year training program before becoming part of the team.

Colorado Heli Ski has a number of offerings. These include a single run as well as the full day with 10,000 vertical feet to be skied. There are other interesting packages.

Magic Mountain offers jeep touring in the summer.

HIKING

Vail Valley offers delightful hiking trails. Look around at the mountains and see the opportunities "to get away from it all". High lakes, waterfalls, wild flower meadows make hiking here a peak experience.

Pay attention to the altitude, the sun, and the changeability of the weather. If you have recently come to this altitude, your blood will not carry the increased number of red blood cells to support the activities you enjoyed at sea level.

Cleaner and less dense air means that the sun's rays are stronger. The sun will really get to you. Remember to bring your sunblock and to use it. Be prepared for the clouds and the rain. Although most mornings begin with a cloudless sky, clouds and thundershowers are common in the afternoon. Temperatures can drop dramatically. Hail and snow are even possible on days that began sunny and warm. Dress in layers.

Remember to carry water. You will need plenty of drinking water. Resist the temptation to drink out of mountain streams, despite the strong temptation.

Bring a map or guidebook. *THE VAIL HIKER AND SKI TOURING GUIDE* by Mary Ellen Gilliland is an excellent choice. You may obtain a U.S. Geological Survey topographical map. If you are going off into an area that is not well marked, you need a compass and a Swiss Army knife. Read the CAUTIONS section of this book carefully.

HORSEBACK RIDING

STEVE JONES' BEAVER CREEK STABLES
845-7770 or 328-6920

The Steve Jones' Beaver Creek Stables offers scenic mountain rides in the Beaver Creek area. One and two hour professionally guided rides are available. There is also a three hour tour which includes lunch. They offer an all day trip to Beaver Lake which includes fishing with equipment provided. In the evenings, a horseback ride or a horse-drawn wagon ride are available to and from Beano's Cabin.

4 EAGLE RANCH
Four Miles North of Wolcott on Highway 131
926-3372

4 Eagle Ranch is a dude ranch offering horseback riding with miles and miles of riding area. The ranch program includes one hour, two hour, half day and all day rides. Horse-drawn covered wagon rides are available for group tours. The scenery is fantastic. I frequently go to the ranch to paint. The ranch operates as a working ranch with cattle, hay fields that will be harvested by hand, and longhorn cattle.

PINEY RIVER RANCH
949-9090
476-3941

Piney River Ranch offers horseback riding right at the base of some of the 13,000 foot peaks of the Gore Range. One hour, one and a half hour, two hour, half day and all day rides are available. Numerous ancillary activities are also available as well as food.

SPRADDLE CREEK RANCH
Vail
476-6941

Spraddle Creek Ranch offers rides from one hour up to three hours. Their rides include the Elk Spring Ride, the Rim Rock Ride and the Ute Trail Ride, among others. They even offer a pony ride for the youngster, primarily for the six and younger crowd.

TRIPLE G
14 Miles North of Wolcott
653-4499
653-4444

Triple G is a riding outfit located at the State Bridge. One or two hour rides are available. Lunch and dinner rides are also available. Guides take the rides through the historical Ute Indian camp areas.

ARROWHEAD
926-3080

Horseback riding is available at Arrowhead.

HUT BACK COUNTRY TOURS

THE TENTH MOUNTAIN TRAIL AND HUT SYSTEM
925-5775

Part of the Tenth Mountain Trail and Hut system operates out of Vail. It extends to Aspen and beyond. The trail system is for hiking and cross-country skiing. The name Tenth Mountain Trail and Hut system honors the Tenth Mountain Division which trained at Camp Hale before entering World War II in Italy. It offers breathtaking views and plenty of exercise. You need reservations to stay in the communally used huts. No dogs allowed.

PARAGON GUIDES
926-5229

VAIL/BEAVER CREEK CROSS-COUNTRY SKI SCHOOL
949-5750 ext. 4313

I

ICE SKATING

DOBSON ARENA
479-2270

VAIL GOLF COURSE
479-2260

NOTTINGHAM PARK
949-5648

BEAVER CREEK
(Below Promenade)
949-9090

Indoor ice skating is available at Dobson Ice Arena on Meadow Drive across from the public library. Call for times for public skating. You can also watch hockey matches there.

Outdoor skating at Vail Golf Course and Nottingham Lake include hockey areas as well as free skating.

INFORMATION

The *Vail Daily* is Vail's free daily newspaper, published seven days per week. *The Vail Trail* is a weekly. *The Vail Trail*, published on Friday, features extras like real estate news and an inner section providing restaurant and entertainment information. Unlike this volume, *The Vail Trail* reviews one restaurant per week. *The Avon/Beaver Creek Times,* a weekly, comes out on Wednesdays.

TV 8 is *The Vail Channel.* Weather and slope information begin at 7:00 a.m. Channel 12 shows a lot of ski movies. Channel 13 provides visual information with music in the background. Channel 23, a local channel, carries more educational and political information. A number of Vail businesses advertise on *ESPN,* Channel 16; they know what the average Vail skier and tourist/athlete is watching.

Vail operates Information Booths at the Vail Village Parking Lot and the Lionshead Parking Lot.

Vail Valley Hotline phone number is 476-TOWN (476-8696). This phone number sponsored by Visa will lead you to a great deal of information. Access numbers to specific information all begin with **#, the pound sign.** Daily updates 3245; sports news 7267; entertainment 3683; restaurants 7378; lodging 5634; sports shopping 7767; shop till you drop 4363; athletic facilities 2845; skiing information 7544; tours and excursions 8687; transportation 8726; child care 2445; churches 5342; local professional care 5622; medical services 6334; automotive services 2886; how to use the hotline 4357.

J

JEEPING

Jeep the old stagecoach roads; visit ghost towns; enjoy picnics on picturesque backcountry roads, and don't forget to look at the wildflowers.

ADVENTURES IN JEEPING
476-7645
(800)247-7040

ALPINE JEEP ADVENTURES
476-5678
(800)488-5678

A.T.S. ADVENTURES
476-7576

DISCOVER JEEP TOURING
949-6411
476-9359

MAGIC MOUNTAIN
476-9359

NOVA GUIDES, INC.
949-4232

K

KAYAKING

BALANCE KAYAK SCHOOL
476-6176

RAFTMEISTER
476-7238

Yes, Vail has kayaking, from beginner experiences and lessons up to spectacular white water kayaking. The Dowd Chutes portion of the Eagle River features a thrilling experience for the expert. Also, there's a gated course for those with experience.

Try the Eagle, Colorado or Arkansas rivers from your Vail "basecamp."

Memorial Day Weekend watch the best kayakers in the country on the Eagle River at Dowd Chutes.

L

VAIL PUBLIC LIBRARY

479-2183

Vail Public Library is a cozy place to relax. Its lovely setting beside Gore Creek, combined with its attractive, peaceful interior, make it an ideal respite. While you need to be a Vail resident and have a library card to take books out, there are a number of comfortable sitting places to relax and read. There is also a wonderful children's section. Parents may want to call for dates of story times for small children. Magazines and periodicals have their place. The library has an art exhibition space often used by local artists, such as myself, and art groups. Public lectures are presented here, as well. If you took that Level 1 lesson just to please your spouse and decide that you need a break before venturing back onto the slopes, check out the Vail Public Library. The Library has a copy machine and typewriters for public use.

M

MINATURE GOLF

Kids love minature golf; adults enjoy it. Vail Valley has three spectacular courses. One operates at Lionshead near the Gondola building and next to the Born Free Express Lift; another is at Nottingham Lake in Avon; additionally you will find a course at Beaver Creek Resort west of the Centennial Express Lift. The courses at Lionshead and Beaver Creek Resort are eighteen holes. The course at Nottingham Lake is nine holes. All holes are par 15 (at least by my experience).

MOUNTAIN LIFT RIDES

During the summer Vail Associates operates the Vista Bahn Express Lift from Vail Village; the Centennial Express Lift on Beaver Creek Mountain; and the Lionshead Gondola. Hiking trails, biking trails, and outdoor lunches can be enjoyed at the top.

N

NATURE CENTER

479-2291

The Vail Nature Center is operated by the Vail Recreation District. It is located to the east of Golden Peak beyond Betty Ford Alpine Gardens and the Gerald R. Ford Amphitheatre.

Activities include wildflower walks; bird walks; beaver pond walks; youth hikes; adult hikes; and nature discovery workshops. Special programs are also provided.

NIGHTLIFE AND APRES SKI

ALFIE PACKER'S
Lionshead Mall
476-9732

Alfie Packer's frequently offers music and nightlife entertainment. They call their aprés ski operation the "Bad Attitude Club," but insist they are "the friendliest bar in town."

ALTITUDE CLUB/250 SOUTH
Evergreen Lodge
476-7810

The Altitude Club/250 South is a disco bar with big screen TV. Enjoy Country Swing here.

BEAVER TRAP TAVERN
Saint James Place
Beaver Creek
845-8930

The Beaver Trap Tavern is alive for aprés ski and nightlife fun.

BOOCO'S STATION
Minturn
827-4224

Booco's Station in Minturn offers jazz and country swing. Check the newspapers for current entertainment.

CASSIDY'S HOLE IN THE WALL
Avon
949-9449

Cassidy's has a strong nightlife program, frequently providing live music. Their excellent country swing program is exciting.

CHAMPION'S
Edwards
926-2444

Live music and dancing weekends in a restaurant atmosphere.

THE CLUB
Vail Village
479-0556

The Club, located at the top of Bridge Street, frequently offers live music.

Doors open at 8:00 p.m.

THE COYOTE CAFE
Beaver Creek
949-5001

The Coyote Cafe is a fun place for après ski and late night entertainment. You cannot miss it as you walk down the stairs from the slopes.

CROOKED HEARTH TAVERN
Hyatt Regency
Beaver Creek
949-1234

The Crooked Hearth Tavern offers après ski and evening entertainment.

CYRANO'S
Bridge Street
Vail Village

476-5551
Cyrano's offers exciting music and après ski enjoyment.

D.J. McCADAMS
Concert Hall Plaza
Lionshead Mall
476-2336

D.J. McCadams is open 24 hours a day, usually.

DAILY GRIND
Bridge Street
Vail Village
476-5856

The Daily Grind presents evening opportunities for poets and musicians.

4 EAGLE RANCH
Four miles north of Wolcott
926-3372

Barn dances with country swing will reward your trip to 4-Eagle Ranch.

THE GASHOUSE
Edwards
926-3613

The Gashouse has open microphone nights.

GONDO'S
Gondola building
Lionshead
479-9929

Gondo's provides aprés ski and late night entertainment.

HONG KONG CAFE
Vail Village
476-1818

The Hong Kong Cafe comes alive at night. It is a jumping place with loud music to excite you.

HUBCAP BREWERY
Crossroads Shopping Center
Vail
476-5757

Enjoy Vail's own brewery.

HYATT REGENCY LOBBY
Beaver Creek
949-1234

Peter Grewe plays his special blend of instrumental piano in the lobby of the Hyatt Regency.

JACKALOPE
West Vail
476-4314

The Jackalope is located in West Vail between Gart Brothers and Safeway. Loud, danceable music provides fun entertainment. They also have pool tables and multiple televisions.

LOUIE'S
Wall Street
Vail Village
479-9008

Live jazz and blues music most weekends nights.

MICKY'S
The Lodge at Vail
Vail Village
476-5011

Micky's offers piano music by Micky Poage.

NICK'S DANCE CLUB
Bridge Street
Near the Covered Bridge
Vail Village
476-3433

Nick's is located on Bridge Street near the Covered Bridge, beneath Russell's Restaurant. Nick's is a late night place to be, especially if you like to dance to "mainstream" music. Catering to 21 to 40 year olds, Nick's has been successful for a number of years and seems to be quite in tune with its clientele. Nick's is open seven days a week from 8 p.m. to 2 a.m. It usually starts rocking about 10:30 p.m.

PADDY'S SPORTS BAR
North Side of U.S. 6
Eagle-Vail
949-6093

Paddy's offers sports oriented television and a game room.

PALMO'S CAPPUCCINO AND SPIRITS
Gateway Plaza
Vail
476-0646

Palmo's is a great place for evening relaxation.

RED LION
Vail Village
476-7676

The Red Lion is located at the top of Bridge Street, frequently offering live music. Their multiple televisions are sports oriented.

SARAH'S
Christiana Lodge
Vail Village
476-5641

Sarah's presents Helmut Fricker, "Vail's favorite entertainer." Helmut plays the pipes and the accordion. He is a wonderful man. You may notice Helmut entertaining elsewhere in Vail. He loves to perform outdoors and entertain the children.

SHEIKA'S
Vail Village
476-1515

Sheika's is located on Bridge St. beneath Pepi's Bar in the Gasthof Gramshammer. Sheika's plays great disco music.

SONNENALP (KING'S LOUNGE)
Vail Village
476-5656

Gene Johnson plays the piano.

STATE BRIDGE LODGE
On the Colorado River
14 Miles North of Wolcott on Highway 131
653-4444
653-8888

Located north of Wolcott, State Bridge Lodge offers excellent entertainment. Check the newspapers. Door to door transportation service is provided 7 days a week at special charter prices. Call 524-7684. Don't drink and drive. A restaurant and cabins are on site as well as other adventure activities. Closed in winter.

SUNDANCE SALOON
Lionshead Mall
476-3453

The Sundance Saloon is "Vail's Neighborhood Bar," offering dart boards, pool tables, foosball, and air hockey.

traMONTI
Charter at Beaver Creek
949-5552

traMonti offers the piano music of Brett Riggin.

TURNTABLE RESTAURANT
Minturn
827-4164

Open from 5 a.m. to 3 a.m.

VENDETTA'S
Vail Village
476-5070

Vendetta's frequently has music in the upstairs bar.

WESTIN LOBBY LOUNGE
Westin Hotel
Cascade Village
476-7111

Peter Vavra plays Broadway show tunes, classical works, and contemporary pieces.

P

PARKS

NOTTINGHAM PARK
Avon
949-5648

This lakeside park in Avon might be just the kind of relaxing place you and your family need on a bright blue warm sunny day. Grab your suntan lotion and bring your lunch.

Here playground equipment provides great fun for children. You can enjoy miniature golf; a paddleboat; windsurfing; or kayaking. Or you can play volleyball; tennis; soccer; football; frisbee; tennis; or croquet. Roller skating and roller blading make for good exercise. A number of equipment items are rented at the cabin on Nottingham Lake. If you don't know how to windsurf or kayak, lessons are available.

Fishing is a favorite way to relax away the day. The lake is stocked and fishing is allowed from the shore during boating hours or from the dock before 10 a.m. and after 8 p.m. Fishing licenses are required and may be purchased at many Avon retail stores. For more information, call the Forest Service in Minturn, 827-5715.

July 4th fireworks at Nottingham Lake are fantastic. The festivities begin in the early afternoon. Food and drinks are available. Alcohol cannot be brought into the Nottingham Lake area.

Skating is a wonderful winter sport on the pond.

BIG HORN PARK

Located in East Vail on East Meadow Drive, Big Horn Park has a pond as its central attraction. The playground offers swings, slides, and other activities. Plenty of green grass is also available for frisbee or flying kites.

FORD PARK

Ford Park offers a playground and manicured lawn, surrounded by magnificent trees. Gore Creek, Betty Ford Alpine Gardens, Gerald R. Ford Amphitheatre, and the Nature Center are within its bounds. You will find an historic schoolhouse in good repair. Ford Park has public tennis courts.

LIONSHEAD PARK

There is a playground area in the Lionshead area just across the bridge spanning Gore Creek and to the East. Miniature Golf is nearby.

PIRATE SHIP PARK

Pirate Ship Park is located just to the east of the Vail Mountain base in the Vail Village Area.

PEPI'S WEDEL WEEKS

476-5626
(800)323-4386

Austrian ski champion Pepi Gramshammer has organized early season ski instruction with Vail Ski School's "very best instructors." Sessions are limited in size, so you'll get personalized attention.

PINEY RIVER RANCH

476-3941
476-9090

Piney River Ranch and Piney Lake are located about one half hour by car from Vail via Red Sandstone Road. It is a dusty drive and you need to drive carefully. Views along the way and the splendid lake scenery are worth it. You can bike to Piney Lake; it may be dusty because of passing autos.

Piney Lake (60 acres) is situated at the base of the magnificent Gore Range with 13,000 ft. peaks. It is a beautiful lake and a wonderful place. You can rent rowboats or canoes and venture forth onto the lake. Fishing is also allowed. You can even rent fishing equipment. Outdoor meals are available for breakfast, lunch and dinner. There is a pleasant trading post to browse. If you wish to hike, the trails begin beside the lake. Guides are available for the hikes.

Horseback riding is a thrilling feature of this unique Western location. One hour, two hour, half day and full day rides are available. There is even an overnight horsepack trip for those who really want to get away from it all.

During the hunting seasons, guided hunts are provided. Three different base camps are strategically located in the 117,000 acre area.

Snowmobiling and dinners at Piney River Ranch are offered winters.

R

RAFTING

A.T.S. OF VAIL
476-7576
(800)247-7074

A.T.S. of Vail utilizes the Colorado, Arkansas, and Eagle Rivers. They also offer jeep trips.

ADVENTURES IN RAFTING
476-7645
(800)247-7074

Adventures In Rafting offers rafting on the Colorado River at State Bridge or at Shohone Rapids.

ALPINE RAFT ADVENTURES
476-5678
(800)488-5678

Alpine Raft Adventures utilizes the Colorado, Arkansas, and Eagle Rivers. Alpine Adventures also offers Alpine Jeep Adventures.

COLORADO RIVER RUNS, INC.
653-4292
(800)826-1081

Colorado River Runs, Inc. has provided raft trips since 1973. They utilize the Colorado River at State Bridge, the Eagle River at Eagle, and the Arkansas River at Buena Vista.

EAGLE RIVER/TIMBERLINE TOURS
476-7487
(800)339-RAFT

Eagle River Whitewater/Timberline Tours offers the hottest, hot, moderate and easy rafting experiences. They have half day and full day offerings. They utilize the Colorado River and the Arkansas River. Even young children can go on the easiest trips.

IMPULSE RAFTING
476-8680
(800) 339-7238

Enjoy Browns Canyon, Royal Gorge, and Clear Creek trips.

NOVA GUIDES, INC.
949-4232

Nova Guides, Inc. offers rafting experiences on the Colorado River, the Eagle River and the Arkansas River. They have different trips for excitement seekers and scenery seekers. Half day, three quarter day and full day excursions are available.

Other offerings include ATV (all-terrain vehicle) and jeep tours to get way up and away from it all. Fishing trips are also provided. In winter, they offer snowmobiling.

RAFTMEISTER
476-RAFT (7238)
(800)274-0636

Raftmeister offers rafting experiences on the Arkansas River, the Eagle River and the Colorado River. They have half day, full day and overnight adventures. All levels of thrills are available. They offer a combination hot air balloon and rafting experiences. They also offer backcountry mountain bike tours and hut-to-hut bike tours. Additionally, they have a kayak school. Furthermore they have nature photo hikes and wildlife tours.

STATE BRIDGE LODGE
653-4444

State Bridge Lodge offers rafting on the Colorado River. Here they have a restaurant; bar; cabins; and horseback riding. Biking and hiking are also available. Live bands provide entertainment. Check for the schedule. Express Vail, Inc. will provide door to door travel service.

TIMBERLINE TOURS
476-1414
(800) 831-1414

Timberline Tours advertises itself as Vail's "oldest guide service" (Est. 1971). It offers all levels of rafting trips on the Colorado, Eagle, and Arkansas rivers. Many of their guides work for the Ski Patrol at Vail and Beaver Creek.

RUNNING, ROLLER BLADING OR IN-LINE SKATING

There is plenty of running, roller blading or in-line skating going on in the Vail Valley. It is a great place for these sports. But if you are a flatlander take note of the effects of altitude and dehydration on your system.

Vail has a number of running contests throughout the summer. These include a warm-up 2 mile run; the Vail Hill Climb of over 2,000 ft.; a half-marathon out to Piney Lake; plus the Vailfest 5K and 10K which winds through the Vail area, starting in Lionshead.

S

SHOPPING

Next to skiing and dining, shopping may be the most active pursuit in the Vail Valley. Vail Village is renowned for fine shops in a charming pedestrian setting. The Village, designed after European resort areas St. Anton, Zermatt and Megeve, houses quaint shops amidst its Tyrolean architecture.

Vail shopping features intriguing clusters of stores in Vail Village Center, Crossroads Center and Vail Village Inn Plaza. These three are within easy walking distance from the heart of Vail Village. The Gateway building is Vail's indoor mall.

Lionshead Mall features shops ranging from art and gifts to climber-oriented Vail Mountaineering.

Beaver Creek boasts the Promenade with elegant shops. Minturn hosts offbeat shopping and the upscale Two Elk Gallery.

SKI HERITAGE MUSEUM AND SKI HALL OF FAME

Vail Transportation Center
476-1876

The Colorado Ski Heritage Museum and Ski Hall of Fame presents exhibits dealing with the evolution of ski equipment; military skiing (the 10th Mountain Division); cross-country skiing; ski fashions; and the 1989 Vail/Beaver Creek World Alpine Ski Championships. There is a Gift Shop.

SLEIGH RIDES

Horse drawn sleigh rides enchant winter evenings. Sleigh rides are available at the Vail Golf Course (through Seasons at the Green Restaurant, 479-2350); Eagle-Vail Golf Course (through Whiskey Creek Restaurant, 949-4942); another at Eagle-Vail (via Rocky Mountain Sleigh Company, 476-9422); at Avon's Nottingham Park (operated by the One Horse Open Sleigh Company, 949-9072); at Arrowhead (through the Bristol Restaurant, 926-2111); and at 4 Eagle Ranch (926-3372). The sleigh rides at the Bristol and Seasons at the Green are provided by Steve Jones Beaver Creek Stables (845-7770).

SNOWMOBILING

PINEY RIVER RANCH
476-9090
476-3941

Vail Associates offers exciting snowmobile tours. You can be picked up at your hotel. They also offer the Lift-Doo Tour, which allows you to ski half day and snowmobile the second half of the day on a special ticket. Furthermore, you can have an exciting and unique Twilight Dinner Tour. All of the tours range from two hour to full day.

NOVA GUIDES
P.O. Box 2018
Vail
949-4232

Nova Guides skimobile tours commence two miles south of Minturn on U.S. Highway 24. They offer hourly, half day or full day excursions. On the Top of the Rockies excursions you will reach 12,000 feet altitude, weather permitting.

TIMBERLINE TOURS
476-1414
(800)831-1414

Timberline Tours offers 80 miles of groomed trails. Trips for beginners through experts include suits, boots, and helmets. Families are welcome. Free pick up service is provided.

SUPER STAR STUDIO

Downstairs from Gorsuch
Vail Village
479-9512

Super Star Studios offers you the opportunity to be a Super Star. We know that you already are. This studio lets you record it for time eternal on audio or video cassettes. They have plenty of background music to accompany you. Or you can lip sync. Your cassette be a memorable document of a memorable vacation.

SWEETS

HAAGEN DAZS
Crossroads Center

LAURA'S FUDGE SHOP
Gore Creek Drive

MOUNTAIN MAN NUT AND FRUIT CO.
Avon Market Center

ROCKY MOUNTAIN CHOCOLATE FACTORY
Top of Bridge Street

SWEET LIFE
Top of Bridge Street
Lionshead Mall

T

TENNIS

Over 20 public tennis courts in the Vail are operated by the Vail Metropolitan Recreation District, 479-2279. For tennis information or reservations call 479-2294 for Ford Park; 479-2296 for Gold Peak; and 479-2295 for Lionshead. The phone number for the Eagle-Vail Tennis Club is 476-5636.

Additionally, numerous hotels and clubs have private courts. These include the Radisson Resort (476-4444); Vail Run (476-1502); the Cascade Club (476-7400); Vail Racquet Club (476-3267); and Vail Athletic Club/Potato Patch Club (476-8060 or 476-0700).

Indoor courts include those at the Cascade Club; Vail Racquet Club; and Vail Run. Outdoor courts are available at Beaver Creek and Cordillera.

Bill Wright's Summer Tennis Camps can be contacted at P.O. Box 1462, Vail, CO 81658

At this altitude you may have trouble keeping up with the pace of the balls; the pros do.

W

WILDLIFE TOURS

COLORADO SAFARI
Vail Rod and Gun Club, Ltd.
476-1880

Join outdoor columnist Chuck McGuire in a ten passenger van touring the great Colorado River Basin.

NOVA GUIDES, INC.
949-4232

Enjoy guided tours in the White River National Forest to view wildlife in their natural habitat.

WINEMAKING

MINTURN CELLARS
Minturn
827-4065

Minturn Cellars offers their own products and wines from other Colorado wineries. Their wine tasting room is open afternoons and evenings. Catering is available.

TRANSPORTATION
TO VAIL AND WITHIN THE VAIL VALLEY

The Drive To Vail From Stapleton Airport

The drive from Stapleton Airport to Vail Valley can be entertaining, beautiful, and educational. The positive side of this drive will be covered in the first portion of this text; following will be some cautionary statements which you should heed to maximize the joys of this trip.

Coming out of Stapleton make a right turn onto Quebec. Get in the left hand lane of Quebec as you will soon come to the left turn onto I-70 West. The drive to Vail is straight ahead 100 miles on I-70 West. Allow two and one half hours. Note that the mileage markers and exit numbers go down, rather than up, as you go west on I-70.

I will be describing some alternatives to a straight through drive which could add up to a half hour to your drive. Undertake these expeditions only if the day is crystal clear with a blue sky.

Get ready for some intriguing sights as you drive west.

First, you will note an interesting geologic formation at Exit 259 just before you enter the foothills at Morrison. Farther along, if you look carefully high up on your left as you pass Exit 256, you can view the interesting looking Sleeper house, the house that was utilized in Woody Allen's film, *Sleeper*. Some see it as a "space ship;" others see a "clam."

If you are in the mood to view Buffalo Bill's Grave, use Exit 256. After this, you will climb a significant grade on the highway. Suddenly you will encounter a perfectly designed bridge as the Rockies come into view in their magnificent splendor especially on one of our typical clear sky blue days.

Speaking of clear weather, you may not see any snow until you reach the high mountain country. Do not worry that there is no snow en route. Plenty awaits in ski country.

You will notice just past Exit 254, there is a rest area named Buffalo Herd Overlook. Look carefully; you may experience the joy of seeing live buffalo.

Many locals get off in Idaho Springs at Exit 241 for a short rest, in order to buy some gas or take a rest stop. A favorite here is the Sunrise Donut Shop which bakes a variety of fresh, fresh donuts. My favorites are the pine cones; the pumpkin bars; and the buttermilk bars. Hmm. Maybe I will stop off after all. There is also a mineralized hot springs in Idaho Springs.

Georgetown at Exit 228, an 1870s silver mecca with historic buildings and the famous Georgetown Loop Railway, is approximately half way to Vail using I-70. There are places to eat and a street mall atmosphere. In the summer take the historic railway ride to Silver Plume which penetrates the mountains above Georgetown. It's a lot of fun.

As you drive farther west on I-70 you climb a significant incline on your way to Silver Plume. Unlike Georgetown, Silver Plume has done little to encourage tourists. This has been a purposeful decision by the residents to have a historic place with a real small town character. As you drive on towards the pass, you may notice that your car doesn't pick up as fast as before the climb out of Georgetown. This is due to the high altitude and relative oxygen deficiency for the car. You may notice a little feeling of oxygen deficiency in yourself. Read the Cautions section of this book which is about the effects of high altitude.

It is here that you have a choice to make about whether to drive through Eisenhower Tunnel on I-70 West or to drive over Loveland Pass. Providing you have a well equipped car, a knowledgeable driver vis a vis driving in the snow and on ice, a clear day, and time to spare, you can drive over Loveland Pass. If you cannot meet all of these conditions, just continue driving through Eisenhower Memorial Tunnel.

Just before you enter the tunnel you will see Loveland Basin Ski Area, one of the smaller ski areas. It may be small but the slopes are steep enough to make you wonder, especially if you can get a good look at Avalanche Bowl or Cats Meow.

If you decide to go over Loveland Pass you will get a closer look at Loveland Basin. On a clear day you will see magnificent mountain vistas as you drive over the pass. Cars may stop and park at the top of the pass. Passengers will enjoy the views. A treat will be your first view of Arapahoe Basin Ski Area and the famed Pallivacini run or "Palli" for short. Steep, isn't it?

Down the road six miles below A-Basin you will find the flatter terrain of Keystone Ski Mountain. Have a good look at its intermediate runs. You will not be able to see its North Peak or Outback which are excellent for advanced skiers. Note that a significant portion of Keystone is lighted and can be skied until 10:00 p.m. It may be interesting to stop and have a few runs. You reconnect with I-70 West at Dillon/Silverthorne, Entrance 205.

Leaving Dillon/Silverthorne, you will see beautiful Lake Dillon on your left. Then you will come to the town of Frisco, which has two exits. The turnoff for the Breckenridge ski area is the first of these exits, Exit 203. After you leave Frisco, you will be entering Ten Mile Canyon. The canyon leads to Copper Mountain ski area at Exit 195. From here driving over Vail Pass takes approximately a half hour.

Approaching Vail, you will see a sign stating Vail has three exits. If you are a first timer to Vail, do not get off at Exit 180, unless you have been given clear directions to do so. This is East Vail. If you do exit here and feel lost, there is an outdoor pay telephone to your right.

For best orientation get off at Exit 176. Make a left turn. You will then come to the "famous" four way stop. The Vail Village Parking Structure is to the east and the Lionshead Parking Structure is to the west. If you are unclear as to what to do now, I advise going straight ahead and stopping at the Food and Deli market, the second left parking lot after the four way stop. There are outdoor phones here. Also, you can grab a quick snack or a few supplies and ask directions of the check out people.

A third and final highway exit for Vail is the West Vail Exit, Exit 173. Farther down the road is Exit 171 for Minturn or Eagle-Vail. The next exit is Exit 167, for Avon and Beaver Creek. Make a left turn here to reach Beaver Creek Resort. Keep going straight. After a couple lights, you will come to a security gate. You will be asked where you are heading. The guard can be helpful in guiding you to your destination. If you are a day skier, you may be directed to park at one of the two parking lots just to the west of the guard house. A free bus will take you up to Beaver Creek Resort.

CAUTIONS ABOUT DRIVING IN THE MOUNTAINS

Make sure the car you are driving is a mountain car, preferably a four wheel drive vehicle. Tires should be in good condition with either studs or at least all-season radials. If you are renting a car, be sure to ask all of these relevant points, so that everything important is included. Also, be sure to have an AAA card (or its equivalent). I recommend that you arrive at Stapleton as early as possible to avoid driving after dark. There are a few descents both heading towards and returning from Vail where cautious driving is especially indicated. On the way to Vail take care on the descent into Idaho Springs; the descent into Dillon/Silverthorne from Eisenhower Memorial Tunnel; and the descent into Vail from the top of Vail Pass. Returning watch out on the descent of Vail Pass; the descent into Dillon/Silverthorne; the descent from Eisenhower Tunnel; the descent from Silver Plume into Georgetown; and the descent on I-70 East as you approach the outskirts of Denver.

Shuttle Vans, Taxis & Limousines

Airport shuttle vans transfer many Vail and Beaver Creek guests to their lodgings. Visitor don't need a car due to an excellent public transportation system. Taxis and limousines are often used for local transportation. The following are airport shuttles and other transport systems.

SHUTTLE VANS

COLORADO MOUNTAIN EXPRESS
949-4227
(800)525-6363

VAIL WEST TRANSPORTATION
476-1223
(800)538-8633

VAIL VALLEY AIRPORT EXPRESS
476-8008
(800)882-8872

VANS TO VAIL
476-4467
(800)222-2112

GREYHOUND BUS

476-5137

TAXIS

VAIL VALLEY TAXI
476-8294
476-8008
(800)882-8872

LIMOUSINES

CONTINENTAL DIVIDE LIMOUSINE SERVICE
476-0310

GATEWAY LIMOUSINE
476-0762

PRESIDENTIAL LIMOUSINE, INC.
(303)698-1114
(800)442-5422

Vail's Bus And Parking System

WITHIN VAIL

Vail's bus system is simple, quick, and efficient. The automobile is virtually abolished. Free buses are provided by the Town of Vail within the town limits. Buses leave from the Vail Transportation Center in the Vail Village parking structure for East Vail and West Vail. This parking lot houses the Ski Heritage Museum.

Vail proper relies on a bus system that runs from Golden Peak to Lionshead. In the winter, the buses run frequently, essentially one bus just behind the other. It only takes 10 minutes to get from the Vail Village stop to the Lionshead stop and vice versa. The bus drivers are courteous and often entertaining. Skis are kept on the side of the bus.

It does pay to watch your skis, however. A man once took my new skis off the rack, mistaking mine for his. I was able to yell, get the bus to stop, and resolve the situation. I was lucky in this regard. While this was simply a mistake, you should watch your skis to prevent thievery.

Where do all the cars go? A good question. Cars go to either the Vail Village parking structure or the Lionshead parking structure. From these parking structures it is a short walk to the ski ticket purchase locations. Some cars go to lots at Golden Peak or at Cascade Village.

Hotel or condo guests can usually park in small lots next to the hotel or condominium complex.

VAIL TO BEAVER CREEK

An inexpensive bus system connects Vail and Beaver Creek. At Beaver Creek some cars can park for a fee at the parking lot at Beaver Creek Resort. The majority of cars park free at the base of the mountain and skiers need to take a bus from the parking lots to Beaver Creek Ski Resort. Small parking lots at lodges accommodate registered guests.

The phone number for the Vail system is 479-2172; the number for the Beaver Creek system is 949-6121.

VAIL ARCHITECTURE

Vail Village's Tyrolean architecture mirrors the charm of St. Anton, Zermatt and Megeve. Six intriguing Vail structures are sketched here. You can savor some delightful expressions of Bavarian interior design at Ambrosia; the Tyrolean; Ludwig's (Sonnenalp Hotel); and the Villager (Vail Village Inn). Masterworks of wood at the Villager create a wonderful feeling of harmony, design and environmental awareness.

Vail Interfaith Chapel

Swiss Chalet

Clock Tower/Ore House

Gasthof Gramshammer

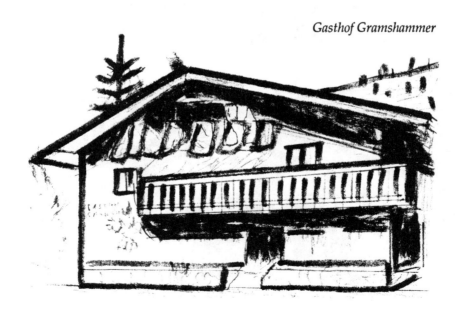

La Tour's Glockenspiel

Ambrosia

INDEX

ORDER ANOTHER COPY OF

You can order additional copies of **EXCITING VAIL AND BEAVER CREEK** by mail.

This insider's guide enables a visitor to Ski Vail/Beaver Creek like a local. How to avoid crowds... locate the best powder... escape (or find) steep spots... navigate North American's largest ski area with ease.

And more. Nearly 150 Vail Valley restaurants critiqued. Every activity from whitewater rafting to wildflower walks highlighted.

A great gift!

Send mail orders to:

Harley Press
P.O. Box 4577
Vail, CO 81658
(303) 476-1521

Please send **EXCITING VAIL** to:

Name: _____

Address: _____

City: _____ State: _____ Zip: _____

___ **EXCITING VAIL** book(s) at $14.95 each $_____

     Local tax   (Vail only)   1.22
     Colorado tax   (Colorado only)   .45
     Postage & handling   3.00

       TOTAL ENCLOSED $_____

Mail to: Harley Press, P.O. Box 4577, Vail, CO 81658